NGOs and Transnational Networks

D1611936

NGOs and Transnational Networks

Wild Cards in World Politics

William E. DeMars

Pluto Press

LONDON • ANN ARBOR, MI

First published 2005 by Pluto Press
345 Archway Road, London N6 5AA
and 839 Greene Street, Ann Arbor, MI 48106

www.plutobooks.com

British Library Cataloguing in Publication Data
A catalogue record for this book is available from the British Library

ISBN   0 7453 1906 8 hardback
ISBN   0 7453 1905 X paperback

Library of Congress Cataloging in Publication Data applied for

10   9   8   7   6   5   4   3   2   1

Designed and produced for Pluto Press by
Chase Publishing Services, Fortescue, Sidmouth, EX10 9QG, England
Typeset from disk by Stanford DTP Services, Northampton, England
Printed and bound in the European Union by
Antony Rowe Ltd, Chippenham and Eastbourne, England

Contents

TABLES

Acknowledgements

Along the way I have incurred many debts, in the first instance to the many mid-level NGO professionals on several continents who have explained to me the complexities and paradoxes of their work. My admiration for their courage to act is undiminished by my revealing what I take to be the inadvertent consequences of their actions. The ideas here have germinated in intellectual dialogue with many, most particularly Georges Abi-Saab, Bertha Amisi, David Forsythe, Pierre Gassman, Tony Lang, Gil Loescher, George Lopez, Mark Peterson, Jackie Smith, Alex de Waal, and Thomas Weiss. My students at the American University in Cairo, the University of Notre Dame, Earlham College, and Wofford College have helped me by their experience and research as well as their questions and confusion. I thank the Feris Foundation of America, Refugee Policy Group, American University in Cairo, the University of Notre Dame, the Institute for World Politics, Sophia University in Tokyo, and Wofford College for supporting research travel and writing. While acknowledging the help of others, I accept full responsibility for the interpretations in this book and for any errors of fact that remain. Finally, I am grateful to my wife, Therese, for both her patience and well-justified impatience as the project developed, but most of all for her companionship along the way which makes the whole adventure worth having.

Introduction

Observing world politics at the beginning of the twenty-first century, international non-governmental organizations (NGOs) seem to be everywhere, and they often work in mysterious ways. If omnipotence remains yet out of reach, it is not for lack of effort, since NGOs cumulatively claim to be able to do almost anything in world politics, from feeding famine victims and protecting endangered species, to eliminating nuclear weapons and AIDS, to democratizing Russia and the Arab world.

NGOs are both prominent and obscure in world politics. They are prominent, for example, in organizing massive street protests in February 2003 against the U.S. "War on Terror."[1] NGOs are also obscure, for example, as shadow partners in international legal maneuvers. Chilean General Augusto Pinochet found himself stranded in London for more than a year—from November 1998 to January 2000—while the British government considered whether to extradite him to Spain. Spanish judge Baltasar Garzon had charged Pinochet with crimes against humanity for acts of torture and killing after the 1973 coup, which overthrew Chilean President Salvador Allende. While the affair was ostensibly a negotiation between two governments, the deeper political process was catalyzed at every stage by human rights NGOs. Operating largely behind the scenes, a network of NGOs had initiated the original indictment in Spain, and promoted Pinochet's extradition across Europe and North America. However, Amnesty International—the prominent human rights NGO based in London—had penetrated the case so deeply that a decision by a panel of British law lords was reversed when personal links by one of the lords to Amnesty were revealed.[2] Britain finally denied the extradition and returned Pinochet to Chile for health reasons. Nevertheless, a spokesman for Human Rights Watch declared, "The Pinochet decision was a wake-up call to dictators around the world. If you torture somebody today, you can get arrested for it tomorrow almost anywhere."[3]

NGOs are actively engaged at both the top and the bottom of world politics. At the top, the U.S. National Security Council guiding American foreign policy consisted of 99 policy assistants in 1999, more than a third of whom were on loan from non-profit think-tanks and NGOs.[4] During the Rwandan genocide from April to July 1994, Alison Des Forges of Human Rights Watch briefed both the UN Security Council in New York and the U.S. National Security Council in Washington, DC with real-time information on the course of the killings.[5] The bottom of world politics is so densely populated with grassroots NGOs operating in every region that counting them has become a cottage industry among scholars and officials. For example, Charles William Maynes, president of the Eurasia Foundation, reports that 80,000 NGOs have somehow sprung up in Russia since the demise of the Soviet Union in 1991.[6] UN Secretary General Boutros-Ghali pleaded for help from tens of thousands of grassroots NGOs to persuade member nations to support United Nations activities: "I wish to state, as clearly as possible—I need the mobilizing power of NGOs."[7]

The NGO organizational form has become so irresistible that a broad assortment of notables, missionaries, and miscreants are creating their own NGOs. Middle-power governments are privatizing some of their diplomatic functions to NGOs. For example, International Crisis Group, an "early warning" NGO headed by former Australian Foreign Minister Gareth Evans, strives to head off emerging conflicts by collecting and analyzing information whose sensitivity ranges somewhere between investigative reporting and strategic intelligence.[8] Christian churches in Africa undergo "NGO-ization" as African clergy rely on networks of international relief and development NGOs for communication, transportation, and general support.[9] At the same time, some of the shadier operators in world politics cloak criminal activities under NGOs to gain the veneer of respectability. Before his mysterious murder in January 2000, Arkan, the Serbian paramilitary leader, indicted war criminal, and smuggler/businessman, founded and supported his own charitable foundation, "The Third Child."[10] The U.S. government has frozen the assets of certain international Islamic charities, accusing them of channeling aid to terrorist groups.[11] Top Israeli leaders have been accused of illegally passing foreign campaign donations through non-profit organizations.[12]

NGOs do work in mysterious ways. While they sometimes achieve much more than promised, frequently they accomplish much less. Their real significance is that *NGOs often create inadvertent political consequences whose impact is more important than either success or failure in reaching official goals.* The influence of NGOs in world politics is greater than either their boosters or their detractors claim.

If NGOs are rarely what they seem, then political analysis of NGOs ought to include a measure of skepticism, even irreverence, concerning the sacred global norms they claim to serve. For example, NGOs are conventionally categorized according to the norms articulated in their mandates. Government officials, international organizations, scholars, journalists, and the general public all follow this lead and conceptualize NGOs within issue-areas of related normative goals, such as human rights, humanitarian relief, or environmentalism. With a dose of agnosticism introduced into our internationalist faith, we may find it conceivable that these issue-area boundaries are not the best points of departure for analyzing the politics of NGOs.

This book aims to analyze NGOs across all these issue-areas. The point of departure here is not the norms NGOs proclaim, but the structure of transnational action they share, a common structure that forms the basis of seemingly infinite tactical variations. Norms and ideas are not disregarded (this is not a materialist analysis), but neither are they taken at face value.

This structure of transnational action shared by all NGOs is spelled out in chapter 2. One element of that structure may be touched upon here, however, to indicate the unconventional approach taken in this book. Whatever its issue-area, every NGO articulates a promise of future progress and gives supporters a taste of that promise today. NGOs move people and influence events as much by evoking a progressive future as by taking action in the present. To make a better future *feel possible*, or at least a bit less impossible, may be enough to sustain an NGO project. For example, Amnesty International and the Mothers of the Disappeared in Argentina promise a world of universal respect for human rights; CARE, Oxfam, and Save the Children promise a better life for the poor; Greenpeace promises protection for endangered species and ecosystems.

With all due respect to these authentic human aspirations, which I happen to share, the NGOs that evoke them take rather tiny steps toward utopia in any particular year or decade. Moreover, at the level of NGO operations, to make even these small steps requires amalgamating the conflicting self-interests of societal and political partners in several countries. One core challenge for NGO professionals, therefore, is to infuse very small steps with very large meanings, and thereby either to transform or obscure the self-interests of partners.

This challenge is to evoke a progressive future and to make that future present today. In this view, the NGO pledging "sustainable development" by distributing condoms is attempting something like the sacramental rite of the priest evoking the Kingdom of God, the revolutionary praxis of the agitator prodding history toward the classless society, or the medieval alchemist mixing base ingredients to make gold.

And yet—if it would not ruin the magic—one is tempted to ask a few political questions: Who benefits from faith in progress in this particular form? What alternate political faith is displaced? What is the impact on local society of importing money, ideas, and international linkages? I would suggest that another metaphor is most apt: NGOs are wild cards in world politics—their impact is up for grabs, and they attract local and global actors who compete, and sometimes cooperate, to play, capture, or neutralize them.

As NGOs have proliferated in numbers and influence, especially in the last decade, a growing body of scholarship has addressed the NGO bloom (see chapter 2). However, many analysts tend to celebrate and promote the NGOs they profile. The tendency by scholars to credit utopian promises based on mundane practices reflects the self-understanding of NGOs themselves. Such scholarship identifies too closely with NGO goals and reiterates in theory the self-legitimating discourse of NGOs. The tunnel vision of such approaches fails to reveal the politics of NGOs in its full range and complexity. This book, in contrast, portrays NGOs and their networks as international institutions in which political conflict is inherent, not incidental. Instead of tunnel vision, it cultivates "peripheral vision" to perceive unintended side effects. The proliferation of NGOs does indeed transform world politics, but often not in the directions that NGO advocates claim.[13] In sum, this book seeks neither to bury NGOs nor to praise them, and still less to reform them. Its purpose, rather, is to understand the actual consequences and uses of NGOs in world politics.

Chapter 1 begins with examples of NGO action from several fields, in the form of "Your NGO Starter Kit." It spells out the claims and contradictions involved in initiating any international NGO. Specific examples of NGO politics illustrate the need for a fresh analytical approach formulated with greater independence from the worldviews of NGOs themselves. Chapter 2 offers a new structural theory, portraying NGOs as sites of institutionalized political conflict at three levels: within themselves as organizations; in the networks they create; and in the regional and global systems they inhabit. Chapter 3 examines historical origins of NGOs prior to 1945, emphasizing the religious roots of modern NGOs, the stamp of American government and society on NGO origins, and the shifting norms of progress that NGOs have enacted.

Chapters 4, 5, and 6 illustrate three distinct power relationships between state and society embodied by NGOs, the most significant consequences of which fell outside official NGO goals. Human rights and other NGOs inadvertently transformed the authoritarian regime in Argentina during the 1970s and 1980s (chapter 4). NGOs permeated the wars of Yugoslavia's collapse during the 1990s, shaping the conflicts by being incorporated in the strategies of all the warring parties and outside powers (chapter 5). Several groups of NGOs are joined in a growing "NGO war" to reengineer sexual relations, women's fertility, and families on a global scale (chapter 6). Chapter 7 addresses the future of NGOs, including emerging trends of NGO–corporate partnerships, the resurgence of religious identities in NGOs, the post-humanist trend, and NGOs in the "War on Terror."

1
Your NGO Starter Kit

"Mister," he said with a sawdusty sneeze,
"I am the Lorax. I speak for the trees."
Dr. Seuss, *The Lorax*, 1971

NGOs are increasing in number and influence in all regions of the world, and across a growing roster of issue-areas.[1] The primary geopolitical focus of their normative agendas is to influence the "Third World" of former European colonies, and the "Second World" of former (and remnant) communist states. The broad turn to NGOs reflects a largely unexamined faith that they are the most effective vehicles for social and political transformation. Does NGO proliferation necessarily contribute to progressive change? This chapter examines an assortment of NGO claims and discovers some contradictions lying just beneath the surface.

NGOs are so numerous, operate in so many countries, and address so many disparate issues that most accounts of NGO politics follow conventional approaches to partition the NGO world for easier study.[2] Four well-worn premises frequently serve. First, NGOs are divided between international agencies based in prosperous Western countries and local or "grassroots" organizations working directly with the poor or the victimized. Second, much is made of the "issue-areas" that are assumed to be hermetically sealed from influencing each other. Third, there is a strong assumption that NGO influence on how the world works follows automatically from NGO participation in formulating "global norms" in international conferences and treaties. Finally, a sharp distinction is drawn between service NGOs presumed to work in partnership with governments, and advocacy NGOs presumed to challenge government policy and legitimacy. All four premises, which are drawn directly from NGO self-understandings, conceal much more than they reveal of the politics of NGOs. NGO cases and vignettes recounted in this chapter illustrate why these conventional premises are illusory and misleading for research.

Most observers assume that the best answer to the question "What do NGOs do?" can be found in their normative principles, that is, in what NGOs say. This assumption is fundamentally misleading for understanding NGOs in world politics. For example, the development fundraising technique of individual child sponsorship, pioneered by Save the Children Fund U.S. in the 1940s, provides the donor with a photo of the sponsored child, a family history, and even personal letters. Implicit in the idea of sponsorship or adoption is a direct line between one donor and one child. This approach is fraught with controversy, however, even among the NGO professionals who use it. In reality, the organizations themselves often have no way of tracking whether or how the contributions affect individual children. Nevertheless, NGOs are unable to give up the direct mail and televised appeals because child sponsorship raises an estimated $400 million each year in the United States.[3]

In this case, and generally in international NGOs, the beneficiaries are separated from financial donors by thousands of miles, and the NGO staff is positioned between beneficiaries and donors, controlling the flow of information, funds, and services. In this far-flung organizational formation the professional NGO staff wields tremendous discretionary power, unaccountable to either beneficiaries or supporters, to massage information to reflect the expectations of the partners rather than the reality of the mission. No NGO can continue to exist for long without the generosity of donors, the cooperation of home and host governments, an identifiable beneficiary population, and a societal pool from which to draw committed staff members. Each partner must be given a plausible rationale for cooperation with the NGO, or nothing happens. To make far-reaching normative claims is built into the structure of NGO action. It is simply the price of admission to the NGO game. NGOs must mislead in order to exist.

At the theoretical level, leading interpretations testify to the primacy of *principled ideas* about right and wrong, justice and injustice, in NGO activity, with *causal ideas* about how the world works taking a decidedly secondary place. From this premise, much of the leading research proceeds logically to emphasize how NGOs and their networks frame normative appeals and implant their principled ideas in the minds of target audiences. Such research, while interesting and useful, does not, in my view, reveal the full significance of NGO activity in world politics. Instead, I would argue, all transnational NGOs make causal claims about the structure of the problems they address and the solutions they offer, but these causal claims are veiled behind their normative appeals. The causal claims must be obscured because they cannot sustain close scrutiny.

In the debate on normative frames versus causal claims, I argue for the primacy of the latter. This chapter shows how NGOs smuggle in implicit causal claims under the noise and fury of their powerful normative appeals.

Following these insights, we can identify the essential components of "Your NGO Starter Kit." Imagine you are creating your own NGO. Whatever your personal motives—to make a better world, make a name for yourself, or simply make a living—what must you possess to get started, even before you seek out partners? Joining the NGO game requires four normative claims: a global moral compass, a modular technique, a secular sanction, and a representative mandate. Each of these normative claims serves in part to mask an underlying causal claim about how the world works.

GLOBAL MORAL COMPASS

A *global moral compass* says something about the world and something about the people initiating the NGO. Concerning the world, it makes a claim of universal, cosmopolitan human needs or rights (or biological rights in the case of environmental causes). It also says something about the NGO leaders—the integrity of their conscience and the intensity of their commitment to spread the universalist faith.[4] A moral "compass" provides direction to NGO strategy, and also encompasses a potential global constituency of rights or needs bearers to whom the NGO is dedicated. In this way an NGO is commissioned for a global scope of action, to be able to go anywhere and assert confidently, in effect, "We already know what is needed here, and we have been sent to help provide it." Claiming a global moral compass is, therefore, an act of self-authorization, appointing oneself as a moral authority in a given issue-area.[5] ("I am the Lorax. I speak for the trees.")

However presumptuous the moral compass asserted by an NGO leader may appear, organizational progress depends entirely on the voluntary assent to this claim by a cluster of partners in several countries. No one is forced to support an NGO. In gaining this cooperation, some NGOs have the advantage of a persuasive and emotionally moving origin story. For example, Amnesty International began in 1960 when London attorney Peter Benenson read a news report of two Portuguese students sentenced to seven-year prison terms by the Salazar dictatorship for raising a toast to freedom in a Lisbon restaurant. Angry at the injustice and frustrated by the lack of a means to respond, Benenson and friends fashioned the innovative tactic of an international letter-writing campaign to pressure governments to release "prisoners of conscience"—people imprisoned for their beliefs who had never used or advocated the use of violence.[6] In the decades since, tens of thousands of Amnesty International letter-writers have been moved to imitate Benenson's spontaneous response to injustice. In so doing, they have accepted the authenticity of Amnesty's global moral compass.

Within an NGO's global moral compass is hidden an implicit causal assumption about how the world works. There is always some form of claim that progress can be achieved in a selected issue-area with autonomy from the contingencies of the local political and social context. Every NGO must assume this, whether they are addressing infant feeding, peacemaking in civil wars, whale species survival, or any other issue-area. The causality of both the problem itself and the NGO solution must be autonomous from the social context in both directions: the context must not invade or disrupt the circumscribed issue-area, and action on the issue must not produce significant negative effects in the local context. This claim of *circumscribed causality* is essential to NGO action because, if the claim fails, so too does the normative authority of the NGO's global moral compass. If issue causality cannot reliably be circumscribed from the local context, then an NGO's moral commission to go anywhere and generate progress becomes impossibly presumptuous. The normative claim depends utterly on the causal claim, but also serves to screen the causal claim from scrutiny.

Your NGO Starter Kit must include a global moral compass, which comes with a claim of circumscribed causality attached. You will want to keep the latter in the background by drawing attention to moral issues. To see how this can be done, there are no better examples than the Titans of recent NGO history.

NGO TITANS

A handful of individuals have achieved global influence through the power of a persona—projected onto the world stage by an NGO, conveying a contagious moral conviction, and offering a simple and readily imitated technique for action. Peter Benenson provided such a persona for Amnesty International, until he was forced out of the organization in 1965.[7] In half of the 26 years from 1974 and 1999, the Nobel Peace Prize was awarded to either an international NGO or an individual closely associated with an NGO cause.[8] In 1997 the prize went to the International Campaign to Ban Landmines, whose influence owed much to highly publicized visits to landmine victims in many countries by Diana, Princess of Wales.

"NGO Titans" illustrate the complex interplay between the projection of a global moral compass and the claim of circumscribed causality. Norman Borlaug won the Nobel Peace Prize in 1970 for his research on high-yield wheat at the Center for International Maize and Wheat Improvement, an NGO in Mexico City. Borlaug not only contributed to the scientific development of high-yield strains, he personally promoted their adoption by India and Pakistan during the 1960s. Despite recurrent famines on the subcontinent, India and Pakistan resisted Borlaug's proposals until their 1965 war created emergency conditions. Progress was rapid after both governments put their full support behind the "Green Revolution" strains of wheat and rice. India had become self-sufficient in all cereal production by 1974 and eventually multiplied its wheat production six-fold.[9] The specter of recurrent famine disappeared from the Indian subcontinent as a consequence of the work of Borlaug and his colleagues.

Borlaug's achievement grew out of his personal commitment to feed the hungry and his technical expertise. His persona fused the authority of science and humanitarianism, both of which reside "above politics." Because he had no political agenda, his innovations could be more acceptable to political actors. At the same time, however, the Green Revolution both depended upon political support and profoundly transformed the context of politics on the subcontinent. The high-yield wheat and rice required new farming techniques and greater use of chemical fertilizer and herbicides, the distribution, finance, and implementation of which, in turn, demanded governmental action on a large scale reaching into the hinterland. The Indian civil service was well placed, relative to many other newly independent countries, to effectively implement such an ambitious bureaucratic program.

The political consequences of this success have been enormously far-reaching, if rarely remarked upon. Had India continued to be plagued by recurrent famine until today, its internal stability would have been severely and chronically shaken, and its relations with outside powers would have been supplicant rather than assertive. India's bold leadership of the Non-Aligned Movement, its military buildup and effectiveness in wars with several neighbors including China, its playing off the superpowers from a position of strength during the Cold War, its economic and technological achievements in the 1990s, and its credible appeal for a permanent seat on the United Nations Security Council—all of these would be almost inconceivable for a country unable to feed its own population.

The irony is that Borlaug's narrow, apolitical concerns for crop science and feeding the hungry transformed the internal and external politics of the second most populous country in the world. His avowed goal to create a tightly circumscribed effect instead generated the broadest possible scope of influence. Borlaug deserves to be called an NGO Titan because his actions shaped nations and fortified governments.

Yet Borlaug did not work alone, either scientifically or organizationally. His research center in Mexico City had been established in the 1940s by the Rockefeller Foundation, which sent him to India and Pakistan in the 1960s to promote the wheat strains he had developed. More broadly, the Green Revolution as a global phenomenon can be traced to the initiative of the Rockefeller and Ford Foundations, which together established a loose, global network of similar nonprofit agricultural research centers, cultivated additional funding for them from the World Bank and major governments, educated a generation of agricultural scientists from throughout the developing world to understand the technical innovations, and directly promoted the high-yield seeds.[10] The vast growth in agricultural productivity to which the Green Revolution made a crucial contribution means that "Despite a doubling of world population since 1960, the food supply per head for the world has increased, calories by 13%, protein by 8%, and both by even greater margins in the developing countries as a whole."[11]

The executives and program officers of major foundations are anonymous NGO Titans, who project no public persona, but can dramatically shape the ideas, institutions, and even the physical sustenance of nations and governments. Borlaug learned this anew in 1984, when he came out of retirement to team with Ryoichi Sasakawa of Japan and former U.S. President Jimmy Carter to promote high-yield agriculture in sub-Saharan Africa. The Ford and Rockefeller Foundations now opposed bringing the Green Revolution to Africa, under the influence of environmental activists who believed that the chemical inputs would destroy the fragile ecology. For a time, the three veteran NGO Titans found themselves outside the Ford and Rockefeller consensus, and therefore without donors beyond Sasakawa's own Peace Foundation. A *modus vivendi* was reached when the environmentalists ascendant in the Foundations were convinced by Borlaug and others that higher crop yields would help Africa protect its remaining forests.[12]

NGOs can profoundly shape ideas, institutions, and practices on a global scale even when they claim to pursue only a narrow, circumscribed agenda. The key protagonists of the Green Revolution in Asia were NGO Titans like Borlaug, whose persona projected a global moral compass. Ironically, he used the apolitical authority of science and humanitarianism to promote a profound economic and political revolution in the subcontinent.

A global moral compass is an essential tool in Your NGO Starter Kit, but it also reveals something about NGO research. The top-down power of NGOs based in the global north to shape societies in the global south is no less real when development theory emphasizes the opposite, bottom-up relationship—the power of the "grassroots NGOs" and "transnational civil society" in the south. Such discourse about empowering global civil society often originates precisely with the foundation managers, think-tank intellectuals, and northern NGO leaders who are empowering themselves to reshape the south.[13] The discourse masks the real flow of power. This is why the conventional distinction between international NGOs and grassroots NGOs is misleading: the distinction prejudges the flow of power, which should be a matter for empirical investigation. This distinction may be accepted uncritically by researchers who want to promote a particular NGO project, but should not be followed by scholars who want to reveal the politics of NGOs.

MODULAR TECHNIQUE

The second component of Your NGO Starter Kit, a *modular technique*, is a set of practices (such as writing letters, organizing street protests, boycotting products, "adopting" a child, conducting environmental assessments, or running conflict resolution seminars) that an NGO can bring to bear to alleviate the unmet needs or unprotected rights of its target population. The practice must be easily replicable in diverse and far-flung settings; that is, readily portable or modular.[14] A modular technique is essential to Your NGO Starter Kit because it allows a central organization to coordinate worldwide activities and presents an acceptable face of the NGO to partners in many different countries. The efficacy of an NGO practice to influence the target issue should be self-evident, or as close to it as possible, in the eyes of observers. Why? Because debate about the efficacy of NGO technique disrupts the impact of its normative and symbolic appeal. This is why a "short causal chain" between the problem and its proposed solution is so highly recommended for effective NGO advocacy.[15]

The role of causal claims is more obvious here than anywhere else in conventional NGO practice. Building on the claim that the issue-area can be circumscribed from the social context, the NGO must also assert that its modular technique will create only the intended consequences and no others. In short, the modular technique implicitly claims *magic bullet causality*. This claim relies on some combination of the technical expertise of NGO professionals and their good intentions. The precise mix between the two varies widely. Alex de Waal decries the misleading "citadel of expertise" that disaster relief practitioners build around their various specialties to create an aura of technocratic efficacy and a rationale for ignoring the local context.[16] But technique is not enough to assure the accuracy of the global gunfighter's magic bullet; he or she must also have the pure intention that the bullet will strike the heart of the villain (the global problem) and not hit innocent bystanders. That is why much literature by and about NGO activists portrays them as moral heroes. The force of their good intentions must be combined with the power of their technical mastery to hold the observer's gaze on the gunfighter and distract attention from the actual path of the bullet. Much of NGO discourse about modular technique, therefore, is on the order of normative claims designed to elicit admiration and to deflect critical thinking about the veiled claim of magic bullet causality.

These first two claims are closely linked, and both are essential to Your NGO Starter Kit. First, a global moral compass tells the world that you know what is important in any new operational environment. It says that your conscience, as institutionalized in the NGO, can be trusted to prioritize action on the NGO mandate anywhere. Just as essential, a global moral compass presses the hidden causal claim that a particular issue-area can be isolated or circumscribed from its social and political environment anywhere in the world. Second, when you have a modular technique in Your NGO Starter Kit, you can claim not only that you know what must be done, but also that you know how to do it. For a technique to be truly modular, it must function similarly anywhere in the world regardless of social context. Therefore, a modular technique also presses the hidden causal claim that it will work like a magic bullet to hit the target with no collateral damage.

THE POLITICS OF A HUNGRY CHILD

At stake in the consideration of hidden causal claims is whether the "issue-area" conceptualized at NGO headquarters, and implanted in the minds of donors, really holds up in the field. When the NGO exports its moral compass and modular technique to many countries, how well do they travel? The standard claims of circumscribed causality and magic bullet causality assert that they travel very well, thank you. In practice, this is often not the case. The account of Borlaug's experience promoting high-yield wheat in South Asia points to one variation in which the NGO succeeds spectacularly in achieving its official, circumscribed goal, but the consequences of success overflow to transform regional society and politics. A second variation is where the NGO fails to achieve its official, primary mission, but nevertheless keeps all its partners reasonably satisfied and sustains the life of the project. Two examples of this second variation can be found in NGO missions to Ethiopia after the 1984 famine.

Film of starving children in northern Ethiopia shocked and moved millions of viewers when it was shown on worldwide television in October 1984.[17] Before these images appeared, the Ethiopian government had curbed news of the famine, and Western donors, particularly the United States, had little desire to abet the Soviet Union's largest ally in Africa to manage its internal problems. The film, shot with government permission in feeding camps run by British NGOs Oxfam and Save the Children, signaled the Ethiopian government's desperation for food aid to stabilize the migrating population, which threatened to overrun its cities. The same film rendered it politically impossible for Western donors to ignore the crisis. Concern was so pervasive that rock musicians launched "USA for Africa" and "Band Aid" to raise funds for the famine. Public opinion demanded Western governmental action. U.S. President Ronald Reagan, in order to justify a major American relief operation that seemed to contradict his determination to make life difficult for communist regimes, proclaimed, "A hungry child knows no politics."

While the statement is true at the human level, the process of moving relief aid from the West to Ethiopia did enmesh hungry children in politics. After the film appeared, the Ethiopian government decided to accept greater Western relief assistance, and Western governments decided to provide that assistance as surplus food. Savvy policymakers on both sides understood the real terms of the transaction: food aid would keep some Ethiopians alive while bolstering the short-term stability and coercive capacity of the Ethiopian government.

High-level political decisions by donor and recipient governments were not sufficient to make the aid flow, however. Institutional bridges had to be built to span the East–West chasm. And the real terms of the affair had to be obscured to satisfy essential bureaucracies and constituencies. NGOs played essential roles in legitimizing and delivering the aid.

Western donor bureaucracies were paralyzed by a lack of numbers. It was necessary to quantify malnourished people and the required aid tonnage in order to catalyze bureaucratic planning and mobilize political support for aid. However, the donors did not trust the numbers offered by the Ethiopian government's Relief and Rehabilitation Commission, whose data and calculation process were never fully explained. A modular technique was needed to generate numbers that would move the donor bureaucracies. The solution was simply to agree on an arbitrary planning number, somewhat below whatever the RRC was seeking, but without gathering any additional data. As cover for such political agreements, the UN Food and Agricultural Organization sponsored "Joint Donor Assessment Missions" in which groups of politicians and bureaucrats traveled to see some hungry people and dry fields, and then negotiated an arbitrary but politically acceptable number.[18]

Another solution was to seek additional data through a proliferation of "famine early warning" schemes. One of the most effective, measured by the power of its data to move donor bureaucracies, relied on precise measurements of the bodies of malnourished children in scattered rural villages. Save the Children Fund UK pioneered this technique of "nutritional surveillance" in Ethiopia. Save the Children Fund nutritionists selected a sample of villages in each region, and then a sample of children in each village, and periodically measured each child's height and upper arm circumference.[19] Analyzed statistically, and arranged in time-series, such data could create a picture of deteriorating nutrition that effectively moved relief bureaucracies in London, Paris, Brussels, and Washington.

The appearance of hard, technical data, the professional expertise radiating from nutritionists, and the symbolism of emaciated children's bodies all combined to give these data a powerful political impact. The almost complete absence of a scientific basis for the meaning of the information did nothing to reduce its effectiveness in facilitating the movement of food aid to Ethiopia. Many of the nutritionists involved in the practice knew that they could neither predict nor warn of anything significant using such "anthropometric" assessments, and that the narrow, technical scope of the methodology guaranteed that they would never understand the causes of malnutrition. Two disillusioned NGO practitioners later complained:

> We have been seduced by anthropometry, which is easy to measure, easy to manipulate and can be easily taken out of context to mean just about anything! This has stunted our analytical skills, and created a strait-jacketed approach to famine relief; high rates of malnutrition equal famine equal food distribution.[20]

For NGO politics, however, the technical blinders worn by NGO nutritionists in Ethiopia during the 1980s were absolutely essential for their modular technique to be accepted by the Ethiopian RRC. The government that encouraged foreign NGOs to measure its children's bodies did not allow NGOs to survey adults for their views on the causes of their hunger. Anthropometry worked as a kind of NGO wild card—maintaining the appearance of technical efficacy while becoming what powerful patrons wanted it to be. Anthropometry fitted well with the government's official theory that hunger was caused by drought and soil erosion. Alternate theories—supported by overwhelming evidence after the end of the civil war in 1991—attributed famine to the government's coercive agricultural policies and its counterinsurgency violence against the rural civilian population.[21] In reality, the government itself caused the famine through massive and various forms of violence against its own people.

To stay in Ethiopia—and continue to play a role in keeping the food flowing to some hungry Ethiopians—international NGOs had to carefully avoid drawing conclusions about the causes of famine that diverged from theories acceptable to the government. To play it safe, they remained strictly confined to the relief and development issue-area. Venturing beyond acceptable issue boundaries, particularly in the direction of framing the problem in human rights terms, would and did result in the government's termination of NGO operations and expulsion of expatriate staff.[22]

Ethiopian children—whose bodies were measured to create the numbers to bring the food—were indeed enmeshed in a political process of deception and persuasion. If they did not know politics, politics knew them. The modular technique of nutritional surveillance in Ethiopia concealed the nature of the nutrition problem in order to satisfy partners and preserve the project.

Was this an isolated case of fictitious causal claims by NGOs? During the same period, 1985 to 1991, international donors channeled an enormous quantity of surplus food to Ethiopia for the largest food-for-work program in Africa. In projects arranged by the Ethiopian government through its official peasant organizations, international NGOs paid peasants with food and supervised their labor to plant millions of trees and construct 1.5 million kilometers of soil terraces and bunds. The goal of all this was to prevent soil erosion, which prevailing theories identified as a major cause of the famine. Erosion, according to conventional development theories, was caused largely by the peasants themselves—their aggressive population increase, their misguided tree-felling which had deforested large areas over the previous century, and their irrational attachment to traditional farming practices.[23]

If the peasants were the problem, then it made no sense to consult them, and it made perfect sense to use international food aid to bribe them and Stalinist agricultural policies to coerce them to do the right thing in their own long-term interest. The donors, NGOs, and Ethiopian government could all claim that they were not merely feeding people, they were also working to prevent the next famine.

Subsequent research suggests that this prevailing "environmental policy narrative" was wrong on all its major causal claims. Famine was caused by coercive agricultural policies, not erosion. The historical rate of erosion and deforestation had been grossly exaggerated. Peasants possessed extensive knowledge of techniques to conserve soil and promote tree growth. And the food-for-work projects created little benefit, while aggravating environmental damage and reducing agricultural productivity. Allan Hoben summarizes the dismal results of the environmental reclamation program in Ethiopia:

> Today, in retrospect, it is clear that much of this effort was wasted or counterproductive. The long- and short-term soil conservation benefits of the structures and trees are uncertain. The most rigorous research conducted to date shows that under most conditions terracing has lowered agricultural production instead of raising it as had been anticipated ... Farmers have been unwilling to construct or maintain structures without food-for-work or coercion, and many of the structures have fallen into disrepair. Most community wood-lots have been harvested or destroyed. Hillside closures had mixed results. Where they were built best, they tended to

reduce household income from livestock, to cause environmental damage by concentrating livestock on the remaining pasture, and to harbour wild animals and pests.[24]

Not only the causal theories, but the issue-area designations themselves were profoundly misleading. At best, a simple relief program masqueraded as environmental reclamation. At worst, the relief and environmental paradigms together prevented a more appropriate human rights analysis and response.

For Your NGO Starter Kit, two lessons are clear. First, successful NGO operations must please the powerful partners, while it is optional whether they adhere to principles and serve the beneficiaries. Second, when the partners and the principles conflict, the most sophisticated way to finesse the clash is through adopting causal theories, for whatever modular technique is available, that support the claims of circumscribed and magic bullet causality. These two causal claims work together to oversimplify and obscure the complex politics that is always imbedded in NGOs and their transnational networks.

For NGO scholarship, the lesson is that research confined within issue-area boundaries will legitimate the NGO program, because such research will overlook the most important politics of the situation. If your NGO has only a hammer, promote causal theories that portray the world as full of nails and try not to pay too close attention to what is actually getting pounded. Encouraging research on "unpounded nails" will make it easier to ignore social and political realities that look nothing like a hammer or a nail.

So far, Your NGO Starter Kit includes a global moral compass, exemplified by NGO Titans, and a modular technique, illustrated by the politics of a hungry child. Two more normative claims are needed to complete Your NGO Starter Kit: you must justify your transnational activity by claiming the authority of a *secular sanction* from global norms "above" governments, and the authority of a *representative claim* to speak for the people from "below" governments. This ability to claim authority from both above and below governments is your most powerful normative tool. As usual, these normative claims contain hidden claims about political causality.

SECULAR SANCTION

A *secular sanction* is an essential component of Your NGO Starter Kit because NGOs exercise considerable power across national borders.

They channel foreign funding, hire local educated people, select beneficiaries and intervene in their lives, and spread ideas about desirable social arrangements. NGOs need a response to the question, "By what authority do you do this?" Part of the standard NGO answer is to cite global norms that exist somewhere "above" governments; indeed, above politics itself.

Ironically, the norms said to exist above governments are most often statements and agreements made by governments themselves, speaking collectively through intergovernmental organizations. The prototype and model for secular sanctions authorizing widespread NGO action must be the Universal Declaration of Human Rights, passed as a simple resolution of the United Nations General Assembly on December 10, 1948.[25] Since World War II, whenever governmental representatives gather in groups, they tend to make grand proclamations and promises, casting governments as the engines of progress in every field. Of all these documents, the Universal Declaration of Human Rights is perhaps the one that has made the most progressive difference in people's lives.

The Universal Declaration of Human Rights is the model of a secular sanction at work. It began as an intergovernmental statement of global norms, largely ignored by many governments at home, and then slowly stimulated the mobilization of a global NGO movement to "enforce" and "implement" those norms.[26] This model has been recapitulated, and greatly accelerated, in many new issue-areas. For some issues, NGOs themselves have promoted creation of new international treaty instruments to be signed and ratified by governments, as in the recent treaties on the Rights of the Child, Land Mines, and the new International Criminal Court. On many other issues, government representatives gather in enormous world summit conferences (with NGOs lobbying on the side) to negotiate a joint statement that the NGOs can then enforce. Such statements have no legal binding force, but nevertheless exert strong policy influence. This pattern became extremely prominent during the 1990s with the Rio Earth Summit (1992), the Vienna Conference on Human Rights (1993), the Cairo Conference on Population and Development (1994), and the Beijing Conference on Women (1995).

All these strategies and issue-areas utilized a similar political symbolism, which is captured by the vertical metaphor of global norms residing above and being enforced and implemented on governments below. Behind the moral claim of secular sanction there is a hidden causal claim that the norms themselves produce a top-down *enforcement causality* that influences governments to "comply" with the global norms. International norms are efficacious, the claim asserts, producing consistent results when invoked by NGOs.

In the vertical metaphors of previous millennia, a God or gods in the heavens stood above law and government to legitimize and ultimately judge them. The common faith of the twentieth century invested instead in secular promises of material progress through politics and technology. All the major twentieth-century political movements—fascism, communism, democratic capitalism, and Third World nationalism—worshipped at different altars within the same temple of secular material progress. Twentieth-century notions of global authority—whether implemented by the League of Nations, the United Nations, or NGO networks—were made of similar secular stuff.

The claim of NGO enforcement causality attempts to persuade by analogy to domestic politics. NGOs, portrayed as enforcing and implementing global norms, are cast as the global analogs to domestic police, judges, and administrative bureaucrats in a rule-of-law democracy. Within this analogy, international treaties, UN General Assembly declarations, and global summit statements are the equivalent of laws passed by world legislative bodies.

A moment's reflection calls into question this claim of enforcement causality. First, unlike police, judges, and bureaucrats in a government under rule-of-law, NGOs are self-appointed rather than elected or appointed by higher officials. In addition, while NGOs may hold other actors to account, they themselves are relatively unaccountable to either procedural rules or outside actors. Third, unlike government enforcement agencies, NGO networks are inherently fragmented in their coverage and inconsistent in the application of norms. Finally, in most cases the "global norms" that NGOs enforce have been generated by groups of governments, many of which are themselves not accountable to their own citizens through elections or the rule of law.

The anti-globalization movement of the 1990s provides a good example of the linkages between the claims of secular sanction and enforcement causality inherent in NGO action.

DANCE OF THE RIVAL GLOBALIZERS

NGOs took on a significant new role in the late 1990s as leaders of anti-globalization campaigns and protests. "Globalization" is a complex phenomenon, but at the core it is simply the accelerating movement across national borders of goods, services, money, information, and people. International business corporations are the chief protagonists and beneficiaries of globalization, but their way is paved by agreements among governments negotiated through multilateral economic institutions. Before the movement shifted in 2003 to protesting the American-led war in Iraq, it had mainly targeted such international institutions as the World Bank, International Monetary Fund (IMF), and World Trade Organization (WTO).[27] Campaigns by NGO networks upset U.S. Senate ratification of the Convention on Biodiversity in 1994, and also sabotaged negotiations toward a Multilateral Agreement on Investment within the Organization for Economic Cooperation and Development in 1998.[28] A new wave of sometimes violent street protests drew massive media attention when the "Battle of Seattle" disrupted a WTO meeting in November 1999. Similar protests have greeted subsequent meetings in Prague, Melbourne, Gothenburg, and Quebec.

Such spectacles all appear to follow a common choreography of political theater. In the opening scene, limousines deliver officials to a world-class hotel while protestors vie for their attention. In the second scene, nonviolent protesters and rioters are engaged by police on the street, while inside the meeting officials laud the good intentions of the demonstrators and promise to address their concerns. In the final scene, the international institution redoubles its efforts to co-opt the protest movement by offering NGOs a combination of funding and institutional access to decision-making within the organization.

The tactic of street protest attracts a gaggle of invited and uninvited guests, including anarchists and opportunists whose violence is decried by other activists. In addition, there is an element of new political culture as young people express alienation from the impersonal forces of globalization. Nevertheless, the protests are not fundamentally a spontaneous flowering of a grassroots social movement. The Battle in Seattle was carefully organized for a year prior to the meeting by Global Trade Watch, an NGO linked to Ralph Nader's Public Citizen, and NGO partners in 25 other countries.[29] Behind all the protests aimed at multilateral economic institutions are conventional NGO campaigns pursuing instrumental policy goals such as Third World debt reduction, greenhouse gas limitation, increased funding to fight AIDS, and reforming the WTO.

Fundamentally, this is a contest to control the "commanding heights" of international norms, which both sides of the struggle assume are efficacious for global politics. Many of the NGO organizers view multilateral economic institutions and major governments as fronts for global corporations, together establishing "globalization from above" to benefit a narrow elite. They see their own effort as building a coalition of transnational civil society actors to form a movement of "globalization from below" representing the majority threatened by the elite project.[30]

For the sake of discussion, let us accept the broad critique of real globalization: that it benefits a tiny elite, exacerbates poverty and inequality, and is implemented through anti-democratic processes in multilateral economic institutions. Now let us raise questions that are rarely posed: What is the significance of casting NGOs as the leaders in the resistance to globalization? What are the broader consequences of this strategic choice and the lost opportunities of not pursuing other options?

We know that national governments join the WTO, in part, to tie their own hands in the face of domestic opposition to the more painful adjustments required by globalization, and that negotiations on global and regional trade agreements tend to be conducted in great secrecy. Given these anti-democratic trends, NGO opposition is better than no opposition. But there is a serious question of historical counterfactuals—what are the "roads not taken" in opposition to globalization? The international labor movement, for example, is now well past its historical high point of influence. Labor groups appear as junior partners in the NGO-led coalition. More broadly, casting NGOs as leaders in the credible opposition to globalization means that workers are represented, but not through the International Labor Organization, not in a vigorous alliance of thriving national labor movements, and not in an internationale of socialist or workers' political parties. The poor are represented as well, but not by leftist mass movements, not by their own governments, and not through resurgent religious/national movements, whether nonviolent (Poland's Solidarity) or violent (Islamic Jihad). The history of the suppression and marginalization of these alternatives is long and complex. But it is a matter of immediate observation to acknowledge that installing NGOs in the lead against globalization, rather than any of the alternatives, constitutes an historic "switching point" with profound, if not entirely foreseeable, consequences for the future. As a matter of organizational structure, any of the alternate leadership institutions recited above would be more tightly accountable to a mass constituency than are NGOs.

It seems, therefore, that NGO leadership has the effect of channeling organized and credible resistance against globalization into precisely that political arena where it will be most fragmented and most easily co-opted. If this is the case, how could it happen against the determination and good intentions of the NGO organizers?

This leads to an empirical question, which should not be ignored even though all the evidence is not yet in: To what extent can NGOs against globalization mobilize a broad social and political movement in the future? Global Trade Watch is already organizing local lobbying campaigns in congressional districts across the United States; they have a growing web of international NGO allies and one of their goals is strengthening the International Labor Organization. These initiatives may find some success. Nevertheless, preliminary evidence suggests that NGOs are unlikely to mobilize grassroots constituencies for political action *in the Third World*, where it counts.

In a rare leftist critique of the NGO bloom, James Petras argues that the net effect of NGOs is to disempower the constituencies they claim to serve.[31] NGOs, he argues:

- recruit leaders of social movements, guerrilla groups, and popular organizations into NGO positions where they are more accountable to northern donors than to local constituencies;
- co-opt the language of the left while mystifying the divisions, exploitation, and class struggle within "civil society";
- define acceptable research and marginalize perspectives that highlight class analysis;
- provide "social science intelligence" on politically volatile groups to northern donors;
- legitimize government withdrawal from responsibility for welfare; and
- depoliticize and demobilize poor people's movements.

The final charge is the most serious, because it directly contradicts the NGO claim to empower the poor. Petras reflects on his own experience, suggesting elements of an alternate research agenda on NGO influence among the poor:

Most peasant leaders from Asia and Latin America that I have spoken to complain bitterly of the divisive and elitist role that even the "progressive" NGOs play: they, the NGOs want to subordinate the peasant leaders in their organizations, they want to lead and speak "for" the poor. They do not accept subordinate roles. Progressive NGOs use peasants and the poor for their research projects, they benefit from the publication—nothing comes back to the movements not even copies of the studies done in their name! Moreover, the peasant leaders ask why the NGOs never risk their neck after their educational seminars? Why do they not study the rich and powerful—why us?[32]

Can NGOs mobilize a broad social and political movement? Or is the real effect of NGO proliferation in the Third World precisely the opposite? In a study of World Bank funding for *poblador* women's groups in urban Chile, Lucy Taylor finds that the popular movement has not been mobilized but demobilized as funding draws leadership energies from protest into self-help activities that legitimize the government's retreat from responsibility for poverty reduction.[33] This demobilization of popular protest movements, even in a political democracy such as Chile where the opportunity to organize and protest is greater than under many authoritarian regimes, may be the most important consequence of NGO proliferation. Yet it directly contradicts explicit NGO mandates and the intentions of many NGO leaders.

From the perspective of Your NGO Starter Kit, it is clear that Third World poverty is a great opportunity for NGO action. From protesting the architects of globalization at World Bank summit meetings to running World Bank-funded projects among the poorest of the poor, the field is wide open. NGOs are making themselves heard "at the table" where global norms are defined, and are making themselves useful "on the ground" implementing those norms among the poor. In addition, they may perform the added service of drawing Third World intellectuals, popular movement activists, and even guerrillas out of such dangerous and disruptive professions and into safer and more promising careers running (foreign-funded) local NGOs and advocating for the poor at international conferences. The essential qualification to be a leader in this process is the willingness to be someone else's wild card—to fudge or finesse certain contradictions within the project.

From the perspective of research on the politics of NGOs, the heavy focus on studies of NGO involvement in defining global norms is misplaced. Norms defined at global conferences in Beijing or Rio, or economic summit meetings in Seattle or Prague, will certainly be cited in NGO project proposals. However, the impact of those projects on the ground is likely to be something other than advancement of the norms articulated at the summit. The unofficial (intended or unintended) side effects of NGO action will normally be more important than either success or failure in reaching official goals. Therefore, the emphasis of research should be on the real consequences of NGO action in the field.

REPRESENTATIVE CLAIM

The final element of Your NGO Starter Kit is a *representative claim*, to complement authority from above governments with authority from below. Your NGO must plausibly claim to speak for the people (or species) at the grassroots, or to somehow serve or empower them. Your global moral compass, combined with a secular sanction derived from global norms, already tells you what the people at the grassroots really need and want (which is a big help in speaking for them). These deductive approaches must be integrated with some tactic that gives your NGO a plausible bond with the people you claim to represent. The bond may take the form of providing some direct service to the people, or collecting information about abuses of the people.

Like the other three elements of Your NGO Starter Kit, the representative claim also conceals a causal claim, in this case a claim of *empowerment causality*. According to this claim, the NGO acts, not for itself, but to express the power of the grassroots against the elites, or to empower the grassroots. The NGO offers itself to donors and partners as a surrogate for their dealing directly with the people at the grassroots. "By empowering us, you are really giving power to the people," the NGO claims. There are thousands of variations on this theme, across all issue-areas, but all successful NGOs must sound the theme.

The NGO representative claim carries profound political implications. Whatever the NGO's impact on a target population of beneficiaries, the NGO claim to represent a constituency inserts itself into a political context in which other actors seek to speak for and empower (or disempower) the same constituency. The NGO representative claim inevitably impacts the representative claims of other actors.

The NGO is a wild card, and a potentially dangerous one, in the eyes of local political actors. This insight leads to one of the few reliable verities about the effects of inserting international NGOs into Third World situations. Those other actors—governments, legal and illegal opposition groups, and interested foreign actors—will attempt to influence any NGO whose representative claim is influencing them. Typically, other actors will attempt to capture, channel, or neutralize the power of NGO representative claims. These are the terms of the contingent political contest to be fought within and around each international NGO.

To observe the political contest surrounding NGO representative claims, there is no better setting than Egypt, a society with several millennia of transnational experience.

VANGUARD ARAB CIVIL SOCIETY

Egyptian civil society is so lively because it lies between so many other societies.[34] In the words of a travel brochure, Egypt is the gateway to many worlds. Geographically, it borders Israel, controls the Suez Canal through which Persian Gulf oil reaches Europe and North America, and hosts some of the most fascinating archeological sites and coral reefs in the world. Militarily, Egypt has fought four wars with Israel, became the first Arab country to make peace with Israel in the 1979 Camp David Accords mediated by U.S. President Jimmy Carter, and has since received about a billion dollars a year in American military aid. After the 1991 Gulf War, in which a small Egyptian force joined the coalition to fight against Iraq, Egypt emerged as the militarily strongest Arab state.

Egypt is a gateway to all the other societies it engages. Gaining access through the gateway requires establishing relationships with the right people and bringing something to trade. You can get anything you want (oil through the Canal, a swim in the Red Sea, peace with Israel, Egyptian Arabs fighting Iraqi Arabs), but there is a bargaining process and it takes time. Economists, thinking one-dimensionally, call this "rent-seeking behavior." For Egyptians—heirs to 5,000 years' experience living on a narrow strip of land along the River Nile—such bargaining and negotiation are the high civilization of everyday life.

Culturally and socially, Egypt is at the same time secular Arab (with a large Christian minority), Muslim, African, and Mediterranean. It has colonial links (and resentments) vis-à-vis Turkey, France, and, most recently and palpably, Britain. Egyptian society both receives and sends powerful influences in relation to all these transnational societies. Links with American society, with significant roots from the early twentieth century, have greatly expanded since 1980. Many of those mutual societal influences are structured through NGOs, and increasingly so in recent years. Here is the politics: the multiple transnational influences, often mediated through NGOs, bargain and contend with one another within Egyptian civil society. The representative claims and latent agendas of these NGOs merge and clash in complex ways.

Egyptian civil society, in spite of the many restrictions and obstacles it imposes, is the largest, freest, most pluralistic, and most open to foreign involvement in the entire Arab world, and much of the Muslim and African worlds as well. For these reasons Egypt is widely regarded as, in effect, the *vanguard Arab civil society*, where practices and fashions can be established and then diffused to other Arab societies. If you have a social, cultural, or political project you want to advance in the Arab world, you have to be in Egypt.

Since the 1952 revolution, Egypt has been ruled by a succession of authoritarian governments under an ideology of secular Arab nationalism.[35] In this context, much political opposition is displaced from formal political institutions and seeks other means of expression, including underground Islamic militancy and Western-style human rights advocacy.[36] Both tendencies view the current government as corrupt, ineffective, and elitist. Yet they have been unable to join forces because significant sectors of each view the other as an even worse alternative than the current secular authoritarian option. Significantly, both Islamists and human rights advocates operate through NGOs.

It is here that Egyptian civil society produces some surprising politics. Most scholarship assumes that welfare and service-oriented NGOs tend to be politically benign or supportive of governmental legitimacy, while advocacy NGOs tend to challenge government legitimacy and produce social change. This distinction is used to organize research, so that most scholars study either welfare NGOs or advocacy NGOs, but not both together. The distinction is confounded by realities in Egypt, where welfare NGOs can threaten to overthrow a government, while strong advocacy NGOs can reinforce governmental legitimacy in surprising ways.

The most numerous Egyptian NGOs are Islamic welfare societies or associations, which originated in the nineteenth century and have adapted with the evolution of modern Egypt. Linked with a mosque, each society offers social services that may include schooling, skill training, day care, youth activities, and medical care. Islamic welfare associations are found in rural and urban areas, and vary greatly in size and range of services.

Local groups of the Muslim Brothers, or other more radical Islamist movements willing to employ violence, have established themselves as behind-the-scenes partners with a mosque and Islamic welfare association. In these cases, the association articulates into the public sphere a muted form of the representative claim of the Islamic political movement. In addition, the political Islamists may use the mosque and welfare association to provide jobs for activists, to recruit new members, and as a meeting place.

Indeed, even those Islamic welfare associations that are not directly linked with an Islamist political movement can reinforce the latter's cause and legitimacy. The motto of the Muslim Brothers, "Islam is the Solution," is verified in the eyes of much of the public whenever they observe an explicitly Islamic institution outperforming the secular government. The message is simple and embedded in the very existence and identity of the association. It does not have to be made explicit to be understood by the public in clear terms: *If we Islamists can operate this welfare society and treat you with honesty, competence, and compassion, then we can run the government better than the corrupt, inept, irresponsible leaders now in power.*

This scenario, in which Islamic welfare associations indirectly legitimize political Islamists, unfolded in an intense and unexpected fashion on October 12, 1992 when a devastating earthquake struck Cairo leaving hundreds dead and thousands homeless. The swift, competent response of the Islamic welfare societies to the immediate needs of earthquake victims so outshone the official government response that it became an immediate threat to the representative claim of the government.[37] The slogan "Islam is the Solution," became suddenly more believable in light of the evidence at hand. Paradoxically, the representative claim inherent in Islamic welfare associations—*as nonpolitical NGOs*—was amplified to the point that it loudly proclaimed the Islamist political challenge to the government's own claim to represent and serve the people.

Sensing their new legitimacy after the 1992 earthquake, some militant Islamist groups launched a new wave of violence which would continue through much of the 1990s. The role of foreign funding behind the welfare associations and militants was murky, but the government responded by issuing Emergency Law Decree 4 precisely to curtail such funding. The government accurately perceived that some Islamic welfare associations were wild cards through which certain domestic and foreign actors were seeking access to political power in Egypt. The government moved energetically to capture and neutralize that wild card.

In this case, the service activities of welfare NGOs challenged the government with the kind of political punch that most scholars assume to be associated only with "advocacy" NGOs. On the other side of the coin, Egypt also produces conditions under which even strong rights advocacy NGOs may serve the interests of the government at the same time as challenging them.

The human rights movement is one of the most independent and competent sectors of Egyptian civil society. Its leading activists are cosmopolitan in experience, politically savvy, intellectually sophisticated, and highly professional in their investigative and legal tactics.[38] In addition, the number of human rights NGOs, though still small, has been growing steadily since 1990. Nevertheless, their influence on government policy has been slight, whether in ameliorating specific human rights abuses or in promoting democratization.

Why does the government of Egypt permit the existence of human rights NGOs if they challenge its legitimacy? Doing so serves a cluster of subtle but cumulatively significant governmental interests. First, by permitting human rights NGOs to function in a quasi-legal fashion the government can cite their existence in response to foreign critics of their human rights record. Second, allowing them to function openly, rather than to work in secrecy underground, facilitates government intelligence and security surveillance of NGO activities. Third, by permitting the number of human rights NGOs to expand, the government ensures that a growing number of sophisticated activists with international connections are occupied in activities with manageable political impact. Fourth, it should not be forgotten that even human rights NGOs draw welcome foreign funding into the Egyptian economy. Finally, their existence indirectly demonstrates the superiority and sophistication of Egyptian civil society in comparison with other Arab societies, and confirms the image of Egypt as the vanguard of Arab civil societies. By these various subtle causal paths, strong advocacy NGOs can serve government interests even while challenging government policies and legitimacy.

A leading interpretation of "transnational advocacy networks" theorizes that local NGOs can influence their own government through a "boomerang" effect by which an international network of NGOs and governments punish the government with criticism using information and normative frames supplied by the local NGOs.[39] In

Egypt, human rights NGOs have on occasion thrown the boomerang, but the Egyptian government has been adept at manipulating the NGOs themselves in order to pull back their international partners in what might be termed a "bungie cord effect." Political power can flow in many different ways through NGOs, and which way it will flow is a matter of contingent political contention. The value and effect of a wild card is variable and unpredictable.

In mid-August 1998, two Coptic Christian men were murdered in the village of El Kosheh in rural, northern Egypt. Because the village was majority Christian, the police (who were Muslim) decided they needed a Christian suspect. They feared that accusing a Muslim would foment religious conflict, but their own actions had precisely that effect. Using investigative tactics standard throughout Egypt, the police began arresting people and torturing them for information—but they detained only Christians since they were seeking a Christian perpetrator. The local Coptic Orthodox bishop, whose protest to regional security authorities had been rebuffed, finally contacted human rights NGOs in Cairo on September 10.

A leading national human rights NGO, the Egyptian Organization for Human Rights (EOHR), sent an investigator and published a report at the end of September. The EOHR report emphasized brutal police tactics and the violation of individual citizens' rights, without painting a picture of collective religious conflict.[40] However, the Egyptian Center for Human Rights and National Unity—without conducting an investigation—immediately faxed international news offices and expatriate Coptic organizations. Some of the latter trumpeted the religious persecution angle, and a particularly inflammatory article in the British *Sunday Telegraph* angered Egyptian government leaders.[41]

Due to a lack of coordination, two Egyptian NGOs had thrown contradictory transnational "boomerangs," one framed in terms of individual citizens' rights and the other in terms of collective religious persecution. The government reacted largely against the second, asserting in the state-controlled press that there is no persecution of Christians and no police torture in Egypt.[42] In November a newspaper with close ties to the government orchestrated a smear campaign against the Secretary General of EOHR, Hafez Abu Saeda, who was detained for six days in December. Although formal charges were never filed, the government told reporters that he was accused of accepting foreign funding without official approval.[43]

The specter of imprisonment hung over Abu Saeda for more than a year, and the whole affair chilled the human rights and broader NGO communities in Egypt.[44] Allies of the human rights cause in Egypt and abroad were forced into a defensive posture, helping core NGOs to hold their positions rather than launching bold new criticisms of other human rights violations.[45] The issue of torture in El Kosheh receded to the background of debate among activists and pundits in Cairo and foreign capitals. The net effect of the arrest of Abu Saeda was to reverse the "boomerang effect" and create a "bungie cord effect" which pulled back the broader criticism of the government by the transnational advocacy network.

Ignoring the recommendation of the EOHR to hold the police accountable for torture in El Kosheh, the government conducted a belated investigation, never made the results public, and filed no charges against the police. Tragically, on January 2, 2000, the village was beset by precisely the kind of sectarian violence that the government said could never happen, yet had desperately sought to avoid. At the end of that day, 23 people were dead, including 20 Christians.[46]

To keep the international human rights network in a defensive posture, the Egyptian government harasses at least one prominent activist at all times. Three months after Hafez Abu Saeda was cleared, Saad Eddin Ibrahim, director of the Ibn Khaldun Center and promoter of democracy, was arrested and charged with accepting unauthorized funds from the European Union. In May 2001 he was found guilty and sentenced to seven years' hard labor. After a retrial and significant international pressure, Ibrahim was cleared of all charges in March 2003. Yet since his acquittal he has been targeted by a campaign of character assassination in the government-controlled press.[47]

The structure of relations between Egypt and other countries, Western and Arab, is such that Egyptian human rights NGOs can be made to act as a bungie cord, pulling and holding back their transnational network partners from criticizing the government, rather than as wielders of a boomerang that comes around to strike the government through the transnational network. At stake for international partners in the human rights network is not only the future of Egypt's human rights movement, but also the ramifications for the broader Arab world. Events in Egypt—the vanguard Arab civil society—reverberate far beyond its borders.

International advocates of democracy, human rights, or even Islamic theocracy, as well as powerful governments including the

United States, Britain, France, and Saudi Arabia, all want to influence Egyptian civil society. They all seek NGO allies in Egypt, provide funding, and export visions and models. They attach their own latent agendas to the representative claims of different NGOs. The stakes for Egyptian civil society have only increased since President George W. Bush announced in 2003 that democratizing the Arab world was a major goal of American foreign policy.

The broad lesson is that the real consequences of NGO action are determined less by the external distinction between advocacy and service NGOs, and more by local struggles to capture, deploy against others, or neutralize the political impact of NGO operations, whatever they may be. Since both welfare and advocacy NGOs make representative claims, it should not be surprising that the claims of either type may clash or merge with governmental representative claims under different conditions.

To sum up, Your NGO Starter Kit includes four normative claims, to which you should draw as much attention as possible. Unavoidably, each normative claim comes with a somewhat awkward causal claim about how the world works. Your *global moral compass* asserts your confidence to make moral and practical judgments anywhere in the world, but it depends on the veiled claim of *circumscribed causality*— that the causality of both the problem and the NGO solution can reliably be isolated from local social and political contexts. Your *modular technique* is a set of practices that your NGO can bring to bear anywhere in the world to create a self-evidently positive impact on the problem, but it depends on the veiled claim of *magic bullet causality*—that the technique will influence only the problem at which it is aimed. Your NGO's *secular sanction* invokes the moral authority of global norms above governments to justify action, but relies on the hidden claim of *enforcement causality*—that global norms create consistent results everywhere (rather than contingent wild card results that depend on local politics). Finally, your *representative claim* casts your NGO as acting "for the people" with moral authority originating below governments. However, this relies upon another, often unspoken, claim of *empowerment causality*—that NGOs actually mobilize the power of those they claim to represent.

For the sake of getting your new NGO off the ground, remember that NGO causal claims can rarely withstand serious scrutiny. The most effective means to prevent researchers from exposing the messy variations in NGO impacts is to frame their research in terms of the conventional premises of the NGO world. The analytical distinction between international and grassroots NGOs often obscures the influence of the international foundations and donors. The distinctions between issue-areas hide the inadvertent side effects of NGO action on local politics and society. The distinction between advocacy and service NGOs can distract attention from the political uses to which other actors can put NGOs. Whenever possible, send scholars to listen to governments and NGOs moralizing at global conferences (in Rio, Beijing, Vienna, or Copenhagen, etc.), but do not encourage them to do field research on the actual effects of NGO operations.

But what is really going on under these layers of misleading claims and illusory research premises? What are NGOs really doing and with what effects? As already discussed, the first two causal claims (circumscribed and magic bullet causality) serve to hide the *politics* of NGOs and networks. In addition, the second pair of causal claims (enforcement and empowerment causality) generate an illusion of general, uniform progress that conceals the remarkable *particularity* of each local situation, and often obscures the genius of singular NGO responses in the particular historical moment.

To understand NGOs in world politics requires a new theoretical approach to illuminate both the politics and the particularity of NGO action.

Table 1.1   Your NGO Starter Kit

Explicit Normative Claim	Global moral compass	Modular technique	Secular sanction	Representative claim
Implicit Causal Claim	Circumscribed causality	Magic bullet causality	Enforcement causality	Empowerment causality
Illusory Research Premise	Distinction between international and grassroots NGOs	Distinction between issue-areas	Focus on global norms created in treaties and international conferences	Distinction between advocacy and service NGOs

2

Partners in Conflict:
A Structural Theory of NGOs

THE NGO BLOOM

World politics has seen a proliferation of NGOs throughout the twentieth century, with an accelerated burst of growth during the 1990s.[1] Currently, the NGO bloom has three dimensions. First, NGOs are proliferating quantitatively in established issue-areas, including human rights, grassroots development, humanitarian relief, environmental protection, feminism, population control, conflict resolution and prevention, and democratization.[2] Second, the increase in NGO numbers is a global phenomenon affecting all regions, even Asia and the Middle East where governments have maintained relatively tight control over civil society for decades.[3] Third, NGOs are also proliferating qualitatively, by taking the initiative to colonize or create new issues where hitherto they have exerted limited influence. The NGO bloom, in all its dimensions, constitutes a problem for government policymakers everywhere, because the very presence of NGOs alters the context for government policy.

The NGO bloom is not only a problem for policymakers. It is also an unsolved puzzle for scholars of international relations. It is curious that ringing endorsements of the growing influence of NGOs in world politics emanate from widely distant points on the ideological spectrum. From the right, neoconservatives praise NGOs for taking over many of the functions of shrinking government bureaucracies. From the moderate left, political liberals laud NGOs as a democratizing force, holding governments accountable by representing societal rights. Farther left, some radicals look to NGOs to incubate a counter-hegemonic project that could eventually yield revolutionary change.[4] These interpretations foresee mutually contradictory political consequences from the same NGO bloom. All three interpretations share a tendency to extrapolate from extremely modest NGO achievements today to messianically ambitious political goals far in the future. This set of puzzles, and others, remain largely opaque to the current literature on NGOs in world politics. Available theoretical tools fail to capture important dimensions of the current NGO bloom.

THINKING ABOUT NGOs

The prominence of NGOs in the field of International Relations has ebbed and flowed with changing international events and academic fashions. The discipline of International Relations has been called an "American social science" which emerged in the 1940s when the United States committed itself to continuous global engagement.[5] Studies of NGOs have usually found their place on the periphery of the discipline, confined largely to academic ghettos with specialized journals that appeal to the policy concerns of relatively narrow constituencies.

Prior to the 1990s, serious consideration of the broader significance of NGOs has surfaced only once within the central theoretical debates of International Relations.[6] The 1970s literature on "transnational relations" gained popularity among graduate students and young scholars in response to a combination of factors: the decline of security threats with the withdrawal of the United States from Vietnam and a period of relaxation in the Cold War; the rise of economic threats with the 1971 breakdown of the Bretton Woods monetary system and the 1973 oil crisis; and the spread of counter-cultural trends after the transnational student protests of 1968 and the advent of broad human rights and environmental movements. As quickly as it had appeared, transnationalism disappeared from the central theoretical debates of the discipline during the 1980s when security threats returned to the foreground of international affairs.[7]

The first transnationalism of the 1970s broke new ground, but its usefulness for the empirical study of NGOs was limited. John Burton's world society approach concentrated on transnational processes and transactions, particularly communication links, and not on actors such as NGOs. Harold Jacobson viewed NGOs as auxiliaries to inter-governmental organizations like the United Nations and European Community. Robert Keohane and Joseph Nye, as well as Richard Mansbach and his collaborators, cast a broad net to encompass multinational corporations, religious communities, and revolutionary movements, devoting relatively little attention to NGOs themselves. Indeed, Peter Willetts published his 1982 edited volume, *Pressure Groups in the Global System*, "in reaction against the omission of non-economic groups by Keohane and Nye."[8] Keohane and Nye themselves later subsumed transnational relations under their broader theory of interdependence, which was more state-centered.[9] For all these reasons, 1970s transnationalism failed to spawn a sustained agenda of theoretically informed empirical research on NGOs in world politics.

Real NGOs continued to burrow into the nooks and crannies of world politics whether or not scholars paid any attention. Finally, in the early 1990s, NGOs became impossible to ignore, and the decline of security threats made it possible for scholars to see them. "Civil society" actors, including NGOs, were implicated in both the wave of democratization that washed over southern Europe and Latin America and also the peaceful end of the Cold War. For a few years in the early 1990s, almost anything seemed possible. Human rights NGOs promoted humanitarian military intervention in Bosnia and Somalia (see chapter 5). Tens of thousands of NGOs teamed up with the United Nations to change the world by networking and writing statements at a series of world conferences (see chapter 6).

The NGO bloom of the 1990s has been matched by a burgeoning literature on the influence of NGOs and nonstate actors in world politics. This new literature can be viewed as falling into three major schools: pluralist, globalist, and realist. While specific studies often employ a combination of viewpoints, the three frameworks are described here as logically distinct in order to emphasize the conceptual consistency of each school.[10]

In the *pluralist* school, NGOs are understood as the articulate and organized element of civil society, acting largely independently of government.[11] The pluralist view offers a range of variations, portraying NGOs as servants of the poor in grassroots development, or prophetic voices of the voiceless lobbying governments and the UN, or transnational pilgrims in an emancipatory passage from oppressive rule to self-regulating community. Ironically, these secular images derive from biblical narratives in the Hebrew scriptures, particularly the Book of Exodus and the prophets Isaiah and Amos. Such stories of sacred providence, mutated into narratives of secular progress, continue to resonate in Western culture and diffuse into cosmopolitan global culture. This is no accident. The eighteenth- and nineteenth-century predecessors of today's NGOs, beginning with the anti-slavery movement, emerged from communities of Protestant Christians who drew inspiration from the Jewish Covenant (see chapter 3).

It is no secret that many scholars who gravitate to NGOs as a topic of study tend to be personally sympathetic toward the norms and goals embodied by the organizations. As a consequence, much NGO scholarship follows pluralist interpretations. Pluralist theory reiterates in abstract terms the representative claims made by NGOs themselves. From the point of view of scholarship this is both a benefit and a bane—a benefit because pluralist interpretations recognize the importance of transnational NGO partnerships and autonomous tactical choice; and a bane because the pluralist causal narrative truncates the full range of NGO politics, highlighting only the single axis of political conflict between society and state.

For the pluralist school, the cumulative impact of the recent NGO bloom is to democratize world politics through NGOs speaking truth to power on behalf of civil society. This image of civil society challenging the state is applied to studies of varying empirical scope. For Africa, Asia, and the Middle East where democratization seems to be lagging behind, regional specialists produce literatures on the potential of civil society as a catalyst for change.[12] In the society/state drama, the role of society may be assigned to NGOs in a single country, or transnational civil society among several countries, or global civil society. The role of state may be played by a single government, the United States as global hegemon, or an organ of the United Nations.[13]

When NGO researchers mention "sovereignty," they often argue that NGOs are subduing, transcending, contesting, or moving beyond it, or that it is declining on its own. The metaphor may echo Marx on the withering away of the state, but it can be deployed for a wide range of political causes, including class solidarity against global capitalism, international cooperation to solve global problems, and humanitarian military intervention (usually by a major military power whose sovereignty is decidedly not declining) against Third World dictators and warlords.[14] Whatever the political project, the language of subduing sovereignty indicates a pluralist narrative by evoking the imagery of a society emancipating itself from oppression like the Exodus of the Israelites from Egypt.

The theme of emancipation entices the attention of the political left to the NGO world.[15] Both NGO networks and NGO scholarship have an extraordinary capacity to absorb and tame challenges from the radical left, yet some of the most trenchant critiques of this very process emanate from scholars on the left.[16]

If power erupts from the bottom up in pluralist imagery, it flows from the top down in *globalist* accounts. Global norms are "implemented" or "enforced" by NGOs collecting information on norm compliance by states, multinational corporations, and other actors.[17] The imputation of supranational authority to global norms entails an assumption that elements of world government, or at least governance, are emerging above states. Globalist policy analysis is written as if the United Nations were becoming a unitary bureaucracy pursuing rational policy objectives for the sake of global human interests. Under these assumptions, NGOs are the UN's extension agents or Texas Rangers bringing authority and order to the hinterland. Globalism portrays NGOs as rather passively implementing and enforcing the global norms that emanate from UN organs and multilateral agreements.[18] Global norms are the cause, while NGOs are the passive channels. Globalist accounts reiterate in abstract theory the claim of moral authority from above governments that is part of every NGO's self-understanding.

When the United Nations convenes a global conference on an issue deemed to be a global problem, typically the meeting of government representatives is paralleled by a simultaneous conference of NGOs from around the world.[19] Participants in these meetings, and many scholars as well, often portray the parallel NGO conference as the "lower house" whose members represent and speak for global civil society, to complement the "upper house" of official governmental delegations. The implication of this representative claim is that governments and NGOs together constitute a kind of inchoate world parliament.

Globalism views NGOs through the lens of UN institutional interests and reiterates the discourse of UN multilateralism. In this New York view, NGOs may be useful to fill the enforcement gap in multilateral agreements and to lend legitimacy to the UN itself, and NGOs may be criticized according to the same criteria. Globalism is concerned primarily with the politics of building normative consensus within multilateral fora, and secondarily with the politics of enforcing that normative consensus on the recalcitrant subjects of global authority. Empirical studies in the globalist school highlight these two axes of politics. The cumulative impact of the rise of NGOs, in the globalist view, should be to rationalize world politics according to global norms. While this view ignores much of NGO politics, it does call attention to the links between the credibility of norms articulated by governments in international organizations and the moral authority asserted by NGOs.

Both pluralism and globalism take as their nemesis political *realism*, which tends to dismiss the influence of NGOs by arguing that they address issues with which states are not concerned, or that they are political epiphenomena acting on behalf of state interests. For hardline realists, neither NGOs nor other international institutions produce any significant impact on world politics.[20] As a consequence to this position, thoroughgoing realism generates little research on NGOs.

Realism's language of national interests reiterates the discourse of states, and the dismissal of NGO influence preserves the notion that states are the most important actors on the world stage. Ironically, both realism and globalism share the assumption that NGOs are passive channels of causal forces—either state interests or global norms—that originate beyond NGOs themselves.

The politics of NGOs is far too complex and abundant to be contained in any one of these schools, but each one contributes valuable insights that should be retained. Pluralism recognizes the importance of societal partners and NGO tactical choice; globalism points to the influence of international norms and institutions; while realism acknowledges the pervasiveness of political conflict and the likelihood of inadvertent negative consequences from political action.[21]

As an adequate response to the NGO theory deficit, neither eclecticism nor a simple synthesis of the three schools will do. Each of the three leading approaches prejudges the politics of NGOs in a restrictive way that blinds scholars to the complexity of NGO power. Realists prejudge that NGO power is insignificant compared to the power of states; pluralists that NGO power flows from societies upward to states; globalists that it flows from international norms downward to states. To take politics seriously, a workable NGO theory ought to challenge researchers to discover the variable and particular patterns of power relations without predetermining the findings.

No one can study all NGOs at once. But scholars prejudge the politics of NGOs most profoundly, and most invisibly, when they demarcate empirical research according to conventional distinctions adopted uncritically from the world of NGOs and their funders. Pluralist and globalist studies almost invariably demarcate their empirical scope by following one or more of these conventional distinctions—between issue-areas, between advocacy and service NGOs, between international and grassroots NGOs, and between the global conferences that define supranational norms and the NGOs that enforce them (see chapter 1).

Simply by using these distinctions uncritically, scholars commit themselves to accepting the universal moral and causal claims of NGOs themselves. All NGOs claim to know what should be done anywhere in the world on their issues and to possess the technique and moral authority to do it, regardless of local political and social conditions. To accept these claims, which are implicit in the four distinctions above, is to shroud from view precisely the kinds of evidence of variable, local consequences that would challenge the universalist premises of pluralist and globalist NGO theory. The consequences of NGO global operations cannot be known from headquarters. NGOs are wild cards—they may be dealt normatively, but they are played politically.

What is needed is a new theory that is conceptually independent of the social actors that it analyses, that cuts across issue-areas and other conventional distinctions that distract attention from the political impact of NGOs, and that directs empirical attention to the variable and particular consequences of NGO action.

A STRUCTURAL THEORY OF NGOs

Among the conventional views of pluralists, globalists, and realists, John Boli and George Thomas with their collaborators have pursued a line of NGO research that is unique unto itself.[22] Applying insights from historical sociology, they portray international NGOs across a wide range of issues as powerful "enactors and carriers of world culture" since the late nineteenth century. Their arguments bear superficial similarities to globalist accounts, since both approaches identify international norms that exist above states and shape state practice. For globalists, however, norms guide actors by constraining and channeling their behavior from the outside. Boli and Thomas go much farther, arguing that NGOs create the archetypes and principles of "world culture," which in turn constitute actors and purposes, not merely constrain them. In short, world culture shapes governments, societies, and individual persons into particular forms.

In a critical contribution, the sociological approach of Boli and Thomas identifies the *structural* path of NGO influence. In this view the most significant impact of NGOs is indirect, influencing the social and material structure of the international system, which in turn shapes much more powerful actors. However, there are three weaknesses in the historical sociology approach to NGOs. First, it omits nearly all sense of political process from the story of NGOs. The hallmarks of a political story are rivalry, loyalty, and tactical choice—who did what to whom, when, where, and how? Second, the sociological approach lacks any sense of irony, ignoring the inadvertent consequences and hidden agendas that are pervasive in the NGO world. Third, the structural path of NGO influence operates not only at the world macro-level, as Boli and Thomas acknowledge, but also at the mid-level of regions and countries, and the micro-level of the individual NGO.

This chapter proposes a theory of NGOs that is both structural and political, that can generate an open-ended empirical research agenda, and that seeks to incorporate what is best in the pluralist, globalist, realist, and sociological schools while overcoming their weaknesses.

This chapter also avoids wading into arcane social theory.[23] Nevertheless, it should not be forgotten that political action is also social action. And if the human animal is "suspended in webs of significance he himself has spun," as Clifford Geertz suggests, then the challenge of describing social action is to account for both the spinning and the suspending.[24]

The beams of this structural theory are seven propositions, which respond to three basic questions:

- What are NGOs?
- What do NGOs do?
- What difference do NGOs make in world politics?

WHAT ARE NGOs?

Proposition #1: NGOs are private actors pursuing public purposes

If business firms are private actors pursuing private profit, and governments are public actors pursuing public purposes, then NGOs have one foot in each camp. As private actors, NGOs do not seek to control the levers of public power. Therefore, they neither organize for elections like political parties, nor use violence to seize power like terrorists and insurgents. In contrast to firms, NGOs do not pursue the private profit of their owners or shareholders. Instead, they articulate and claim to serve a broad, public purpose based on universal human (or species) rights and needs.

The simplicity and clarity of this definition is useful precisely to highlight the controversy and ambiguity of much NGO practice. What counts as a "private actor" and what is acceptable as a legitimate "public purpose" are contested questions that change over time and differ between societies.[25] Part of the empirical task is to map this variety and contestation.

By their very contestability, NGO private identities and public mandates attract political actors seeking to give veiled expression to political projects. At the extreme, the ostensibly private identity of an NGO may be a front for government action. In the development field, government-organized NGOs, known as GONGOs, have been created by recipient governments to receive foreign grants, and by donor governments to conduct sensitive operations.[26] These are really public actors posing as private. NGO public mandates are subject to an analogous form of outright fraud in the practice of "greenscamming," by which mining and forestry corporations create pro-industry NGOs to challenge environmental NGOs on their own normative ground, as putative representatives of civil society.[27] In greenscamming, a private purpose clothes itself as public—business-organized NGOs, or BONGOs, engage in NGO puppetry attempting to capture some of the aura of NGO moral authority.

This moral authority is rooted in the public purpose that every NGO must claim to serve. The public purpose is a normative mandate through which each NGO asserts a *representational claim* to serve the needs and rights of a particular population. Mainstream theory takes this representational claim as unproblematic, realists by reducing it to an epiphenomenon of state interests, and pluralists and globalists by accepting it at face value. The reality is more complex.

All NGOs are the unelected envoys of civil society. NGO representational claims can clash or mesh with each other and with authority claims by other actors. This elementary observation generates profound implications for empirical research in the wide range of political contexts in which NGOs operate.

For example, because NGOs articulate plausible but contestable representational claims they may pose a particularly acute threat to authoritarian governments whose own claims to represent their citizens are weak.[28] The result is predictable—authoritarian governments with the means to do so attempt either to co-opt or to cripple all NGOs that operate within their territory.

Internal conflicts are another context in which NGO representative claims are guaranteed to be controversial. Where political or military opposition groups challenge a government, each side also articulates a rival representational claim as part of its political program. These adversaries tend to view NGOs as prizes to capture or threats to suppress. The government of Turkey, for example, perceiving Islamic welfare associations as nodes of political opposition, banned them from providing relief to victims of the 1999 earthquake.[29] In the scenario of violent internal conflict, the stakes of NGO alignment are higher and more hotly contested.[30]

Empirical questions

- Who claims to be a private actor, and to serve what legitimate public purpose?
- How do NGO claims mesh or clash with the representative claims of other actors?

WHAT DO NGOs DO?

Proposition #2: NGOs bind themselves to societal and political partners in several countries, and are constituted by their partners

Because NGOs neither produce wealth nor wield military force, they are weak in both productive and destructive power—two of Kenneth Boulding's "three faces of power."[31] If power is based exclusively on material resources, then NGOs as a class are the weakest actors in world politics. However, they have a distinct advantage in Boulding's third face of "integrative" power. NGOs are the most well-connected actors in world politics, with links to societal and political partners in several countries. Large development and environmental NGOs operate in many tens of countries simultaneously, maintaining governmental and societal partners in each. Amnesty International and Human Rights Watch monitor human rights globally, obtaining sensitive information about the societies and governments of virtually every country in the world.

The interest here is primarily with international NGOs that operate along a North–South axis. Their headquarters, funding, leadership, and social base are typically located in the developed, capitalist democracies, while their activities are designed to influence populations in the Third World and former communist world. This is rarely an equal relationship, in spite of the language of partnership. NGOs whose headquarters are based in Washington, New York,

London, or Paris enjoy a relative abundance of funding, expertise, technology, and access to political power.

Links with partners are not simply given; they must be created and sustained through energetic action. For international humanitarian relief and human rights NGOs, the most important link is access to the victims of disaster and conflict. Access is crucial, whether the goal is to export information about the victims of human rights abuse or to import material aid to the victims of famine.[32]

To observe that NGOs depend on their partners does not fully capture the nature of the relationship. A more penetrating insight is that NGOs are constituted by their partners. Without crucial partners a particular NGO would cease to exist or become something else. If Amnesty International were to be banned by the British government, to lose its worldwide membership, alienate core activists, or forfeit the trust of informants who convey information on human rights victims, it would disappear or be transformed into another NGO. The general point is that NGOs are constituted by their principled mandates *and* crucial partners, and perhaps primarily by their partners.

The argument here is *structural at the micro-level*; each NGO is constituted by its immediate operational environment (structure), which consists of essential partners. This claim is more than semantic; it generates distinctive criteria for empirical investigation and research design. For example, whereas a pluralist approach might find nothing objectionable about a profile of a single NGO based exclusively on research at the organization's headquarters, this structural approach demands field research and independent assessment of NGO partners in several countries. A structural research design at the micro-level might compare several NGOs with similar normative mandates operating in the same political context, but with different societal partners.

NGO societal partners are as important, and as constitutive, as political partners. This is a rich and relatively underdeveloped field for empirical research. NGO professional staffs are often recruited from an identifiable societal group, such as a religious faith, a particular ideological tendency, or even an ethnic group. Some NGOs are the organizational expressions of transnational social movements.[33] In parts of Africa during the 1990s, internationally funded NGOs became the single largest source of middle-class jobs at a time when government bureaucracies were downsizing.[34] In Guatemala during the 1980s, some prestigious NGOs with international donors were staffed largely by Guatemalan *blancos*—light-skinned, upper-class descendants of Spanish colonialists.[35] Hence, an NGO societal partner may be a socio-economic class or ethnic group.

Pluralist theory takes NGO links to civil society as given, and not subject to empirical investigation. In contrast, this proposition suggests that NGOs are at least as much partner-driven as principle-driven. This is not only a matter of partner funding, but also a question of loyalty between societal partners. The implication for research is that the journalist's dictum, "Follow the money," should be augmented by the counsel, "Follow the partners."

The most important consequence of bonds cemented by an international NGO between its societal and political partners may not be the achievement of goals defined in the mandate. Whether or not they protect human rights, feed starving people, or promote grassroots development, NGOs do succeed in linking hundreds of societies and governments and other political organizations that would otherwise not be linked. These connections may be made to serve other purposes, and their existence may generate inadvertent consequences intended by no one.

Empirical questions

- Who are the societal and political partners—local and remote, acknowledged and unacknowledged—of an NGO, and how does it reflect the connection to each partner?

Proposition #3: NGOs carry and channel partner latent agendas, becoming institutional sites of both cooperation and conflict between partners

It is not enough merely to assert that NGOs are constituted by their partners. One wants to understand in some detail how this happens. This proposition suggests part of the answer. Partners constitute NGOs by attaching their latent (hidden) agendas to NGO operations. One partner's latent agenda may either mesh or clash with the NGO's salient, official agenda, and with the latent agendas of other partners. Indeed, what international NGOs may do best, whether or not they accomplish official goals, is to carry the contradictory latent agendas of societal and political partners in several countries. In short, each NGO is a bundle of these contradictions. *Each NGO is an institutional site of dynamic cooperation and conflict among its partners.* This is a more profound dimension of a structural theory of NGOs at the micro-level.

It would be unwise to attempt to construct a systematic taxonomy of NGO partners abstracted from any particular setting. The only stable patterns are that NGOs create partnerships and that NGOs are constituted by their partners. Who the partners are, and what they seek from the relationship, are dynamic and malleable. It is precisely this plasticity that makes NGOs so attractive to partners.

Traditional NGO partners have included governments, societal groups and UN organizations. Only in the 1980s did armed insurgents and terrorists become legitimate partners for relief and development NGOs.[36] In conditions of state collapse, particularly in Africa since 1990, the ranks of NGO partners have been joined by multinational corporations, warlords, private security companies, and mercenaries.[37] Some NGOs and foundations working in Russia since the mid-1990s have been forced to negotiate with organized crime entities for security guarantees.[38]

To raise these examples is to suggest the range of possible research on NGOs as sites of dynamic conflict and cooperation among their partners.

The concept of a latent agenda presupposes that most NGO partners bring to the relationship motives other than support for the official mission of the organization. Agendas remain latent to the extent that they do not negate or overwhelm the salient agenda that is articulated in the official NGO mandate.[39] It is the rule rather than the exception, however, that partners attempt to attach latent agendas to NGO operations. More to the point, to carry partner latent agendas is intrinsic to what NGOs do, not accidental. It is constitutive of international NGO work. This claim is profoundly at odds with NGO self-description and with all the schools of NGO scholarship.

A few caveats are in order to respond to the concern that this line of reasoning could be used to legitimize nationalist accusations against responsible NGOs as being "tools of hostile foreign powers." It is easy to overestimate the impact of NGO latent agendas, to exaggerate their importance to the point that every NGO is viewed as the front for an international conspiracy. Latent agendas are not necessarily contradictory to salient NGO mandates, but may be merely collateral to them. Among societal groups, for example, many religious communities find that the repertoire of normative and organizational options available within the NGO sphere offers a rich grammar for expressing their beliefs in muted form, drawing attention to their existence, building transnational solidarity among members, and promoting acceptance of their presence in hostile environments.[40]

By the same token, many of the political agendas attached by states are quite benign. For example, several West European governments fund development NGOs in regions of the world where they have little diplomatic or commercial activity as an affordable means to extend an international presence.[41]

The reality is that NGOs are everyone's second or third choice for pursuing international goals. Religious groups would rather proselytize for new members than run welfare agencies. Human rights activists would rather arrest, prosecute, and punish violators than publish impotent reports. Authoritarian elites would rather repress without international scrutiny than allow NGOs to publish accounts of their indiscriminate violence. By operating through NGOs, most partners have already significantly compromised their maximal agenda. Hence, the latent agendas attached to NGOs are often diluted versions of partners' real interests. The political content is thinned. In addition, one partner's latent agenda may be opposed, and effectively neutralized, by the latent agendas of other partners. In particular, the societal bonds and personal loyalties of NGO professionals account for much of the recalcitrance of NGOs as tools of political partners.[42]

To view partner latent agendas solely as a threat to the purity of NGO missions is to misunderstand the contradictory nature of the relationship. An NGO that carries no latent agenda is one that makes a negligible impact, because it has little money, few projects, and difficulty recruiting staff. Smart NGO professionals develop complex scripts for playing off one partner against another, and using partner latent agendas to fuel the NGO salient mission. In short, partner latent agendas put the "GO" in NGO.

Partners contribute distinct forms of essential organizational capital to each NGO. Societal partners *embody* the airy principles of NGO salient agendas by providing a pool of potential staff members and helping to set country mission priorities. Political partners *empower* NGO salient agendas by granting access to beneficiaries, providing funding, and facilitating field operations. By embodying and empowering NGO operations, partners give substance and shape to the abstract principles of NGO salient missions.

NGOs have the remarkable ability to partner mutual enemies. One of the clearest examples of this was the famine relief operation to the Soviet Union from 1921 to 1923 undertaken by a cluster of American NGOs with funding from the U.S. government. Among the several latent agendas of the United States, the operation succeeded in creating a positive image of the United States among Soviet citizens, and in raising agriculture prices at home by distributing surplus grain, but it failed to spur change in the young Soviet system toward a more liberal economy. On the Soviet side, Lenin used the operation successfully to pacify a starving and potentially rebellious population, but failed to gain diplomatic recognition and trade agreements from the U.S.[43]

The NGOs in this case can be understood as having used the latent agendas of the two governments to empower their own goal of feeding the hungry. The two governments cooperated at the level of famine relief, but competed at the level of their latent agendas. Therefore, each American NGO that operated in Russia can be understood as having institutionalized both international cooperation and international conflict.

This entire discussion of partner latent agendas implies an unconventional perspective on NGO professionalism and ethics. To jettison all partners that attach latent agendas would disembody and disempower the NGO mission; NGO professionals know that to hold crucial partners they must serve latent agendas. By the same token, to allow any latent agenda to spill over and "drown" the salient mission would eventually cripple the organization. Either extreme is unprofessional and unethical. NGO professionalism is found precisely in balancing competing values in a setting of low formal accountability. Indeed, the weak accountability of international NGOs is one of the sources of their widely praised capacity for flexibility and innovation. Measures to tighten NGO accountability are likely to reduce the space for innovation; conversely, steps to promote innovation are likely to broaden the scope for incompetence and abuse.

Empirical questions

- What are the latent agendas of each NGO partner, and how do latent agendas mesh or clash with each other and with the official, salient agenda of the NGO?
- Which latent agendas are achieved, which thwarted, and to what extent?
- How is the merging and clashing of partner latent agendas reflected in the organization, operations, and culture of the NGO?

Proposition #4: NGOs enjoy operational autonomy from their partners

The argument at this stage brings the agency dimension of NGO action back into balance with the structural dimension. The fact that any international NGO must sustain multiple partnerships merely to survive would seem to constrain its freedom of action. Paradoxically, the necessity to hold multiple partners grants the organization a high degree of tactical autonomy vis-à-vis each partner. By defecting, crucial partners can kill the operation; however, each partner is restrained from defecting precisely by the latent agendas it hopes to attach to, and achieve through, the NGO. NGO professionals use their central position in this configuration of relationships to play off partners against each other.

External accountability for international NGOs is inherently diffuse, spread among multiple constituencies and their multiple agendas.[44] Even internal accountability relies heavily on the discretion of organizational staff. Where board members and donors (private or public) reside in one country, while the beneficiaries live in another, NGO staff gain considerable autonomy because they control the flow of information between the two arenas.

The combination of the autonomy of professional staff within the organization and the autonomy of the organization vis-à-vis powerful partners is the source of the much-lauded flexibility and innovative capacity of NGOs in all fields. This usually refers to the capacity for NGOs to accomplish their mandates with less red tape and at lower cost than government or IGO alternatives. However, NGOs also possess extra-mandate forms of flexibility that they do not advertise. They can bend or suspend the official mandate in order to hold a crucial partner. They can forge new norms and embrace new partners "on the fly" as they compete for an operational niche in a new crisis or issue.

When governments do not know what else to do concerning a region or issue, they are tempted to "throw NGOs at the problem." NGOs are inexpensive, they maintain a flow of information to donors, their failures are more easily disavowed than those committed by official government agencies, and their successes may map new government policy options. In short, NGOs do not have to be successful in accomplishing their official mandates in order to be considered useful by governments. U.S. foreign policy toward the most peripheral regions of the Third World in the 1990s, especially sub-Saharan Africa after the Somalia misadventure of 1993, has placed

NGOs in the "front line" precisely as an alternative to either serious engagement or complete withdrawal.[45]

Empirical questions

- How and to what extent do NGO leaders achieve tactical flexibility and operational autonomy from their partners, and with what results?
- Conversely, how and to what extent do key partners control NGO tactics, and with what results?

WHAT DIFFERENCE DO NGOs MAKE IN WORLD POLITICS?

Proposition #5: NGOs make networks, which facilitate the transnational movement of norms, resources, political responsibility, and information

Wherever international NGOs operate in significant numbers, they generate complex networks of relationships between political and societal actors in many countries. Networks, as understood here, begin to form when NGOs share *any common partners*. Since NGOs create societal and political partnerships in their normal operations, they make networks willy-nilly. Overlapping clusters of NGO partners inevitably grow into larger webs of relationships. This unconventional definition does not require that network members campaign together for a common goal or share normative values as in pluralist and globalist theories, nor even that they work within related issue-areas. The point of defining the network in terms of common partners is to emphasize that network relationships exist independently of their mobilization through a particular normative frame for a particular political impact. Once the relationships are in place, their *potential* utility becomes part of the context for political choice by all actors on the scene. NGOs and their networks are wild cards on the table in a political game, with the political players looking on.

In addition to local and international NGOs, network members may include parts of governments, UN agencies, regional intergovernmental organizations, foundations, scholars, religious communities, professional associations, journalists, and even warlords and private corporations. This is not a comprehensive list, because any new NGO partner, by definition, joins the networks of which the NGO is a part. Given this extraordinary breadth of membership, empirical study of networks demands extensive field research, typically conducted on several continents, but rewards the effort by illuminating more of the complex politics of NGOs than is revealed by either narrow NGO profiles or diffuse analyses of global civil society.

At a more abstract level, networks can be analyzed as a distinct organizational form possessing extraordinary capacities for innovating tactics, managing risk, gathering information, and an ability "to flow around physical barriers and across legal or geographical boundaries."[46] With these capacities, networks have proven useful for endeavors as diverse as international business, transnational organized crime, and international terrorism.[47] Consistent with networks in these other realms, NGO network interactions tend to be informal, non-binding, temporary, and highly personalized.

Whether an NGO network is large or small, four kinds of factors can move along its relational channels: normative frames, material resources, political responsibility, and information. In other words, NGO networks are normative, distributive, obligative, and communicative.

The norms articulated in NGO mandates testify to a world that does not exist, but some day may come to be. The norms do not make the utopian vision happen, and the gap is usually quite large between the humble steps undertaken by NGOs and the ambitious goals articulated in their mandates. In this sense the norms are weak—they pull actors from the future rather than push them compellingly in the present. The power of NGO norms flows proleptically from an imaginary future backward into the present. And it is real power. As Marx understood, if you can convince someone in what direction the train of history is headed and then issue him a ticket, you have profoundly oriented his political imagination and aspirations.

Under the umbrella of these aspirations for an imaginary future, partnerships are formed between actors that could not cooperate in any other way. Therefore, one power of norms in networks is constitutive, to form relationships that would otherwise not exist. If the network fails to achieve the aspirations, nevertheless the aspirations create the network. The dream of comprehensive economic development in the Third World has not been powerful enough to raise the living standards of the poorest of the world's population, but it has been powerful enough to create an intricate latticework of NGO-mediated relationships between societies and governments in the north and south. That is an impressive achievement, if an inadvertent and morally ambiguous one. To what use will those transnational relationships be put in the future?

It is in this sense that NGOs are the constitutive actors of networks: no NGOs, no network. This is a *structural approach at the mid-level*. Without NGOs, the other actors with the potential to participate in a network may be present. However, their interactions do not make a network. Without NGOs, the most important relationships are vertical between societies and their own governments, and horizontal in traditional diplomacy between governments. Throwing international NGOs into the mix proliferates horizontal, transnational links between societies, and also transverse relationships between the government of one country and the society of another. These transverse relationships are particularly susceptible to creative political mobilization.

In addition to being normative, NGO networks are obligative and distributive. Political responsibility and material resources are closely related in the network, but not in an obvious fashion. Thousands of humble and ubiquitous development NGOs have worked throughout sub-Saharan Africa during the independence era since 1960. To briefly illustrate how NGOs can implicitly assign and shift political responsibility, consider a stylized history of a single development NGO conducting the same operation somewhere in Africa at three historical moments—1975, 1985, and 1995. The operation might be anything that involved international funding and counted as development in the foreign aid field—for example, drilling wells, or food-for-work to plant trees, or child support and education. The point is that the same operational program operating in three different political contexts can create three different sets of political implications.

In sub-Saharan Africa in 1975, a typical development NGO served as an auxiliary to a government welfare bureaucracy.[48] The NGO operation filled gaps in the *government's* commitment to provide universal welfare. The material resources distributed by the NGO attested to and reinforced the government's acceptance of political responsibility for welfare. In 1985, the NGO found that the government, under pressure from its international donors, was cutting spending and privatizing welfare services to NGOs. The resources distributed through the NGO development project carried a new political meaning: to legitimize and cushion the privatization process.[49] The government relinquished political responsibility for welfare as the NGO assumed responsibility, while international donors reduced their welfare support by shifting to NGO recipients. In the third context, in 1995, the country had fragmented into rival warlord formations, one of which allowed the NGO operation to continue. But the warlord insisted that the NGO hire designated "guards" to protect the security of its operation. The NGO continued to support its immediate recipients, but the context had shifted again. The NGO fueled a form of warlord politics that actively undermined development and welfare through predatory military action.[50]

In each scenario the "apolitical" NGO—claiming to do development anywhere regardless of politics—inadvertently made itself available to absorb and reinforce the existing political context, whatever it was. In three different contexts, essentially the same program of resource distribution carried three different political impacts. Ruling elites and international donors used the NGO, first, to assist in the government's assumption of responsibility for general welfare; second, to legitimize the government's relinquishing of welfare responsibility; and third, to support and legitimize the warlord's anti-development, predatory political economy. Presented here as the stylized history of a single, hypothetical NGO, the actual impact was created by networks of sometimes hundreds of development NGOs operating in each country.

The implications for theory are counterintuitive. The influence of NGO aid operations in assigning and shifting political responsibility may be more important than the material consequences of resource distribution in particular cases. In addition, if it is obvious that the abdication of political responsibility for population welfare by African governments must have involved class conflict and international conflict, we can begin to see how NGO networks absorb political conflict into themselves, thereby institutionalizing it. The flow of information through network relationships is best considered below, in the context of a further discussion of how networks institutionalize conflict.

Empirical questions

- Who are the members of the network, and how do NGOs in the network compare and interact in their public purposes, partners, latent agendas, and tactical autonomy?
- What are the movements of normative frames, material resources, political responsibility, and information among the NGOs and their partners in the network, at whose initiative and with what consequences?

Proposition #6: NGO networks absorb and institutionalize international political conflict

For pluralist and globalist approaches to NGO network analysis, the network is defined by normative consensus among its members. Based on this assumption of normative consensus, political conflict within the network tends to be found primarily at early stages of agenda-setting or issue-framing, and can be overcome by creative and entrepreneurial activists.

In contrast, the structural approach developed here suggests that network linkages among NGOs and other actors are laden with contradictory latent agendas and subject to capture for unforeseen political purposes. In short, both conflict and cooperation are intrinsic to international NGOs, not only as individual organizations but also collectively in networks. Yet NGOs are international organizations, part of the larger universe of international institutions. It follows that NGO networks institutionalize international conflicts.

One of the major implications of the global NGO bloom is that more and more political conflicts are channeled into NGO network contention, to be played out at the level of explicit NGO wars over principled issues and also at the level of latent agendas. The point of the structural insight is counterfactual: any particular conflict that is absorbed into network politics might have been structured otherwise by a different institutional process.

In the global humanitarian network, for example, NGOs, UN agencies, and governments dealing in the normative currencies of famine relief, human rights, and conflict resolution now make it standard practice to cooperate with all adversaries in internal wars. NGOs involved with a particular conflict, who themselves or whose sister agencies are working closely with several military adversaries, view their engagement as an opportunity to draw the adversaries together into a process of conflict resolution that may lead to a negotiated settlement. Occasionally, this is the outcome.[51] More often the adversaries treat the NGO network itself as an institutional battlefield on which they play out the war using the resources and grammar of humanitarianism.[52]

Such "NGO wars" are a typical part of world politics in every region. Political conflict institutionalized in NGO networks evinces enormous complexity and variability in the geographic extension of network linkages and the specific content of norms, resources, responsibility, and information that flow "hydraulically" through the network relationships. Therefore, NGO institutionalization is less rule-governed than partner-driven, and less bureaucratic than hydraulic. The implications for empirical research are challenging. As a first step, it would seem reasonable that research on NGO networks be "multi-sited" in design and execution.[53]

We have seen that the individual NGO is a site of institutionalized conflict and cooperation among its partners at the micro-level of the structure of world politics. Analogously, the NGO network is a site of institutionalized conflict and cooperation among its members at the mid-level of the structure of world politics.

The communicative dimension of network dynamics demands special attention because NGOs play several contradictory roles in collecting and analyzing information. In practice, NGOs simultaneously reveal, conceal, and distort political reality.

All international NGOs collect and convey specialized information, whether to expose abuses through public advocacy, to administer services for selected populations, or to provide technical advice and training. Information is particularly scarce in precisely those arenas where international NGOs tend to be found—in Third World countries, under authoritarian governments, where there is no free press, among remote rural populations, in disaster situations, amidst the fog of war. And NGOs routinely maintain communication channels within and between countries. Cumulatively, NGOs may know more about a particular country than the wealthiest corporations and the most advanced intelligence agencies in the world.

NGO information is extensive, but also flawed by inherent operational constraints. The decentralization of activity that makes NGO information cumulatively more comprehensive also leaves it fragmented geographically and demographically, and narrowly focused according to each organization's particular mandate. Bits of information are scattered in a shifting mosaic, the design of which is unknown. Even when NGOs share raw information with each other, few are capable of integrating the pieces into a coherent picture.

In addition to being narrow and fragmented, much NGO information is also pre-theorized to conform to limited notions of social causality. Many NGOs adhere tenaciously to a voluntarist assumption concerning political actors, holding that they are free of political constraints to respond to the NGO's principled demands. The voluntarist assumption ignores the reality that violence and coercion may be instrumental in political strategies. NGOs cannot acknowledge the political constraints facing actors without undermining the force of their own recommendations. Amnesty

International cannot acknowledge the legitimacy of any excuse proffered by a government to justify its abuse of human rights. Were it to do so, Amnesty would simply stop being Amnesty. The voluntarist assumption is an unrelinquishable requirement for assuming a stance of advocacy. Therefore, the political superficiality of much NGO analysis is not curable.

NGOs may ignore the political context, but politics influences their information because every NGO requires access to a societal partner within each country of operation. Access is gained through a process of bargaining with governmental or other political elites. Inevitably, an NGO's access bargain shapes the information it produces. If not false, the information is at least filtered.

When it is dangerous to know too much, NGOs can turn to a repertoire of methods for concealing sensitive information from others, and even from themselves, through discretion, fiction, or fraud.

Discretion is simply keeping information to oneself. No NGO tells all that it knows; hence "transparency" is a tactical option, not a fundamental ethical principle. Of the three tactics of concealment, discretion is the only one that is sometimes acknowledged by organizations that use it. For example, the International Committee of the Red Cross practices discretion assiduously, and as a matter of principle, particularly in its prisoner visits.[54]

The second means by which NGOs conceal political reality is benign fiction. For example, humanitarian professionals know that to generate an international response to a famine crisis often requires mobilizing both international news media and the aid bureaucracies of major donor governments. Each of these information consumers insists on knowing the *number* of victims who are at risk. Journalists need a number for drama; aid bureaucrats a number for planning. In response, tactical exaggeration has long been a well-established practice in the culture of international relief. Indeed, "Those in the relief business are familiar with such exaggeration, but it has always been considered in bad taste to draw attention to it, for fear of sounding callous."[55]

Finally, NGOs or other network members may engage in outright fraud—fabricating information that covers up or legitimizes an anti-humanitarian operation. They may do so through self-deception, ignorance, or as a conscious choice of a "lesser evil" ethical strategy. Such distortions of reality may be part of the price to be paid to maintain partners who are essential to an NGO's mission to build a better world. During the North Korean "great famine" of the 1990s, for example, most international NGOs were pawns in the strategies of the governments of North Korea or the relief donor nations to base policy on fraudulent theories of the scale, location, victims, and causes of the famine.[56]

The information held by NGOs may be vast, therefore, but it is narrow, fragmented, politically filtered, and often distorted by fiction or fraud. For NGOs to reveal political reality, someone must undertake the tasks of collection and analysis, analogous to the production of strategic intelligence. During the Cold War, this occurred slowly and unevenly in two ways. Embassy personnel of Western governments routinely debriefed NGO staff and collected their gray literature, analyzing it in-country and conveying conclusions to their home governments through traditional diplomatic reporting.[57] Alternately, among the NGOs a gifted and controversial individual would occasionally arise who could gather and synthesize NGO information into a penetrating political analysis. Fred Cuny was the most famous of these rare analysts.[58]

The end of the Cold War set off a decade of stormy experimentation to get NGOs and Western intelligence agencies to collaborate. Do-gooders and spooks found themselves interested in the same war zones that were spawning both the most severe humanitarian disasters and also the greatest transnational security threats. The new diplomacy of "early warning and conflict prevention" became the public face of this experimental collaboration, out of which emerged new NGOs such as International Crisis Group.[59] Behind the scenes, NGOs in several fields and American intelligence agencies experimented with a "hazardous partnership" of more intimate collaboration.[60]

If NGO networks are capable of political learning, their learning is highly politicized in the sense that vital organizational interests of network members are at stake in each step of revealing and concealing political causality.[61] The rubric of "learning," which evokes an image of quiet reflection and steady cumulation of knowledge, is ironic when applied to a process fraught with such conflict and contradiction.

To claim that NGO networks *institutionalize* political conflict is not to argue that they rationalize conflict by subjecting it to rules. NGO networks are not centralized, rule-governed, rational Weberian bureaucracies. The genius of NGO networks is in their ambiguity. NGOs and their networks present themselves as morally principled, yet they are radically available to being mobilized for political purposes, and yet again they resist such mobilization. NGOs promise principles to idealists, and promise politics to manipulators, but fail to gratify either set of suitors. By diverting so much of the world's political ardor and egotism into NGO wars, the net effect of NGO networks may be to protect the status quo by neutralizing both the idealists and the manipulators.

In this way, the proliferation of NGO networks may continue to prove that Robert Cox was right two decades ago when he argued, following Gramsci, that international organizations co-opt radical leaders from the periphery: "Hegemony is like a pillow: it absorbs blows and sooner or later the would-be assailant will find it comfortable to rest upon."[62]

Empirical questions

- How are the adversaries in military or political conflict linked to NGOs in the network?
- How does the political conflict shape the network, and how does absorption into the network shape the conflict?
- How do NGOs and networks conceal and reveal information about the political conflicts they institutionalize?

Proposition #7: NGO networks infuse the structure of the international system, shaping states and other agents of world politics

An NGO network may be created for a particular issue—such as infant formula feeding in the Third World—or an event—such as famine in Ethiopia. After the initial battle it may live on, if activists are eager to recast the network or apply similar techniques elsewhere, if journalists and scholars write stirring accounts of the network's triumphs that recruit new supporters, and if partner constituencies continue to support NGO participation.

When an NGO network grows and persists, it is not only a social *agent* ready to tackle the next issue or crisis. It also becomes part of the social and material *structure* of the international system, regionally or globally.[63] At that point, its potential utility becomes part of the context for political choice by all actors on the scene. An initiative to mobilize a network for a new purpose can be launched from any point within it. The network is up for grabs: Which norms will be invoked on whose behalf? What information will be communicated to whom? How will political responsibility be assigned? And what resources will be distributed to whom? Through the answers to these questions, NGOs residing within the structure of world politics shape the agents of world politics, including states.

Yes, NGOs shape states. When they infuse the international system as permanent inhabitants, NGOs and transnational networks occupy the "commanding heights" of world politics to mold governments and their relations to their populations and territories, though often with inadvertent consequences.

What sorts of evidence could support such an audacious argument? The examples sketched below, some of which are pursued elsewhere in this book, illustrate possible explanatory strategies.

International NGOs can shape fundamental state–society relations. During the 1970s, NGO human rights monitoring and advocacy became densely institutionalized in Latin America, initially through dynamic and innovative action by domestic human rights NGOs in a few lead countries, particularly Argentina and Brazil.[64] The early causal path was inside-out, from domestic politics to the regional international system.[65] After the human rights network became established as part of the regional international system, however, the direction of causality shifted to outside-in. The existence of the regional NGO network seeking information on human rights violations, and offering some protection to human rights monitors if not to all victims, led to the formation of human rights NGOs in other countries of the region, such as Guatemala.[66] The path of influence should be understood as structural because domestic human rights groups did not emerge from the societies of many countries until NGO human rights monitoring became institutionalized as a permanent and expected part of the regional system.

International NGOs can transform governments. The goals of the Latin American human rights movement in the 1970s did not include promoting transitions to electoral democracy. Nevertheless, human rights NGOs made a strong, if inadvertent, contribution to the almost complete democratization of the region. Largely through NGOs, the regional human rights movement altered the ideological and cultural context in Latin America to the point where it drew thousands of radical political activists away from the vision of a socialist future through violent class struggle and toward the vision of a future for individual human rights (see chapter 4).[67]

International NGOs can institutionalize regional warfare, and erode the capacity of governments to maintain statehood. When humanitarian organizations establish a presence in protracted wars—ready to feed the hungry, publicize violence, and aid refugees—the military adversaries learn to adjust strategies and tactics to take advantage of the humanitarian presence. Political victimization and martyrdom, which play a role in any war, take on new significance in the context provided by the humanitarians. As humanitarianism becomes embedded in the structure of the international system, new opportunities are created for the "instrumentalization of the victims."[68] In addition, when international NGOs and UN agencies take on greater humanitarian responsibility, it can accelerate state debility. In Africa, particularly in collapsed states like Somalia or Liberia, humanitarian organizations have taken over governmental responsibility for supporting the national population on its designated territory. Humanitarianism has become the international system's default state maintenance system for much of central Africa, in the process helping to institutionalize warlord conflict (see chapter 5).[69]

Turning attention to powerful states, international NGOs can relieve governments of political responsibilities while appearing to hold them responsible. When a multilateral summit conference on a global issue is accompanied by a parallel NGO meeting, the political significance may be precisely the opposite of what NGOs and pluralist scholars think it is. Under the appearance of global civil society rising up to pressure governments to respond to the public will, the reality may be that political responsibility is shunted to NGO networks while governments release themselves from responsibility for effectively addressing the issue at hand. NGO activism may become, on some issues, an alternative to governmental responsibility rather than a prod to it (see chapter 1). This is a structural phenomenon when the practice of NGO conference diplomacy becomes the accepted institutional forum into which political rivalries are channeled.

In general, I would suggest there are four kinds of evidence for structural causality of NGO networks. Causality may be structural, first, when the evidence points to a direction of influence from the outside-in, from the international or regional system to particular societies or governments;[70] second, when the evidence reveals a path-dependent, historical process of indirect change, in contrast to the purposeful, direct influence that is characteristic of agentic causation;[71] third, when the evidence indicates consequences are inadvertent from the point of view of the NGOs; and finally, when evidence shows that the outcome is counterproductive to the goals of the NGO network.

In sum, evidence of structural causality includes at least two of the following effects: outside-in, indirect, inadvertent, or counterproductive.

These examples and conjectures illustrate a possible strategy of explanation that is both structural and political.

Empirical questions

- How and to what extent does the network influence the origin, or shape the institutional form, of societal or political actors (in addition to influencing their particular choices)?
- How and to what extent does the network influence from the outside-in (from the international or regional system to domestic politics)?
- How and to what extent does the network influence through an indirect, path-dependent route (rather than a purposeful, policy route)?
- How and to what extent does the network bring about inadvertent and counterproductive consequences?

CONCLUSION

The structural theory sketched in this chapter leaves room for the particularity and the politics of NGO operations, in contrast to pluralist, globalist, realist, and sociological theories. This structural theory portrays NGOs not only as agents of social and political action, but also as constituting the structure of international relations at three levels: the micro-level of individual NGOs, the mid-level of the country or regional network, and the macro-level of the international system. The impact of NGOs goes far beyond success or failure in achieving their official goals. Freeing the study of NGOs from both boosters and detractors, this theory shows where to look for empirical evidence of how NGOs institutionalize international conflict and cooperation.

Table 2.1   A Structural Theory of NGOs in World Politics
(three basic questions, seven propositions, and 17 empirical questions)

What are NGOs?

Proposition #1: NGOs are private actors pursuing public purposes

- Who claims to be a private actor and to serve what legitimate public purpose?
- How do NGO claims mesh or clash with the representative claims of other actors?

What do NGOs Do?

Proposition #2: NGOs bind themselves to societal and political partners in several countries, and are constituted by their partners

- Who are the societal and political partners—local and remote, acknowledged and unacknowledged—of an NGO, and how does it reflect the connection to each partner?

Proposition #3: NGOs carry and channel partner latent agendas, becoming institutional sites of both cooperation and conflict between partners

- What are the latent agendas of each NGO partner, and how do latent agendas mesh or clash with each other and with the official, salient agenda of the NGO?
- Which latent agendas are achieved, thwarted, and to what extent?
- How is the merging and clashing of partner latent agendas reflected in the organization, operations, and culture of the NGO?

Proposition #4: NGOs enjoy operational autonomy from their partners

- How and to what extent do NGO leaders achieve tactical flexibility and operational autonomy from their partners, and with what results?
- Conversely, how and to what extent do key partners control NGO tactics, and with what results?

What Difference do NGOs Make in World Politics?

Proposition #5: NGOs make networks, which facilitate the transnational movement of norms, resources, political responsibility, and information

- Who are the members of the network, and how do NGOs in the network compare and interact in their public purposes, partners, latent agendas, and tactical autonomy?
- What are the movements of normative frames, material resources, political responsibility, and information among the NGOs and their partners in the network, at whose initiative and with what consequences?

Proposition #6: NGO networks absorb and institutionalize international political conflict

- How are the adversaries in military or political conflict linked to NGOs in the network?
- How does the political conflict shape the network, and how does absorption into the network shape the conflict?
- How do NGOs and networks conceal and reveal information about the political conflicts they institutionalize?

Proposition #7: NGO networks infuse the structure of the international system, shaping states and other agents of world politics

- How and to what extent does the network influence the origin, or shape the institutional form, of societal or political actors (in addition to influencing their particular choices)?
- How and to what extent does the network influence from the outside-in (from the international or regional system to domestic politics)?
- How and to what extent does the network influence through an indirect, path-dependent route (rather than a purposeful, policy route)?
- How and to what extent does the network bring about inadvertent and counterproductive consequences?

3
Ironic Origins of Transnational Organizing

The NGO world in the second half of the twentieth century simply took for granted that the public discourse of any mainstream international NGO would be secular, universalistic, and progressive. The post-World War II consensus assumed that international NGOs are *secular* rather than religious, *universalistic* and cosmopolitan rather than particular and local, and vaguely *progressive* or moderate left rather than either radical left or right. Given this consensus, it is ironic that many of the historical forerunners to post-World War II NGOs were deeply religious in social origin and motivation, or peculiarly American, or shockingly regressive by more recent standards.

Paying attention to these discontinuous genealogies—these historical skeletons in the NGO closet—reveals two larger conclusions. First, the rise of NGOs has not been a steady, unidirectional ascent. The herd has shifted direction quite radically before, and is likely to do so again in the future. Second, NGOs can be instruments for the exercise of profound political power, to shape states up to their highest aspirations and mold societies down to the most intimate human relationships.

RELIGIOUS ROOTS

To acknowledge any significant role for *non*-governmental organizations, one must assume that society is, or can be, relatively autonomous from the state, and that society tends to struggle for freedom and representation vis-à-vis the state. Within such a view, aspiring representatives of society, including NGOs, can challenge the state by two paths: they can organize social movements from below the state, or they can invoke moral authority from above the state. The two leading theoretical approaches for studying NGOs, pluralism and globalism, are abstractions from these two paths for autonomous society to challenge the state.

This basic model of an independent society in tension or dialogue with government is a characteristically Western view. Two deep historical roots in European history and civilization have intertwined to create this view. One root is classical Greek and Roman political thought, which first envisioned the possibility of better or worse ways to organize the government of any society. This critical stance presupposed the intellectual autonomy from the state of at least a small class of philosophers. The ancients also understood human society to exist in a vertical moral universe between the realm of the beasts below and the realm of the gods and timeless natural law above.

More directly pertinent to the contemporary NGO worldview is the impact of the second root—Christianity—on Western notions of state and society. The interpretation of Christianity's historical influence remains deeply contested. The dominant contemporary view traces the idea of an autonomous society as arising only with European modernity in the sixteenth and seventeenth centuries when medieval models of overarching religious and political authority were rejected in faith by the Protestant Reformation, in thought by rationalist philosophy, and in politics by increasingly sovereign nation-states.[1] This view casts medieval Christendom as the foil for the rebellion and rise of autonomous society in philosophy, religious conscience, and politics.

A contrasting view traces the origins of a distinctive sense of autonomous society precisely to the Catholic Middle Ages. According to Paul Ghils, writing on the origins of international NGOs:

> since the Middle Ages, the Catholic tradition has maintained that the spiritual and temporal domains cannot be subject to the same jurisdiction and that there must be a distinct, autonomous sphere of state authority in which the Prince draws his legitimacy from observance of a strictly temporal natural law.[2]

Ghils argues that the legacy of the Church's efforts to preserve its autonomy from domination by political power encouraged the eventual development of a variety of "extrastatal movements" in a secularizing civil society. This was a common feature of Western Europe, whether the regions eventually became Protestant or Catholic. By contrast, in regions of Eastern Europe with an Orthodox Christian or Muslim historical heritage, "the resulting lack of differentiation between the public and private spheres stood in the way of the emergence of an extrapolitical sphere which was to be one of the foundations of civil society in regions with a Roman Catholic culture."[3]

This debate over interpretations of the historical influence of Christianity in Western concepts of civil society may seem arcane, but it reemerges in early twenty-first-century disputes about the boundaries of civil society, the prerogatives of political intervention in the private sphere, and the foundations of global normative authority (see chapters 6 and 7).

Although the long historical roots of NGOs are contested, there is little debate that the most important forebears to contemporary NGOs were single-issue movements of the late eighteenth, nineteenth, and early twentieth centuries.[4] The irony is that these early universalists came from a highly particular social profile: dissenting British Protestants, in both England and their offshoots in America. These dissenting Christians spawned great trans-Atlantic movements for the abolition of slavery, temperance, and women's suffrage. In America, descendants of dissenting British Protestants constituted more than 90 per cent of the population in the eighteenth century, and continued to set the national reform agenda through most of U.S. history:

> Among the campaigns that they initiated were justice for indigenous Americans, women's rights, temperance, the provision of universal public education, urban reform, the abolition of slavery, and the extension of the franchise to blacks and women. The grassroots movements that they promoted were so powerful that they resulted in seven constitutional amendments and numerous laws at the federal, state, and local levels.[5]

The great campaigns of the eighteenth and nineteenth centuries charted a path that has been trodden since by uncountable movements and campaigns. The anti-slavery campaigns were the first to garner widespread support for a single, bounded issue based on universal moral principles. From the formation of the Society for the Abolition of the Slave Trade in London in 1787, it was only two decades until Britain and the United States withdrew from involvement in the international slave trade (1807), and three more decades until Britain abolished slavery in all its colonies (1838). By 1888, a century after the beginning of the movement, slavery was formally abolished in its last stronghold, Brazil. The anti-slavery campaigns established several other patterns that are followed by contemporary NGO campaigns: "The regime to ban the slave trade was the first regime to be institutionalized in a series of international conventions signed by the vast majority of governments; it was the first in which blatantly moral impulses were a key factor and transnational moral entrepreneurs played leading roles ..."[6] In light of this history, the Society for the Abolition of the Slave Trade and its successor, the British Anti-Slavery Society, may be the most effective NGOs ever launched.

How did this particular religious community generate wave after wave of secular political and social reform? Members of dissenting churches in Britain, though Protestants themselves, nevertheless chafed under the Protestant establishment of Anglican state religion. The dissenters, also called Nonconformists or Free Churchmen, included Puritans, Presbyterians, Baptists, Methodists, Quakers, Unitarians, and Congregationalists. Catholicism was a relatively distant enemy. The dissenters faced two more proximate adversaries in the religious and political establishment of the Church of England, and the advocates of a purely secular Enlightenment. This is one setting for what David Brion Davis calls "the complex and dialectical relation between Christianity and the Enlightenment."[7] In response to the broad sweep of the Enlightenment challenge to religious belief, the dissenters mounted a vigorous and eclectic counterattack, borrowing ideas even from their adversaries. At the same time, the rise of industrial capitalism forced wrenching social changes and introduced new resources that Christianity and the Enlightenment struggled to master and direct. From this confluence of religious, philosophical, economic, and political forces, new alloys emerged that continue to infuse the infrastructure of Western and global politics up to the present day.[8] Among these, three leading ideas are constitutive of NGO politics: the ideas of collective moral progress, supranational authority, and societal autonomy from the state.

The dissenting Protestant notion of *collective moral progress* rested on a complex analogy between the personal and the social. One part of the analogy was the rise of industrial capitalism, which transformed social relations and dominated nature in an accelerating revolution that Protestant faith and Enlightenment reason competed to harness. As industrialization arose in the eighteenth century, the spectacle of capitalist productivity evoked competing visions of progress. What could be accomplished with the cornucopia of industrial production? Could the businessman extend the scope of his conscience as far as the geographical and temporal reach of his investment and marketing? Socialists and scientists, philosophers and religious reformers all dreamed of millennial progress.[9]

Leading philosophers offered some of the earliest critiques of the conventional rationales for slavery. However, philosophy did not generate the antislavery movement. According to some scientific accounts, Negroes were an inferior race or even an entirely different species. Indeed, scientists proffered some of the worst justifications for the racial inferiority of blacks produced in the eighteenth century. The very universality of the antislavery movement was rooted, according to Davis, not in any finding of scientific reason, but in the "continuing ideological importance of the biblical account of a single human race descended from common parents."[10] Davis underscores, "the abolitionist view of progress depended on a Christian and an essentially prescientific, pre-Darwinian anthropology."[11]

If the individual Christian could make moral progress in personal holiness, then national and even global societies could make moral progress as well. Davis suggests that, for abolitionists, "What struck their opponents as a secularization of religion was for them a sacralization of social progress."[12] The possibility of growth in personal holiness was rejected by the Lutheran and Calvinist traditions of the Reformation on the continent. However, England's John Wesley adapted the Catholic idea of sanctification to serve his quest to renew the Anglican Church and British society. Wesley's Methodists transposed sanctification for the monks of the Catholic monastery into moral progress for the citizens of the Protestant city.[13] Wesley himself became an early opponent of slavery, pronouncing in 1839, "The gospel of Christ knows of no religion but social; no holiness but social holiness."[14]

By all these indirect causal routes, the idea of collective moral progress was born of the long encounter between Christianity, the Enlightenment, and historical capitalism.

The dissenting churches comprised a minority on the British scene, with each sect (Methodist, Baptist, Quaker, among them) a smaller minority. Within these communities, the antislavery movement began as a minority within a minority. To be a dissenter was to wield a Davidic slingshot of moral authority against and above the Goliath of the established church and state. The antislavery activists took this a step further, invoking moral authority above all nations and governments of the world to command them—as Moses to Pharaoh—to free the slaves.

Therefore, the *supranational authority* claims of abolitionism were a relatively modest extension of the already ambitious authority claims of the dissenters against the established church and state.

In addition, adopting an antislavery platform strengthened the dissenters ideologically and psychologically vis-à-vis both the Anglican establishment and the secular Enlightenment. In England, Scotland, and even the United States, abolitionism served as an ideological club for Evangelical Christians to beat the established churches, to expose the hypocrisy and expediency of their compromise with the manifest evil of slavery.[15]

Contemplating the enormity of the evil of slavery also provided a rock of psychological certainty against the waves of Enlightenment skepticism and rapid social change. Davis suggests that the Christian abolitionists "were engaged in an enterprise parallel to that of the romantic poets and philosophers: the transposing into 'nonpolitical areas,' as M. H. Abrams has described it, of key concepts of the Enlightenment and ideals of the American and French revolutions."[16] Ironically, according to Davis, borrowing from their secular Enlightenment adversary strengthened the moral and religious convictions of the Christian abolitionists:

> Faced with the same revolutionary events that stirred the romantic poets and philosophers—the Enlightenment's challenge to the traditional Christian view of history and human nature, and the continuing disintegration of the preindustrial social order—the abolitionists recovered moral certainty by confronting the objective existence of human slavery. ... Such moral exercises proved that good and evil were not illusions and that the Creator had endowed human nature with the capacity for historical redemption.[17]

By adapting Enlightenment notions of human freedom and natural rights, the abolitionists reinforced their own religious certainty in the face of all their adversaries.

The third ideational legacy of the dissenting Protestants to Western politics is the notion that society is autonomous in principle from the state and asserts itself against the state in movements, revolutions, and claims of rights. This is another alloy of several metals. Biblical narratives of David against Goliath and Moses against Pharaoh inscribed not only the struggle for freedom by abolitionists on behalf of slaves, but also the dissenters' own struggle for freedom from the British laws that barred them from universities, professions, and public office. John Locke and other philosophers had already absorbed and recast ancient political thought from Greece and Rome into republican theories of natural rights and social contracts palatable to a capitalist age of contractual relationships.

This synthesis of philosophical republicanism and dissenting Protestant culture forged the leading ideas of collective moral progress, supranational authority, and societal autonomy. Exported to the New World, this synthesis formed the cultural foundation for the American founding and held for more than two centuries. Put another way, the abolitionist movement and the American nation, born about the same time, constituted different expressions of a single cultural-ideological synthesis. British NGOs in the nineteenth century, and American NGOs in the twentieth century, became the primary means for exporting the same three ideas to the entire world.

EARLY NGO WARS OVER AFRICA

By the later 1860s, after a string of successes, the antislavery movement turned its sights on the Arab slave trade in Africa and other Islamic regions.[18] In this struggle, several prominent Europeans struck a humanitarian pose on the public stage by their proclaimed opposition to Arab slavery—David Livingstone, Henry Morgan Stanley, King Leopold, and E. D. Morel. Each of these men reflected the contradictions of the age. Each was profoundly dedicated to improving himself, and they projected into Africa their wildly divergent notions of self-improvement. King Leopold and Morel finally faced off, each having established a formal NGO modeled on the British Anti-Slavery Society, and fought a war of public relations and humanitarian advocacy in which the lives of millions of Africans and billions of francs were at stake. This was perhaps the first "NGO war" in which apparently principled advocacy organizations took positions on opposite sides of a high-stakes political dispute and used sophisticated public relations techniques to promote their messages.

New technologies vastly extended the reach of business, politics, and culture in the late nineteenth century. It was culture, surprisingly, that reached first and farthest. The steamship, railroad, telegraph, and mass publication of newspapers and books provided the infrastructure upon which a bridge of the imagination was built. The British and American publics in particular saw themselves in sub-Saharan Africa through the writings of correspondents and explorers well before their business and political classes established themselves there. The leaders of this process were entrepreneurs of the imagination, intrepid explorers with mass audiences for their articles and books.

Born of poor, devoutly Calvinist parents in Scotland in 1813, David Livingstone was zealous to improve both himself and the world. He responded to a call by British and American churches for medical missionaries, and when the Opium Wars frustrated his dream to go to China, he turned instead to sub-Saharan Africa. For 30 years he traversed the continent—from 1841 when he landed at Cape Town at the southern tip, to 1871 when he was famously met and resupplied by Henry Morton Stanley on the shore of Lake Tanganyika. He died two years later in what is now Zambia, frustrated in his search for the source of the Nile, and his body was returned to Britain for a magnificent funeral and burial in Westminster Abbey.[19]

From the start, Livingstone's dreams of progress for Africa had embraced the components of Christianity, commerce, and civilization in a seamless vision. His quest to discover trade routes that would link central Africa to the Atlantic Ocean, the Pacific Ocean, and the River Nile sprung from a belief that legitimate commerce eventually would displace the Arab slave trade. He trusted that enlightened British politics and science would bring great improvement over Arab, Boer, or Portuguese hegemony, a belief that his own observations confirmed.

A missionary—but not only for the Christian Gospels—Livingstone no longer had to rely on support from the London Missionary Society after his first book, *Missionary Travels and Researches in Southern Africa*, made publication history in 1857 by selling more than 70,000 copies. In addition to religious and publishing affiliations, Livingstone maintained an association with the Royal Geographical Society for nearly a quarter-century. His estimates of the prospects for profitable commerce and benevolent politics in Africa proved overly optimistic. Nevertheless, more than perhaps any other single person, Livingstone helped the English-speaking public imagine itself in Africa.

The merger of cultural, economic, and political agendas was characteristic of the European attitude toward Africa in the late nineteenth century. In an atmosphere of pervasive faith in human progress, Europeans saw themselves in the mirror of the undeveloped African continent. It appeared that anything was possible, for themselves and for Africa. The earlier antislavery movement had banned the trade in slaves taken from Africa and was in the process of liberating African slaves worldwide. Livingstone's goal was to bring an analogous moral progress to Africans living in Africa itself. The European readers of Livingstone's books could identify personally with this mission of moral progress.

In 1841 the boy who would call himself Henry Morton Stanley, and 30 years later rescue Livingstone at Lake Tanganyika, was born in Wales, the bastard child of housemaid Elizabeth Parry and local drunkard John Rowlands.[20] Shuffled from relatives to workhouse, he made his way as a cabin boy to New Orleans in 1859, where he took on the name of his employer. In America, Stanley managed to fight on both sides of the Civil War, and made a living reporting from the frontier of the American West to the big city newspapers of the East. As a reporter, Stanley learned that the drama of the story was far more important than the accuracy of the facts.

Stanley's overblown tales of the dwindling Indian wars in the American West led the publisher of the *New York Herald* to assign him in 1868 to cover the wars and explorations on the yet larger and more dramatic African frontier. Just as Livingstone had preached more than the Gospel, so Stanley reported more than the news. From their encounter at Lake Tanganyika, Stanley wove the myth that sealed his reputation ("Dr. Livingstone, I presume?"). Stanley assumed the mantle of heroic explorer, antislavery moralist, and herald of progress from the aging missionary. However, while Stanley easily aped the conventional ideology of progress, he had no personal sense of mission beyond maintaining his own celebrity. Given a mission and funding, Stanley would be a formidable force indeed.

In the conventional ideology that Stanley had inherited from Livingstone, African exploration by Western Europeans was considered progressive in and of itself. The logic seemed plausible: by exploring and mapping a new area, and publicizing the expedition, the European would "open" it simultaneously to several progressive and mutually supportive forces. Since Europe had renounced slavery, legitimate trade could only undercut the Arab slave trade. Christianity would prepare peoples to shoulder the responsibilities of civilization, which could be transferred in discrete sets of practices—scientific medicine, advanced agriculture, parliamentary politics—and "reassembled" in Africa. Among its many problems, this ideology gave presumptive legitimacy to all actions by Europeans in Africa, with no structure of accountability in Africa itself, and little or none in Europe. Such an arrangement could avoid disaster only as long as the Europeans involved were all of the highest moral character and most sound judgment.

In other words, the idea of societal autonomy inherited from the antislavery movement easily became pernicious when applied to the European "opening" of Africa in the late nineteenth century. The idea of societal autonomy led people to assume that unregulated societal relationships between Europe and Africa would be civil and not predatory. Prospective predators were only too willing to use that cultural naïveté to cover their bloody tracks.

When Leopold II assumed the throne of Belgium in 1865, he was 30 years old and bitterly frustrated. He had inherited a small people and a small country, which possessed no colonies and was already outgrowing the monarchy to rule through parliamentary elections. The longing for material progress and personal improvement that pervaded Europe took the ironic form, in the young king, of an unquenchable lust for the wealth and power of a sovereign who stood above the world. Like David Livingstone and John Rowlands, Leopold wanted to "better" himself. The nominal king sought the social status bestowed by the external trappings of sovereignty—on the scale of the palaces of Louis XIV. Before his twentieth year, Leopold had known that he needed a colony of his own to achieve these goals.

Before he located and gained control of a colony, and well before he found a profitable product to be exploited, Leopold identified the method that would make him rich. He pored over archives of the Spanish colonial empire in Seville and studied the finances of the Dutch East Indies. By 1864, a year before being crowned, Leopold had concluded that the level of profit he desired could be met only through forced labor. He was not deterred by the expectation that forced labor might be difficult to institutionalize or conceal after the antislavery campaign had abolished slavery in European colonies and America.

For years Leopold searched the world for a colony that could be bought—perhaps a part of Argentina, Fiji, Abyssinia, the Philippines, some drained lakes in the Nile Delta. Finally, his eye settled on the vast, unexplored, and unclaimed regions of Africa. While Stanley was traversing Africa, out of contact with Europe, following the Congo to its source, Leopold meticulously planned a Geographical Conference to be held in his palace in Brussels. When it convened in September 1876, Leopold had assembled an unprecedented gathering of explorers, geographers, businessmen, military heroes, and humanitarians, including the president of the British Anti-Slavery Society. Renouncing any ambition for himself or Belgium, Leopold in his opening speech charged the participants to decide on the "location of routes to be successively opened into the interior, of hospitable, scientific, and pacification bases to be set up as a means of abolishing the slave trade, establishing peace among the chiefs, and procuring them just and impartial arbitration."[21] As imagined by the participants, each base would combine a school for the natives, a hospitality station for explorers, and an infirmary. For Leopold only two things really mattered: that the proposed string of bases traverse the unclaimed Congo Basin, and that the actual establishment of bases by any European be given presumptive legitimacy under the norms of the conference. He achieved both these goals. Indeed, the meeting voted to establish the International African Association and elected Leopold chairman. This was essentially a shell NGO which attracted positive publicity and even financial contributions across Europe, but which had no specific responsibilities and would operate under no supervision. In practice, the International African Association became a symbolic umbrella under which any action by Leopold in Africa would take on a humanitarian hue.

Through convening a humanitarian conference, which founded a humanitarian NGO, Leopold had performed a profoundly political act. According to Adam Hochschild:

> He had learned from his many attempts to buy a colony that none were for sale; he would have to conquer it. Doing this openly, however, was certain to upset both the Belgian people and the major powers of Europe. If he was to seize anything in Africa, he could do so only if he convinced everyone that his interest was purely altruistic. In this aim, thanks to the International African Association, he succeeded brilliantly. Viscount de Lesseps, for one, declared Leopold's plans "the greatest humanitarian work of this time."[22]

The progressive ideology of Livingstone and Stanley had already conflated economic, political, and humanitarian goals. Leopold's Geographical Conference had magnified the normative authority of that ideology and had endowed the act of establishing bases anywhere near the planned routes with the full weight of that normative authority.

It is important to fully appreciate the intricacy of Leopold's political legerdemain at the 1876 conference. As king, he served as the nominal head of the Belgian government. He used the residual prestige of his office to convene an international conference, which invoked supranational authority—located nominally above all governments—to confer upon himself the identity of the leading humanitarian of European society. He was only nominally humanitarian of course, for this was the cover he needed to be the real government of the Congo. Nominally governmental, supragovernmental, and subgovernmental, and all in service of predatory rule—such was Leopold's strategem at the 1876 conference; such was his pernicious use of the idea of supranational authority inherited from the antislavery movement.

Leopold had defined a mission. He needed only a man with an iron will to carry it out. When Henry Morton Stanley reappeared in August 1877 at the mouth of the Congo, after having spent four years traversing the waist of Africa from east to west, all of Europe and North America were prepared to lionize him for his Herculean achievements of exploration. King Leopold was prepared to offer him a contract. After recuperating in Europe and writing his third book, Stanley finally agreed.

Working for Leopold from 1879 to 1884, Stanley built the physical and legal infrastructure for the king's personal colony in the Congo Basin. According to plan, Stanley constructed a base at the mouth of the Congo, took two years to carve a rough road 220 miles around the string of cataracts that was Livingstone Falls, and then hauled a couple of small steamships in pieces around the Falls to be reassembled upriver. From these steamships, Stanley built a string of stations along 1,000 miles of navigable river. Equally important, he negotiated preposterously asymmetric "treaties" between Leopold's International Association of the Congo and tribal chiefs along the route. In the treaties, unreadable to the chiefs who signed their "X," the Association exchanged cloth and baubles for a monopoly on trade, large tracts of land, sovereign governing rights, and the chiefs' commitment "to assist by labour or otherwise, any works, improvements or expeditions which the said Association shall cause to be carried out in any part of these territories."[23] This clause formed the pseudo-legal basis for forced labor.

Parallel to Stanley's projects on the ground, Leopold mounted a bold campaign of international diplomacy to secure his exclusive right to sovereignty over the Congo Basin. No major power actively sought the expense and trouble of colonizing the Congo Basin; but each desired to exclude the others. By delicately playing major powers against each other, Leopold gained formal recognition from the United States, Germany, and finally the entire Berlin Conference of 1884.[24] His agents misrepresented the new entity as a confederation of "free negro republics" that would grant free trade to individuals from all other states. Moreover, he used the vaguely interchangeable titles of "International African Association," and "International Association of the Congo," which had earlier passed for humanitarian NGOs, as receptacles for recognition of a sovereign state with himself as its only government.

Leopold had successfully carried the humanitarian pose to the extremity of absolute power.

And he got away with it for 23 years, until 1908, barely a year before his death, when he finally succumbed to pressure to sell the colony to Belgium for 200 million francs. During that period, Leopold presided over a regime of forced labor that inflicted violence against Africans on a massive scale. In the early years the main product had been ivory, which, despite the high demand in Europe, failed to fully repay Leopold's expenses. Then the 1890s brought a boom in the rubber market to feed the emerging auto and electrical industries. The jungles of the Congo were full of rubber trees, but extracting, drying, and transporting the sap to steamships was backbreaking work that natives shunned. Leopold's agents and concessionary companies perfected the use of violence to enforce labor. A typical operation would begin by assaulting a village and taking all the women hostage, where they were subject to harsh treatment and rape. To gain their release, the village chief had to deliver a quota of rubber. Alternately, Leopold's police would massacre all the people in one village to gain the cooperation of its neighbors; the police having to account for each bullet used by returning the severed right hand of the man, woman, or child who had received it. Estimates of the population loss in the Congo under the years of Leopold's rule—from murder, starvation and exhaustion, disease, and plummeting birth rate—ran to ten million.[25]

Presiding over all this and reaping its profits, Leopold never set foot in the Congo.

Public opposition to Leopold's misrule was sporadic and isolated for many years. Protestant missionaries from Britain and America took the lead in opposing and exposing the violence through speeches and articles, but no organized opposition emerged until 1898. E. D. Morel was a young businessman in a Liverpool shipping company that held a monopoly on cargo shipped to and from the Congo Free State. Fluent in French, Morel was sent to supervise the company's dock operations in Antwerp. Morel observed that his company's ships arrived filled with rubber and ivory, but departed for the Congo with little more than arms and ammunition. As a businessman and a member of the dissident Protestant Clapham Sect which had produced the antislavery leader William Wilberforce, Morel recognized that there was no real *trade* with the Congo, since nothing of value was shipped in return for rubber and ivory.[26] The evidence pointed to a regime of forced labor. Morel confirmed this conclusion by examining the financial and shipping records of his company and of the Congo Free State.

In 1901 Morel quit his job and dedicated himself to writing and organizing. In 1903 he founded the *West African Mail*, a publication to serve as the organ for a new organization, the Congo Reform Association. Reluctant at first to establish an organization that focused exclusively on campaigning for change in the Congo, when well-established groups like the Aborigines Protection Society and Anti-Slavery Society had intermittently addressed the region, Morel was persuaded by Roger Casement, a member of the British consular service in Africa who served as a covert channel of detailed information to Morel. Moreover, Morel was convinced that the Congo was a unique case of a state founded and sustained on slave labor, and so should be treated *sui generis* rather than as part of a larger category. Thus, Morel's Congo Reform Association in the early twentieth century was a forerunner of contemporary NGO country campaigns.

The Congo Reform Association was really a working NGO that served as the nucleus for a growing movement against Leopold's personal colony. Morel brought great skill to the movement. His *West African Mail* proved a magnet for information from all sources and a measure for the accumulation of evidence against Leopold. Morel held mass rallies and recruited prominent individuals, always emphasizing the unique evil institutionalized in the Congo Free State.

Faced with the growing moral authority of Morel's Congo Reform Association, Leopold created a series of shell NGOs and international commissions to fight on his side: the Commission for the Protection of the Natives, the Committee for the Protection of Interests in Africa, the West African Missionary Association.[27] To counter the information in Morel's *West African Mail*, Leopold bribed editors and journalists across Europe and sponsored books to argue his cause. In perhaps the most significant foreshadowing of the contemporary NGO scene, Leopold and Morel conducted an "NGO war" in which ostensibly principled organizations on opposing sides of a political conflict mobilized international norms and information. Five years after the inauguration of the Congo Reform Association, Leopold ceded control of the Congo.

As a model of moral integrity and dedication to a just cause, Morel has few rivals. With King Leopold well cast as the personification of evil, the characters form a morality play that projects a satisfying clarity on the gulf between good and evil. And yet, ironies emerge around the edges. In fact, Leopold's personal colony was not unique in its reliance on forced labor, which pervaded a broader region of Central Africa where wild rubber thrived, and which continued in the Belgian Congo in modified forms through World War II.[28] Morel was wrong in the factual claim that the Congo Free State was a singular case, and in the causal theory that the use of forced labor would end when Leopold was no longer involved in Africa.

Also intriguing are the curious parallels between the lead characters in our morality play, Leopold and Morel. Neither man ever set foot in the Congo. Yet from their vantage points in Brussels and London, they vied with each other like Titans to understand and shape human lives and commodities there. Each man arrived at the same crucial insight concerning the economics of colonies—the centrality of forced labor in a profitable colonial enterprise. Leopold grasped this in 1862 by studying the archives of the Spanish empire and the financial history of the Dutch East Indies. Morel made the same inference in 1898 on the docks of Antwerp. Equipped with the same causal insight, the major difference between the two men was that Morel applied his personal moral compass to correct what Leopold's distinctly amoral compass had wrought.

Both Leopold and Morel were bilingual in French and English, and both were masters of public relations, often playing on the same humanitarian themes to influence their audiences. Ironically, both built on the prior success of the antislavery movement to garner broad public allegiance: Leopold posed falsely as an opponent of the Arab slave trade and Morel honestly condemned Leopold's forced labor, but both appealed to the same diffuse longing in the European public for moral progress in their relations with Africa. Neither man had ever seen Africa. Nevertheless, each was taken seriously when he appointed himself as a humanitarian representative of African society.

Why was the public so easily fooled by Leopold's lies, and also so readily mobilized by Morel's accurate facts but partly illusory notions of the cause and cure for forced labor? Given the distance between Europe and Africa and the few channels of information, a resourceful individual could powerfully shape the flow of apparently authoritative stories about the continent. In addition, the European and American publics cared far more about the image of themselves in Africa than they did about what was really happening in Africa. For the public, to celebrate any combination of the achievements of exploration, the spread of Christianity, the suppression of the Arab slave trade, or the expansion of free trade was to project themselves onto the empty canvas of the imaginary future of Africa. It is difficult to avoid the conclusion that the cultural narcissism of the middle class plays a role in this tragedy, even when the best men were leading the NGOs.

THE CHANGING FACE OF PROGRESS

When everyone believes in "progress," who defines what counts as progress? Who sets the agenda for progressive action? These are essentially political questions. In the history of NGOs, the arbiters of progress have realigned with the rise and fall of major powers and shifted with changes in world cultural fashions. At times, NGOs have promoted "progress" according to ideas that would now be considered reactionary and repugnant. The prominence of eugenics in the first half of the twentieth century is a clear example. In the rise of eugenics, NGOs and transnational networks played crucial roles by transmitting authoritative norms and innovative policies between societies, through international conferences, and to governments.

Programs to manage and control human population, as international political phenomena, have taken several distinct forms over the last century or so. Recent research by Deborah Barrett throws new light on the links between national and international levels, and between non-governmental and governmental actors, in the formation of population policy.[29] Four distinct discourses or models have vied for dominance since 1880, and three of these have reigned across leading states and international society for a time. According to Barrett and Frank:

> Our argument is that the content of international population-control discourse has changed in step with changes in the wider global institutional environment. Thus, pronatalism, which promotes population growth for national strength, dominated in the imperialistic pre-World War II period; eugenics, which promotes population management for national purity, dominated in the nationalist, corporatist interwar period; and neo-Malthusianisn, which promotes population control for national and individual development, has dominated in the recent nation-state period.[30]

More simply, pronatalism seeks a *greater quantity* of "us" and fewer of "them" conceived according to empire; eugenics seeks a *higher quality* of persons within a nation with quality conceived in terms of race or class; and neo-Malthusianism seeks a *limited quantity* of persons in order to manage economic and political development. A fourth discourse, individual choice, seeks *enhanced quality* of individual lives by giving adults, especially women, greater control over reproduction through the availability of contraceptive and abortive technologies. Individual choice has flourished to some extent since World War II as a "subordinate discourse" under and within neo-Malthusianism.[31]

These discourses on population policy have shaped billions of human lives for more than a century. Nothing could be more political. In the rivalries and shifts between these alternative ideologies, it turns out that NGOs and the supranational authority invoked by NGOs at international conferences have wielded critical influence.

To trace the influence of international discourse and institutions, Barrett employs a double methodology. One component involves counting and charting the number of international population conferences devoted to each of these models (a total of 428 between 1880 and 1990). The other involves a close reading of speeches and papers from many of these conferences.[32] From her quantitative and historical analysis, it is clear that the most effective strategy to change government population policy across many countries has been first to get people talking—NGO advocates, scientific experts, and government policymakers—at international conferences to frame the problem in your preferred terms.

This is an example of the structural path of NGO influence at the macro-level. NGOs infused the structure of the international system to shape the standards by which the most powerful governments competed for prestige and power. NGOs shaped states.

Pronatalism was a traditional ideology that rested on established assumptions about imperial strength and religious beliefs about family and sexuality. Because it did not rely on international legitimation, pronatalism was not evident as a theme for international conferences. However, to overturn the deeply embedded ideas of pronatalism, advocates of all three contending alternative models have utilized the same essential strategy. The common path to power has passed through three stages. In the first stage, NGOs and foundations articulate the new model. In the second, experts and NGOs assert the new model at a series of international conferences to establish its supranational authority. In the third stage, government policymakers implement the new global norms, competing with other governments for the prestige of leading the march toward progress. By following this path to structural power, NGOs occupied the "commanding heights" of world culture. NGOs infused the *Zeitgeist* that dictated how to build a powerful state.

After its origins among scientists in Britain and the United States, the eugenics movement spread quickly to other countries in the early twentieth century. Daniel Kevles evokes the atmosphere of dynamism and progress around the eugenics movement, which appeared to sweep all the advanced nations and to command the respect of the top leaders in politics, academia, and religion:

> After the turn of the century, eugenic efforts—often called "race hygiene"— had also developed in Sweden, Norway, Russia, Switzerland, Germany, Poland, France, and Italy; in the nineteen-twenties, the movement spread to Japan and Latin America. In 1912, some seven hundred and fifty people from Britain, Europe, and the United States attended the first International Eugenics Congress, in London, where the Right Honourable Arthur Balfour delivered the inaugural address, receiving hearty applause when he mentioned the "dignity of motherhood." Participants in the congress delivered some thirty papers, and its sponsoring vice-presidents included the Lord Chief Justice of Britain, the Right Honourable Winston Churchill, the Right Reverend the Lord Bishop of Ripon, Alexander Graham Bell, and Charles William Eliot, the former president of Harvard University.[33]

How could so many smart and respectable people be wrong? The "science" of eugenics, which combined early findings of genetics with unexamined assumptions about society and progress, gave an aura of intellectual authority to the idea of more children from the "fit" and fewer from the "unfit." Most important, the movement fitted the *Zeitgeist* of nationalism and the expectation that the state should radically reshape and improve society. As difficult as it is to believe today, eugenics defined what was progressive for many politically aware people in the early twentieth century. Eugenics promised to make an entire people qualitatively better, and it came highly recommended from the most reputable supranational authorities. All the best people were supporting it. To spurn such an opportunity seemed to mean abandoning one's commitment to moral progress.

Eugenics discourse dominated international conferences for several years before governments began to adopt policies for mandatory sterilization. The "unfit" were variously defined as "feeble-minded," mentally disturbed, criminals, or "inferior races." Denmark and several U.S. states had already initiated some of these policies when

Germany did so in 1933. By 1940, a dozen countries had implemented some mandatory sterilization and another dozen were considering doing so.[34] The dynamic of interstate rivalry pushed governments to conform to the new model lest they be left behind.

Hitler and the Nazi regime carried the assumptions of eugenics to their logical conclusion—to eliminate rather than merely sterilize those designated as "unfit." With the defeat of the Nazis and full exposure of their racial policies, the eugenics movement lost international legitimacy. After World War II the United States launched a new *Zeitgeist* by its own example of prosperity and human rights, and by the agenda of "national development" institutionalized in the United Nations. In the new environment, NGO advocates of neo-Malthusianism and individual choice promoted their agendas for population control through the same stages that eugenics had followed (see chapter 6).

The rise of eugenics illustrates the structural power of NGO networks. A handful of NGOs and scientists called a series of international conferences, which transformed the world cultural assumptions for how advanced countries conceived their interests, which influenced the selection of citizens who were allowed to conceive children.

Eugenics played fast and loose with the intellectual legacy of earlier social movements. The eugenics movement utilized the idea of supranational authority to influence government policy, and redefined collective moral progress to mean improving the genetic quality of the nation. However, eugenics turned the idea of societal autonomy on its head by authorizing states to intervene coercively in society to repress reproductive freedom and to violate the right to life. Whereas the antislavery campaign had extended the shelter of universal rights to marginalized groups, the eugenics movement stripped protection from the weakest members of humanity.

THE AMERICANIZATION OF TRANSNATIONAL SOCIETY

It is no accident that British movements and organizations have played leading roles in this account so far. When British military and political power peaked in the nineteenth century, the transnational influence of British society also surged. Indeed, the first achievement of the antislavery movement—banning the international slave trade—relied on the British Navy for enforcement. But the other secret of British transnational influence was the particular character of its society—its relative prosperity, its relative freedom of association and communication, and the cultural and religious confidence that enabled some of its citizens to challenge sovereigns.

The same pair of factors—state power and societal character— also explain the Americanization of transnational relations in the twentieth century. Historian Akira Iriye argues that the twentieth century was aptly named "The American Century," not only for the global extension of U.S. military power, but also for the worldwide spread of the NGO, "a uniquely American experience in social organization."[35]

To generalize these observations, at any historical moment leading states are privileged in their influence on both the governments and societies of other states. Three sets of factors, each of which is complex and variable, interact to make this happen. First, governments of leading states exercise disproportionate influence on the rules and customs of international relations, and introduce models of state–society relations drawn from their own domestic experience. Second, the societies themselves within leading states are privileged by their own relatively greater wealth, confidence, and organizational ability to project their values and practices into the societies of other countries. Third, the societies of leading states are also privileged by the attractive appeal they exert on the societies of less powerful states, whose members seek the prestige, power leverage, personal security, and sense of human dignity that mimesis toward, and alliance with, elements of a leading society can bring.

The first factor can apply equally to any rising power because cultural prestige tends to follow military success. As Stephen Krasner observes, "In the contemporary world transnational fascist and racist organizations are weak; this would hardly be the case if Germany had won the Second World War."[36] However, as the Nazi Party illustrates, not all powerful countries are equal in the capacity of their societies to attract admiration and mimesis.

The particular character of American society developed long before the United States became a global military power. Nineteenth-century foreign observers were struck by the distinctive propensity of Americans to form voluntary associations, and by the wide range of tasks that such private associations took upon themselves. Alexis de Tocqueville, writing in the 1830s, noted that political associations constituted only a small slice of the rich associational life of America:

> Americans of all ages, all stations in life, and all types of dispositions are forever forming associations. There are not only commercial and industrial associations in which all take part, but others of a thousand different types— religious, moral, serious, futile, very general and very limited, immensely large and very minute. ... In every case, at the head of any new undertaking, where in France you would find the government or in England some territorial magnate, in the United States you are sure to find an association.[37]

Tocqueville's much-quoted observation underscores that both the tendency and the ability to form associations have long been pervasive in American society. American people view such associational practice simply as effective human behavior and tend to become baffled, exasperated, or moralistic when faced with other peoples to whom such behavior does not come naturally.

Every American organization abroad carries such assumptions within its organizational culture and the minds and hearts of its American staff. That human society can and should be self-regulating to the point of autonomy from government is an ideal cherished in American culture. American faith in this ideal is an anthropological reality quite independent of the question of where in the world, or by what means, the ideal might be achievable. A classic statement of this faith, written after the American Civil War had sorely tested it, is Walt Whitman's "Democratic Vistas":

> I say the mission of government, henceforth, in civilized lands, is not repression alone, and not authority alone, not even of law, nor by that favorite standard of the eminent writer, the rule of the best men, the born heroes and captains of the race, (as if such ever, or one time out of a hundred, get into the big places, elective or dynastic)—but higher than the highest arbitrary rule, to train communities through all their grades, beginning with individuals and ending their again, to rule themselves.[38]

This idea—that the mission of government is to train communities to rule themselves—would not remain confined to America, Whitman knew. Those who believed it would at least try to spread it to all "civilized lands."

This book provides many examples of the disproportionate influence of particular American NGOs in particular issues and campaigns. Here I want to examine more closely what is peculiarly American about NGOs and their global proliferation. At the heart of American transnational influence is a paradox. On one side of the paradox, the extraordinary autonomy of society from government in the United States is the key to both the assertiveness and the attractiveness of American society in the rest of the world. From this point of departure, the primary stake in the global spread of NGOs would seem to be the changing balance between state and societal prerogatives within each country. However, the other side of the paradox is also at play. As the American model of state–society relations diffuses abroad, it not only influences domestic politics in each country to which it spreads, but also generates certain relative advantages for American power in the world. In short, the spread of NGOs changes power relations not only within each country, but also between countries.

An obscure 1973 essay by Samuel Huntington offers surprisingly penetrating insights into the American content of transnational NGOs.[39] The conventional 1970s literature understood the term "transnational" to refer to *relations between societies* of different countries. Idiosyncratically, Huntington defined "transnational" as referring to the *cross-border scope of operations* by any "relatively centralized, functionally specific, bureaucratic organizations," whether governments, corporations, churches, or international NGOs.[40] He asserted categorically, "The principal sources of the transnational organizational revolution are to be found in American society and in the global expansion of the United States during the two decades after World War II."[41] In spite of the fact that Huntington dismissed the influence of transnational NGOs as trivial in 1973, three of his American sources of transnationalism can be applied to NGOs today.

First, the technological precondition for the development of transnational operations was the development of communication and transportation technology that allowed an organization to exercise central control over far-flung operations. The jet aircraft and communications satellites that made this possible on a global scale were largely developed by industries originally based in the United States, and were first utilized by American organizations abroad. All modern NGOs make extensive use of global communication and transportation technologies, from CARE transporting relief food to European refugees after World War II, to Amnesty International monitoring and reporting human rights violations since 1961, to Greenpeace broadcasting its whale rescues over global media since the 1970s, to Global Trade Watch using the Internet to organize protests against the World Trade Organization in 1999. Each of these activities is a "modular technique" that an NGO claims can be used anywhere in the world with the same effect on a designated global problem (see chapter 1). Earlier generations of NGOs and social movements had used the technologies of commercial printing in the eighteenth century, and faster, cheaper transatlantic shipping in the nineteenth century.[42] NGO modular techniques all depend on Huntington's technologies for transnational operations.

Second, the political precondition for the development of transnationalism after World War II was political access guaranteed within the "Free World" security zone by the influence of the United States:

> The governments of countries within this zone found it in their interest: (a) to accept an explicit or implicit guarantee by Washington of the independence of their country and, in some cases, of the authority of the government; and (b) *to permit access to their territory by a variety of U.S. governmental and non-governmental organizations pursuing goals which those organizations considered important.* ... The great bulk of the countries of Europe and the Third World ... found the advantages of transnational access to outweigh the costs of trying to stop it.[43]

This American form of expansionism was entirely compatible with the independence of former colonies in the Third World. Under American rules, according to Huntington, all organizations that operated with transnational scope—whether the U.S. Navy, or IBM, or CARE—negotiated their access to developing areas. Rather than leading to the decline of sovereignty, Huntington realized, this system reinforced the bargaining power of Third World governments:

> In this sense, the growth of transnational operations does not challenge the nation-state but reinforces it. It increases the demand for the resource which the nation-state alone controls: territorial access. Within the nation-state, those groups which dominate the national government are similarly able to use the increased value of their control over access to the national territory to strengthen their own position vis-à-vis other groups in their society.[44]

The lucrative bargaining position of Third World governments positioned them to reap payments for access by transnational actors and to use those resources to dominate domestically.[45] What do NGOs offer Third World governments in bargaining for access? The question leads into the complex and variable interplay between the salient agenda of each NGO and the latent agendas of its partners, including the government that controls access to the beneficiaries (see chapter 2).

Finally, Huntington argues, the "implicit rationale for transnationalism" derives from American political ideology. Due to its founding experience as a colony that gained independence, America never developed an ideological justification for colonialism. American transnational expansion after 1945 had a different rationale:

> The American case was rarely based on a claim to political or racial superiority which would give Americans the right to rule other peoples, but rather on a claim to technological or economic superiority, which gave groups of Americans the presumed right—and even duty!—to perform certain specialized functions in other societies. Through this sort of rationale, Americans could reconcile the overseas operations which their economic dynamism warranted with the absence of formal political control which their anticolonial history proscribed.[46]

The right to rule based on technological or economic superiority, and moral superiority one might add—we have seen this before (but not exclusively from America). This is a key to understanding Livingstone's mission to spread Christianity, commerce, and civilization to Africa in the nineteenth century. It is a key to understanding the determination of Amnesty International in London and Human Rights Watch in New York to tally other governments' human rights abuses around the globe today. This is the "global moral compass" that every transnational NGO must claim in order to assert confidently its moral principles anywhere in the world (see chapter 1).

In addition, Huntington understood how transnational NGOs could simultaneously reinforce the status quo and also promote change in the domestic politics of Third World countries. In the short term, the access bargain of any transnational organization would tend to reinforce the position of the dominant groups. In the long term, however, the transnational organization "tends to be a major transmission belt for new styles of life, new ideas, new technology, and new social and cultural values that challenge the traditional culture of the local society."[47] So it may be quite reasonable for some partners to expect an NGO to preserve the status quo, while other partners of the same NGO hope to upset the status quo.

All this can be explained more plainly. The realm of "global civil society" operates according to rules and practices that are largely

American in origin and style, as do the realms of the global economy and global security. In all three realms, the power of American rules is the extent to which they are eagerly imported by peoples of other regions. American rules are attractive because they are more open and inclusive of new players than those of any other hegemon in world history or on the contemporary horizon. In security, any former colony can gain independence and play the state game. In the international economy, any corporation can compete on a relatively level playing field. In global civil society, anyone can launch an NGO and start stumping for publicity, funding, and partners. In all three realms, American rules reflect what Joseph Nye has labeled "soft power"—the ability to make others want what you want.[48]

There are only a few catches under American rules. First, in all three realms, because Americans have been playing by these rules longer than others and generally have access to greater resources, while anybody can play, Americans tend to win. Second, to the extent that elites in much of the rest of the world freely choose to organize their ambitious schemes by shaping themselves into independent states, corporate firms, and NGOs, they have already shaped their conceptions of interest to be either compatible with American interests, or at least intelligible to American leaders and amenable to bargaining in an American style.

It is clear that the secular, universalist, and progressive NGOs considered the norm today sprang from historical movements that were devoutly religious, highly particular in their cultural and national identities, and sometimes regressive in their politics. To what degree might NGOs change direction again in the future? Is it possible they already have?

Beyond highlighting the discontinuous genealogy of contemporary NGOs, this chapter also illustrates the potential scope of NGO power. NGOs can occupy the commanding heights of the political-cultural landscape, inhabit the global *Zeitgeist*, infuse the international system, to define what it means to be a state—not merely ideologically but also materially. To ban the trade and ownership of slaves is to transform the political economy of international and domestic society. To implement eugenics is to manipulate the bodies of citizens. To extract natural rubber from a continent by spilling the blood of its people, and to do so in the name of humanitarianism and progress, is to make an impact that is simultaneously economic, political, military, ideological, and demographic.

This chapter also illuminates, through example, who can mobilize the structural power of NGOs, whether for good or for ill. NGOs can be mobilized by leading states or by determined religious or ideological or (pseudo-) scientific minorities, or by determined individuals. By what authority do any of these transform the state and the human person?

4
NGOs versus Dictators:
Argentina's Dirty War Revisited

Argentina's Dirty War, 1976 to 1983, left a long trail of dashed political hopes and ironic political consequences. A revolutionary movement joined by thousands of Argentine students mounted a powerful strategy to duplicate the Cuban Revolution in Argentina, only to be crushed and annihilated by a brutal military response. Argentine generals cleverly eluded international scrutiny of their clandestine tactics of torture and killing for a time, only to have their crimes exposed to unprecedented global reproach by a new network of human rights NGOs. The human rights network failed to restrain the abuses of the Argentine military that it exposed, yet the network served inadvertently as the midwife for the transition of the entire Latin American left from the Cuban line of Fidel Castro to the democracy line of Ronald Reagan. Finally, the images and interpretations of the Dirty War promulgated by the human rights network inspired a generation of scholars and activists who continue to take the Argentina campaign as a template for NGO advocacy, and therefore continue to *misread* both the Argentine case itself and broader patterns of NGO politics.

The NGO network that coalesced for Argentina in the 1970s lived on and developed into the global human rights network of today. However, contrary to the standard accounts by human rights scholars, the achievements of the NGO network for Argentina are not readily transferable to other countries or issues, whether through tactical formulas or universal norms. The Argentina network can better be understood as a brilliant and courageous response tailored to a particular political moment; a response that failed to achieve its own goals but that contributed to a larger process of regional transformation.

VICTIMS, TORTURERS, AND NGOs—THE HUMAN RIGHTS ACCOUNT

In human rights accounts of the Argentine case, there are three imperatives: first, to highlight as the primary axis of political conflict the confrontation between the human rights network and the dictatorship; second, to ignore the military and political contexts of the human rights abuses, which would complicate the story with other axes of political conflict; third, to portray the victims as the innocent targets of insane brutality. In mainstream human rights accounts of the Argentina case, therefore, NGO activists within that country are the central protagonists who establish links with international allies to bring pressure on the dictatorship, forcing it to curb its brutal tactics, and strengthening international norms.[1] This section outlines a mainstream human rights account, introducing the major components of the human rights network, but bracketing out the military and political contexts.

The towering figure of Juan Perón embodied the tumult of Argentine politics, weaving in and out of government from the 1940s to the 1970s with his glamorous wives, Evita and Isabel. Coming to power once by military coup and three times by election, and ousted from power twice by coup and finally by his death, Perón stirred a volatile mix of authoritarian populism that appealed at times to both left and right.[2] His Perónist movement politically mobilized the Argentine population through massive street demonstrations, extremist promises, and recurring economic crises. When Perón died in 1974 the presidency passed to his widow Isabel, whom he had insisted on installing as vice president the year before. She inherited a hornets' nest of political challenges, including two major guerrilla movements and an economic crisis.

The military officers who overthrew Isabel Perón in 1976 were resolved not to conduct merely one more coup in a long series (the ninth since 1930). This dictatorship instituted the ambitious Process of National Reorganization ("Proceso"), designed to crush the leftist guerrillas in a "Dirty War" and tame tumultuous Argentine politics by politically demobilizing the population, fixing the economy, and remaining in power indefinitely. From 1976 to 1983 the military took control of every part of the government and civil society. With an inflated sense of mission, the officers thought they could transcend Argentine politics by instituting a near-totalitarian form of violent repression.

Once in power, the military began abducting victims at night from their homes, torturing and killing them in secret detention centers, and burying the bodies in unmarked graves or dropping them from aircraft into the Atlantic. The government officially denied any knowledge or involvement in the disappearances, leaving families powerless to recover their loved ones alive or even to grieve their deaths. The disappeared—*los desaparecidos*—ultimately numbered in the tens of thousands. In 1984 the Argentine National Commission on the Disappeared (CONADEP) accounted for 8,960 forced disappearances ending in death, but the human rights movement has insisted that the real total was closer to 30,000. The true scale remains disputed after more than two decades of reports, commissions, and trials.[3]

Among their other brutalities, the military disappeared more than 100 children under 15 years old, and several hundred pregnant women, some of whose infants were born in prison and adopted by military families before the mothers were killed. The numbers, the categories of people disappeared, and the gratuitous cruelty of the torture far surpassed what might have been warranted by any conceivable military or political goal. The military attempted to justify these policies with a bizarre National Security Doctrine that claimed it was acting to defend "Western and Christian Civilization." In short, the Argentine military appeared to have been gripped by a kind of political insanity.

The military was rational enough, however, to silence all domestic protest and elude international scrutiny, at least for a time. Indeed, all governmental institutions and established societal groups—including labor unions and the Catholic Church—were either terrorized by the repression or acquiesced in it. Nevertheless, a human rights movement emerged and became the sole source of enduring resistance; it broke the silence and ultimately brought down unprecedented international opprobrium on the regime.

As the Argentina human rights movement emerged it organized into NGOs, whose formation and rise trace some of the most fascinating stories of NGO history.

The Permanent Assembly for Human Rights was formed by a group of Argentine attorneys in December 1975, three months *before* the coup. It coined the term *los desaparecidos* and played a crucial role by collecting files on the disappeared, which later informed international and national investigations.[4] One of its founders, Emilio Mignone, established Centro de Estudios Legales y Sociales (Center for Legal and Social Studies, or CELS) in 1979 with close links to the International League for Human Rights in New York and the International Commission of Jurists in Geneva.

Large numbers of well-educated Argentine exiles first brought the lurid stories of disappearance and torture to the outside world, and pointed out the systematic pattern of repression. The Argentine

Human Rights Commission (CADHU) was founded in Argentina in 1975, but moved abroad in 1976 after the disappearance of two founders. It quickly opened offices in Paris, Rome, Geneva, Mexico City, and Washington, DC. CADHU members testified before the U.S. House Subcommittee on Human Rights and International Organizations in September 1976. According to Iain Guest, "CADHU was not only the best, it was the only source of information on Argentina during the first terrible year of killing."[5]

A network of Catholic and Protestant NGOs concerned with peace, nonviolence, and social justice developed in parallel with the human rights network, and later joined it. Latin American activists had formed friendships during the 1960s with European and North American members of a cluster of Christian NGOs devoted to peace and nonviolence, including Fellowship of Reconciliation, War Resisters League, and Pax Christi. At a continental meeting of Latin American Christian activists in 1974, Service for Peace and Justice (SERPAJ) was formed. Adolpho Perez Esquivel, an Argentine, was named Coordinator General of the group, which would be based in Buenos Aires.[6] In response to growing repression that followed military coups in Brazil, Uruguay, and Chile during the early 1970s, Perez Esquivel launched the International Campaign for Human Rights in 1976. Just three days after the military coup in Argentina, he left Buenos Aires for a four-month tour to publicize the campaign in 17 countries in Europe and the Americas.

The campaign was pitched at an abstract normative level, and only took on the aspect of a prisoners' rights movement only when Perez Esquivel himself was arrested in Buenos Aires in April 1977. During his 15 months' imprisonment and torture, his thousands of contacts on three continents coalesced into a network to pressure the government for his release.

One of the most dramatic origin stories in NGO history traces the rise of the Las Madres de Plaza de Mayo—the Mothers of the Disappeared in Argentina. After months fruitlessly petitioning government officials for news of their missing children, 14 apolitical, middle-aged women who had met each other waiting in government offices decided to take their petition to the central political space of Argentina.[7] On April 30, 1977, Las Madres began what became a weekly vigil of walking silently around the Plaza de Mayo in Buenos Aires, every Thursday at 3:30 p.m. Later, they donned white headscarves, to evoke the diapers with which they had clothed their lost children, and to symbolize the innocent sorrow of their motherhood. The grandmothers of infants born to women in prison, Las Abuelas de Plaza de Mayo, organized as part of Las Madres in 1978.

The family groups ran great risks, and three leaders of Las Madres were disappeared and killed. Yet the group survived and eventually achieved enormous international prestige, which it used to draw attention to the brutalities of the dictatorship. Among their honors, Las Madres

> visited the United States, Canada, and Europe in 1978 (at the height of the dictatorship), were delegates to the Catholic Church's Puebla Conference, the OAS, and the United Nations in 1979, testified before the U.S. Congress in the same year, and were nominated for a Nobel Prize in 1980. When Las Madres toured Europe during the year of the transition to democracy (1983), they were received as visiting dignitaries by the prime minister of Spain, French president, and the pope.[8]

Although Las Madres ultimately attracted the broadest international attention, they did not organize and begin to act until 13 months after the military coup of March 1976.

Christian activists and former missionaries established some of the first international human rights NGOs in Washington, DC and thereby laid the groundwork for bringing parts of the U.S. government into the network. In response to the September 1973 military coup in Chile, a coalition of American churches established the Washington Office on Latin America (WOLA). Joseph Eldridge, formerly an American Methodist missionary in Chile, settled in Washington in September 1974 as WOLA's first permanent director. Around the same time a new wave of Democratic members of Congress, dubbed "Watergate babies" for the scandal and impeachment of President Richard Nixon which helped them get elected, arrived eager to challenge the White House on foreign policy and to insert a principled commitment to human rights into the American global profile.

Cooperation quickly developed between Eldridge and several new members of Congress, particularly Don Fraser (Democrat from Minnesota) and Tom Harkin (Democrat from Iowa). Fraser used his power as Chairman of the House Subcommittee on International Organizations to convene a series of hearings on human rights beginning in 1973. Joseph Eldridge at WOLA worked with Edward Snyder at the American Friends Service Committee to bring in witnesses for Fraser's hearings from the affected countries themselves. In addition, the historic Harkin Amendment to the Foreign Assistance

Act of 1975, which denied U.S. economic assistance to any country committing gross violations of international recognized human rights, was "first drafted in 1975 by staffers of the Quakers and WOLA."[9]

In 1977, the U.S. National Council of Churches formed a Human Rights Office in Washington directed by William Wipfler, who developed a repertoire of responses to information from church workers in Latin America.[10] The timing of a more intense focus on Washington by human rights NGOs was no accident; it responded to the January 1977 inauguration of President Jimmy Carter, who had campaigned on a promise to make human rights a "cornerstone" of U.S. foreign policy.

Amnesty International—the NGO icon of human rights respectability—brought crucial dimensions of unity and legitimacy to the network. Only six months after the coup, while CADHU was still the only source of human rights information to the international community, Amnesty requested permission of the government to send a mission to Argentina. This initiative was modeled on Amnesty's intervention following the 1973 military coup in neighboring Chile.[11] Surprisingly, regime leaders accepted the visit, thinking they could use it to learn the contacts and practices of the human rights activists who were opposing them. For ten days in November 1976, despite intimidation by military "escorts" and slurs in the local press, mission members conducted interviews with family members of the disappeared, newspaper editors, and government officials.[12] It published its report in March 1977, a year after the coup and a month before the formation of Las Madres. Amnesty also opened a liaison office in Washington, DC in 1977.

The Amnesty mission became the catalyst for a cascade of links between Argentine and international NGOs.

The most important contribution by Amnesty was the idea of impartiality and all that it implied. The network became unified under Amnesty's official normative agenda which focused on individual victims of human rights violations, regardless of who committed the abuses. Under this approach, the network was officially indifferent to whoever rules a country, simply challenging all rulers to adhere to universal human rights. Today, it is no longer novel or shocking to suggest that NGOs might undermine dictatorships or nudge them toward democratization. It is easy to forget that the very idea that NGOs might overthrow or undermine authoritarian regimes was anathema to NGOs themselves as late as 1988. Indeed, such a charge was heard only from the dictators.

The credibility and visibility of Amnesty International's testimony on Argentina was enhanced in December 1977 when the NGO received the Nobel Peace Prize. Three years later, the Peace Prize was awarded to the previously obscure figure of Adolpho Perez Esquivel. These twin honors from the Norwegian Nobel Committee endowed the entire Argentina human rights network with tremendous prestige and moral authority.

The human rights network was never more unified than when it was confronting the Argentine dictatorship, and it never confronted the dictatorship more forcefully than when it acted through the U.S. government under the Carter administration. Shortly after Carter's election in November 1976, Congress created the position of Assistant Secretary of State for Human Rights and Humanitarian Affairs. To fill the new position Carter nominated Patricia Derian, a non-diplomat with experience in the Georgia civil rights movement.[13] He also appointed a small corps of veteran NGO activists to positions within the State Department and National Security Council.

President Carter himself, and his Secretary of State Cyrus Vance, personally criticized the Argentine dictatorship. Citing human rights grounds, the administration cut military aid to Argentina, Uruguay, and Ethiopia in early 1977.[14] Derian hammered the Argentine junta in bureaucratic battles within the administration, in press conferences, and in official reports. During three visits to Argentina during 1977 she met with all the human rights groups as well as government leaders. Roberta Cohen and Jerome Shestack, appointed to the State Department directly from the International League for Human Rights, led the effort by the U.S. government to censure Argentina for its human rights violations in the United Nations Commission on Human Rights in Geneva, and in the human rights institutions of the Organization of American States.[15]

For human rights accounts of the Dirty War, the impact of the network is analyzed strictly in terms of human rights outcomes, whether within Argentina or beyond it. Disappearances declined over several years within Argentina, which some observers attribute to the pressure brought on the government by the human rights network. According to data from the 1984 Argentine National Commission on the Disappeared (CONADEP), there were about 4,000 disappearances in 1976 and in 1977, just under 1,000 in 1978, 181 in 1979, 83 in 1980, and a total of 40 over the next three years.[16] Beyond Argentina, the human rights campaign for Argentina contributed to innovations in forensic investigative techniques, and helped to create global norms against torture and extra-judicial execution.

How the human rights network might have been linked to war and political conflict in Argentina and Latin America is not seriously considered in human rights accounts. To do so would be to lose the tight focus on the axis of political conflict between the innocent network and the brutal dictatorship. Would pursuing such questions mean that one does not care about human rights? Or could it help unravel the complex origins and influences of the human rights network?

In any case, the next section examines broader military and political conflicts within which the victims of the Dirty War were caught, and which their fates came to shape.

THE CUBAN LINE IN ARGENTINA

The Dirty War was a war, whatever else it may have been, and the strategy of the guerrillas in that war is incomprehensible without considering Cuba.

The Cuban Revolution of 1959 led by Fidel Castro and Che Guevara electrified the politics of Latin America. Fidel and Che aggressively exported their revolution to the rest of Latin America and beyond.[17] In a region hungry for change, thousands of idealistic, generous, and ambitious young people welcomed the opportunity to drag their nations kicking and screaming into equality and modernity. According to Jorge Castañeda, himself a veteran of the Latin American left, "For more than a decade, the urban, middle-class, university-educated, politicized youth of an entire continent was mesmerized by the armed struggle."[18] As a result, according to Timothy Wickham-Crowley, "Guerrilla movements appeared in virtually every nation in Latin America in the 1960s, even in revolutionary Cuba."[19]

The Latin American left largely abandoned the strategy of its traditional communist parties, which had competed for power through elections. Instead, the "Cuban line" dominated the region, dictating four elements of a new revolutionary strategy.[20] First, the revolution must be hemispheric in its scope and concurrent in its timing, with no waiting for local conditions to ripen. Second, the revolution must be resolutely socialist by expropriating the means of production from private hands. Third, the revolution must be achieved through armed struggle, renouncing all peaceful paths to power. Finally, the revolution must be led by the enlightened, urban middle classes, such as students, intellectuals, professionals, and teachers, and must exclude all old-line party, union, or bourgeois alliances.

In virtually every Latin American nation the local left was permeated by the influence of the Cuban line, creating a regional social movement and organizational network that pre-dated the human rights network.

In Argentina, the leftist political opposition comprised mass organizations, political parties, and two significant guerrilla groups, the Montoneros and the People's Revolutionary Army (ERP), both founded in 1969. By 1975, the Argentine left had mounted what appeared to be a powerful political-military strategy which was on the brink of victory. The strategy combined four elements.

First, the Montoneros and the ERP mounted successful recruitment campaigns through the early 1970s, expanding their combined guerrilla forces dramatically from 600 in 1972 to 5,000 in 1975.[21] This blistering, nearly nine-fold expansion in three years showed no signs of coming to an end. In addition, the guerrillas did their best to project an image of even larger forces to the public and the military.

Second, by 1975 the guerrillas were mounting hundreds of military operations each year, mostly in large cities, including attacks on property, bombings, kidnappings for ransom, hijackings, and seizures of buildings (including military installations). These were often spectacular actions designed with a theatrical flair to gain maximum attention. According to data synthesized by María José Moyano from numerous Argentine news sources, documents of radical groups, and interviews with surviving guerrillas, the Montoneros and the ERP were not already in retreat at the time of the 1976 coup. They staged 723 operations in 1975, and managed 662 in 1976. And they continued to mount military operations while under heavy repression after the coup, with almost 200 in 1977 and almost 100 in 1978.[22]

Third, a number of mass organizations and political parties on the left staged hundreds of their own acts of collective violent protest each year, including riots and bombings, independent of the military operations of the guerrillas. Leaders of both the guerrillas and the military assumed that the bonds of organization and loyalty between the mass organizations and the guerrillas were much stronger than they turned out to be.[23]

An exclusive focus on military elements does not capture the larger potential for political dynamism in a guerrilla struggle. This is the fourth element of the strategy, the political element, designed to magnify the impact of the other three elements. Guerrilla "military" operations in Argentina usually had no specifically military objective as such, and were staged to achieve the *political* goals of rallying the masses to their cause, and humiliating and discouraging the government and its allies. For many years a highly receptive audience welcomed this military-political theater. According to Moyano's analysis of survey data, political discourse, news coverage, and political memoirs, during the early 1970s a majority of the general public in Argentina supported the left's armed struggle, and this support extended across all economic classes and the urban/rural divide.[24]

The elements of this powerful strategy converged so that by the mid-1970s both the guerrillas and the military believed that Argentina had reached a "revolutionary situation" in which a determined attack by revolutionary forces could set off a general mass insurrection and cause the government to fall like a house of cards.[25] The Cuban line appeared to be working in Argentina.

POLITICS IN THE NETWORK

One way to understand the politics around the NGO network is to begin with the politics within the network. If the network was unified by a common target and common normative agenda, the network was also divided by conflicting latent agendas pursued by its members and their partners. Such agendas may conflict with the salient agenda of the network as a whole, and with each other. Again, the salient agenda of the network was provided by Amnesty International, which sought to hold governments accountable, not to replace them.

For the emergence of the Latin American human rights network in the 1970s, Chile and Argentina were intimately linked. The human rights response to the coup in Chile served as a kind of rehearsal for the response to the coup in Argentina three years later.

The 1973 coup by General Augusto Pinochet to oust the elected socialist government of Salvador Allende became a "watershed event in the creation of the Latin American human rights network."[26] The human rights frame became a sort of halfway house for groups with various concerns to ally against the Pinochet regime and against U.S. government support for the coup. These activists were motivated by principled outrage over the violation of universal human rights in Chile. At the same time, for many this cosmopolitan concern was mixed with left-of-center political commitments, and often with a personal imperative to protect friends and colleagues who were being tortured or killed by Pinochet. Hundreds of solidarity groups in the United States arose to protest the coup.[27]

The human rights network created a political space that could embrace leftists who sought other allies against Pinochet, international church people exiled after the coup, and veterans of the Vietnam antiwar movement in the United States and Europe who opposed American intervention in the Third World. Chile became a pariah state in the UN human rights institutions in Geneva before Argentina came under criticism there.[28]

The new wave of human rights NGOs in Washington, DC expressed a strong commitment to universal human rights, but also carried the latent agenda of political solidarity with revolutionary groups in Latin America. Leaders in this field included the Council for Hemispheric Affairs, the Chile Committee for Human Rights, and the Coalition for a New Foreign and Military Policy.[29]

The Washington Office on Latin America was particularly important for solidarity links. Joseph Eldridge, WOLA's executive director from 1974 to 1986, had been an American Methodist missionary in Chile. According to his ministry supervisor, Eldridge "had to get out of Chile" after the coup in 1973.[30] Pinochet's military government expelled much of its Chilean political opposition, as well as many expatriates who sympathized with it. Indeed, WOLA was so effective in providing witnesses of human rights violations in Chile and Argentina for Representative Don Fraser's House Subcommittee on International Organizations precisely because WOLA was "the only NGO with specific connections with the Solidarity movements involving Chile and Argentina."[31]

A massive political exile of the left from the southern cone of South America set the stage for the rapid globalization of the human rights movement in the 1970s. Up to 1 million people fled Chile, Uruguay, and Argentina in the wake of successive military coups during the 1970s. Military governments in all three countries brutally repressed the left, while encouraging international organizations to resettle abroad those who were willing to accept exile. Labor unions and leftist parties in Western Europe strongly lobbied their governments to accept these migrants in what became a political diaspora of the left from the southern cone to 44 other countries.[32] By this stratagem, military governments in Chile, Uruguay, and Argentina successfully reduced their domestic opposition, but inadvertently sowed the seeds for a transnational human rights network that would expose their domestic repression to the world.

It was in this context that CADHU, the Argentine Human Rights Commission, was able to rapidly shift its operations from Buenos Aires to abroad in 1976, and quickly open offices in Paris, Rome, Geneva, Mexico City, and Washington, DC. In short, CADHU rebuilt itself abroad on the massive political diaspora of the Argentine left.

We have seen that CADHU became the first NGO in the Argentina network, and the exclusive source of information on human rights abuses in Argentina for the first year of the dictatorship. It could play this role only because its leaders came out of the radical left in Argentina, and maintained links with armed groups. It carried a strong latent agenda of solidarity with the Argentine left. Although this was largely a defensive imperative to keep comrades alive, it was combined with a political offensive designed to discredit the dictatorship for its human rights abuses in order that the left might somehow take power either politically or through armed struggle. Of course, other NGOs and parts of the U.S. government within the human rights network were well aware of the political sympathies of CADHU activists, but relied on them nevertheless as the source of the best human rights information on Argentina.[33]

In effect, the political solidarity groups, and the human rights NGOs with strong links to armed guerrillas, succeeded in attaching a watered-down version of the Cuban line to the human rights network as a latent agenda. This generated an undercurrent of conflict within the network. But who was capturing or transforming whom?

The official Catholic Church in Argentina took no public role in challenging the dictatorship or promoting human rights, in sharp contrast to the Catholic Church in both Brazil and Chile.[34] In the deeply Catholic society of Argentina the silence of the Church left a cultural void. Other voices with a moral or religious message were amplified by the official Catholic silence.

Perez Esquivel and his global network of Christian activists in SERPAJ were not politically ambitious, but their commitment to nonviolence contrasted sharply with the dictatorship's heavy reliance on violence. By arresting and torturing Perez Esquivel, the Argentine military only highlighted his innocence and their own brutality, thereby reinforcing the message of the human rights movement. The 1980 Nobel Peace Prize awarded to Perez Esquivel constituted a sharp blow to the regime's international legitimacy.[35]

Las Madres de Plaza de Mayo never defined themselves in religious terms, but in the context of official Catholic silence, they projected a powerful symbolic indictment by embodying the Madonna searching for her martyred child. Their explicit demands were modest: "We do not ask for anything more than the truth." Yet, at the same time, they employed a symbolic "political theater" to target the root of the Proceso's claim to legitimate rule. According to Alison Brysk:

> The Mothers consciously contested the imagery being promoted by the "Western, Christian" Proceso; they made pilgrimages to sites of popular Marian devotion and evoked the suffering of mothers seeking children crucified by a state that claimed to be Christian but did not even allow the family to bury its dead. Las Madres' challenge was particularly directed at the military, which had historically styled itself a Marian institution. The legitimacy of Las Madres was such that it even mitigated street level repression. Mothers would turn on the police sent to break up their protests, saying, "Aren't you ashamed to attack defenseless mothers? Don't you have children?"—often causing the police to hang back.[36]

In addition to their Marian drama, the Mothers drew upon a layer of Western culture older than Christianity by evoking the ancient Greek figure of Antigone. Where Antigone defied the king to bury the body of her brother in the name of the unwritten law, Las Madres defied the military to recover the bodies of their children in the name of human rights.[37]

Like CADHU, both Las Madres and Perez Esquivel's SERPAJ carried latent agendas that challenged the legitimacy of military rule in Argentina, but unlike CADHU, which sought a government of the left, Las Madres and SERPAJ did not favor any particular alternative rulers or form of government. It is important to note that none of these NGOs advocated democratization for Argentina, whether in their salient or latent agendas.

Beyond the human rights network, the broader regional network included NGOs and parts of governments committed to goals and norms far removed from what is considered in conventional accounts of the Argentina case. Human rights NGOs were not the only ones to form international linkages—operating alongside was a counter-network of anti-communist NGOs.

The Unification Church, led by Sun Myung Moon of South Korea, established CAUSA (Confederation of Associations for the Unity of the Societies of the Americas) as a political action wing. The Moonie organizations provided direct support to the Nicaraguan Contras and the governments of El Salvador and Guatemala, and also networked with Religious Right NGOs in the United States which were lobbying

Congress to fund the Contras in their efforts to overthrow the Sandinista government of Nicaragua.[38] These NGOs expressed the anti-communist beliefs of their members, while maintaining solidarity links with anti-communist governments and revolutionaries.

This sketch of the politics in the network shows that political conflict was not located exclusively, or even primarily, on the axis between the human rights network and the Argentine regime. The Argentina human rights network was linked much more intimately to national and international conflicts and wars than standard human rights accounts would reveal. Although each side of the war in Argentina had some NGOs more or less aligned with it, they were not aligned in the same way. Solidarity with the guerrilla struggle was a latent agenda for some human rights NGOs, while solidarity with the right-wing dictatorships was part of the official, salient agenda of the anti-communist NGOs.

Moreover, the NGOs in the human rights network are far more interesting than the anti-communist NGOs for the complexity of their internal contradictions and the paradoxes of their ultimate impact. Such nuances are rife in the role of Amnesty International.

THE AMNESTY LINE

Revealing the tensions and contradictions that pervaded the Argentina NGO network only underscores the importance of the common human rights agenda that held these strange bedfellows together in the same bed. This brings us again to Amnesty International. As the first truly global human rights NGO, Amnesty virtually defined the human rights movement for more than two decades. From its founding in 1961 until 1989, Amnesty was the only NGO to monitor continuously human rights abuses for all countries of the world.[39] Throughout this period, the humanitarian aspiration toward truly universal norms was embodied in Amnesty's global research and reporting.

Beyond norms, or rather embedded in them, Amnesty made two implicit, strategic commitments on behalf of the larger human rights movement. In its first strategic commitment, Amnesty was resolute in its deference to existing governments. In its second strategic commitment, Amnesty consistently ignored the political context of both human rights violations and their suppression. Together, these two strategic commitments might be considered the "Amnesty line," which coexisted in the human rights network with the Cuban line of violent, socialist revolution.

The degree to which these commitments were tailored for a particular, limited period in world politics has not been recognized. Known as the champion of normative *universality*, Amnesty gained its success by matching a set of tactics to world political conditions at an extended moment of historical *particularity*.

By its identity and tactics, Amnesty International accorded overt deference to existing regimes and their officials, whether communist or non-communist, and regardless of their brutality to their own citizens. To bring "pressure" on a government, Amnesty mobilized members worldwide to send letters, as well as telegrams and later faxes, politely requesting officials to release "prisoners of conscience" or to stop torture. This central tactic of letter-writing, while demanding certain behavior from governments, also acknowledged their right to rule. Each local Amnesty International "adoption group" would typically be assigned to work for the release of two prisoners of conscience—one held by a communist government and another held by an anti-communist government. In this way, each local group verified and embodied Amnesty's impartiality—its dedication to the rights of individuals, not to the goals of the political opposition movements to which they might belong. In its own self-understanding, Amnesty was not in the business of influencing who held power, but only influencing the adherence of those in power to international norms.

Amnesty's deference to existing governments represented a brilliant adaptation to international political realities that emerged around the historical moment of Amnesty's founding in 1961 and persisted for the next two decades.

The norm of "sovereignty"—deference to internationally recognized governments and borders—commanded international respect from weak countries to ensure their survival from invasion or recolonization. Middle-power and superpower countries affirmed the norm in order to avoid any conflict that could escalate into World War III. Both of these time-bound concerns peaked in the early 1960s with accelerating decolonization and the Cuban missile crisis. Therefore, Amnesty International was not promoting a timeless norm in its consistent deference to existing governments. Instead, its genius was to devise a timely tactic that used national sovereignty as a lever to pry respectable behavior from existing rulers.

Amnesty International provided the salient, normative agenda for the entire Argentina human rights network. By its deference to existing governments, Amnesty served to obscure the latent agendas of other NGOs in the network that sought to undermine military rule. Again, neither Amnesty nor any of the other NGOs in the human rights network sought the democratization of Argentina, whether as a salient or latent agenda.

Amnesty's second strategic commitment, to ignore the political context of human rights issues, also emerged from a creative adaptation to international realities. If the early 1960s saw the growth of norms to restrain war between countries, the same period also witnessed the escalation of violence within countries. As the superpowers drew back from direct confrontations with each other, they developed a taste for proxy wars in the expanding Third World. Strategies of armed revolution diffused throughout the Third World from the Chinese Revolution of 1949 and the Cuban Revolution of 1959. Governments responded to these revolutionary challenges by increasing military and police repression. These historical conjunctures displaced a large share of both national and international politics into the prisons and torture chambers of Third World governments.

In this historical context, Amnesty's response was to invent the idea of *prisoners of conscience*—persons "imprisoned, detained, or restricted for their political, religious or other conscientiously held beliefs, their ethnic origin, sex, color or language who have not used or advocated violence."[40] This definition excluded armed revolutionaries from Amnesty's protection, but did not necessarily exclude their political sympathizers who had not directly advocated violence. This normative frame abstracted from the ideologies of particular prisoners of conscience and their placement on the spectrum of Cold War ideology, just as it abstracted from the Cold War alliances of the governments that imprisoned them.

As a side effect of this commitment, the challengers or conflicts that threatened a particular government simply fell outside Amnesty's circle of concern and analytical attention. In other words, embedded within the definition of prisoner of conscience was an intellectual commitment to ignore the political context and causality of both the violations of human rights and their suppression.

This aspect of Amnesty's strategy was imprinted upon the Argentina human rights network and strongly reinforced by it. The Proceso military government claimed in its propaganda that the Dirty War was justified by a mortal threat to Argentine society from the communist insurgency. Rather than engaging this self-serving propaganda claim, Amnesty and the whole network simply abstracted from the particularities of the political and military conflict, and appealed to the universal standards that all governments must respect.

This argument continues today within Argentina and the global human rights movement, and explains why human rights accounts of the Dirty War tend to ignore the strategies and tactics of the warriors. To analyze the war seems tantamount to justifying the dictatorship and the brutal disappearances.[41] In this chapter I am seeking a path through this moral and intellectual logjam, because the politics of the network, and of Amnesty International's role in the network, are not fully intelligible without violating Amnesty's taboo against analyzing the war.

Nothing illustrates this paradox better than Amnesty's strategic interaction with the leaders of the successive military coups in Chile and Argentina.

After the 1973 coup in Chile, General Pinochet launched a violent repression of the political left, employing massive arrests, torture, and executions. Because the Pinochet regime publicly acknowledged holding most of its political prisoners, the fledgling human rights network, led by Amnesty International, was able to generate thousands of letters and telegrams demanding their release. The generals in Argentina observed across their long border how General Pinochet was pummeled by human rights publicity and humiliated by pariah status in the United Nations. When the Argentine generals staged their own military coup three years later, they chose to rely almost exclusively on the repressive tactic of clandestine disappearance and killing in part to circumvent or delay the response of the human rights network.[42]

Intriguingly, the published literature only acknowledged in the 1990s the choice made in the 1970s by the Argentine generals to use the tactic of disappearances to deflect the international pressure of the human rights network. For us to understand the impact of this history on the Argentine human rights campaign, we have only to grant that *human rights leaders understood this perfectly well at the time*, even if they did not then discuss it publicly. I would suggest that the leaders of human rights NGOs, including Amnesty International, all knew by 1977 that thousands of people were disappearing in Argentina partly as a consequence of the generals' strategic response to their own human rights tactics against Chile.[43]

This was a double defeat for the NGOs: not only were the generals evading NGO pressure, but more people were dying due to the heavy use of disappearances inadvertently triggered by the NGOs. Fully aware of this, human rights NGO leaders were absolutely determined to bring maximum pressure on the Argentine generals. To be sure, other circumstances favored a campaign focused on Argentina: there were human rights groups with good information within the country and in exile; the Chile network was still in place; Jimmy Carter had just been elected president, and the middle-class victims in Argentina would be regarded sympathetically by publics in Europe and North America.[44] Notwithstanding these other factors, however, the Argentina campaign was not a cool application of universal norms; it was a crusade, and it was personal.

This argument ought to be explored in further documentary and interview research.[45] But there is already significant evidence to confirm it. Emilio Mignone, an Argentine human rights activist, recalls, "One phrase I heard repeatedly in that period from the mouths of Generals, Colonels, Admirals, and Brigadiers was, 'we aren't going to do it like Franco and Pinochet who executed people publicly, because then even the Pope will be asking us not to do it.'"[46]

In short, Chile and Argentina were singled out for the human rights treatment. If the Argentina campaign was about creating a catalyst for building universal human rights norms, it was just as much or more about using norms as tools to build a coalition to punish the Argentine generals and get them out of power. The campaign was about particular political struggles in a particular historical moment. Therefore, Amnesty itself carried a latent agenda in conflict with its own strategic commitment to defer to existing governments.

This is not to argue that Amnesty International was biased in some crude sense. But the Argentina case does illustrate that Amnesty's universalism—and that of the human rights network as a whole—was in the service of its country campaigns against selected targets chosen for particularistic motives.

The overall picture is a transnational human rights network that is officially indifferent to who rules Argentina, but is pervaded with latent ties of sympathy and solidarity to various groups on the political left—the armed left following the Cuban line, the nonviolent left of the religious and family groups, and human rights activists dedicated to opposing the leading right-wing governments of the region. So it is doubly ironic that the most important consequence of the human rights network was neither to ameliorate the human rights abuses in

Argentina nor to serve the left, but instead to transform the left in the whole region. In its inadvertent historical mission, the Amnesty line seduced the Latin American left away from the Cuban line and prepared it to embrace the democracy line. To discern this larger storyline, however, we must first take off our Amnesty blinders and study the war.

THE NETWORK AND THE DIRTY WAR

To make a judgment about the impact of the human rights network in stopping the disappearances also requires examining, and making a judgment about, the military strategies of the dictatorship. The question of why the military stopped the disappearances entails the question of why they chose to use the tactic in the first place.

The tactic of disappearances emerged as a variation of "counterterror" strategy drawn from French counterinsurgency experience in Indochina and Algeria. The U.S. military also used counterterror techniques in Vietnam. In spite of the failure of counterterror in all three of these conflicts, the United States encouraged its use in Latin America after the Cuban Revolution. The Argentine National Security Doctrine that justified counterterror in the minds of the military was a concoction of French National-Catholicism, German geopolitical thought, and U.S. Cold War ideology.[47]

The Proceso military dictatorship set out to achieve three narrow military goals and two broad political goals by the use of the counterterror tactic of disappearances. In the military sphere it sought, first, to eliminate acts of collective violent protest by mass organizations and parties, second, to eliminate guerrilla military operations, and third, to annihilate the Montoneros and ERP as fighting forces. The military succeeded in achieving all three military goals, but only because of major strategic blunders committed by the guerrilla leaders.

The dictatorship sought to employ disappearances to accomplish two broad political goals: to elude international scrutiny for its repression, and to pacify and politically demobilize Argentine society. It failed in both these political goals, due to its own strategic blunder.

The failure of the human rights network to stop the disappearances is entangled with the military goals of the dictatorship, while the inadvertent influence of the human rights network to promote democratization in Argentina and the region is wrapped up with the failure of the dictatorship's political goals.

According to Moyano, guerrilla leaders in both the Montonero and ERP could have discerned that by 1974 Argentina was no longer in a revolutionary situation—ripe for a mass insurrection—as it had earlier appeared to be. In 1973, partly in response to previous guerrilla actions, the military allowed democratic elections and permitted Juan Perón to return to Argentina after an 18-year exile in Spain. When Perón regained the presidency, he gave amnesty to the guerrillas and offered them positions in his government. Instead of shifting to a predominantly political strategy, guerrilla leaders decided to exploit the more open environment by intensifying the armed struggle and staging more military operations. Argentine public opinion, which had supported the armed struggle in the early 1970s, shifted against it with the chaos the guerrillas created during Isabel Perón's presidency. This first guerrilla strategic blunder set the stage for escalating military repression.[48]

In their second and even more ruinous strategic blunder, guerrilla military operations became "militarized" in the sense that they lost any political purpose and became ends in themselves. After the 1976 coup, according to Moyano, "armed organizations should have turned to a defensive strategy involving sabotage and small-scale attacks. Instead, guerrilla groups continued to expose their forces in frontal attacks, with predictable results."[49]

This is where the three military goals of the Proceso dictatorship come into play. Acts of collective violent protest by mass organizations and parties ended quickly after the 1976 coup, revealing the weak links between these groups and the guerrillas. However, the Montoneros and ERP continued to mount large numbers of military operations even after the coup, with almost 200 in 1977 and almost 100 in 1978.[50] These operations gave the military the opportunity to annihilate the guerrillas as fighting forces over several years.

Moyano estimates changes in guerrilla membership using "a combination of internal guerrilla documents, guerrilla press releases, and personal interviews with former combatants and members of the security forces."[51] Counting the Montoneros and the ERP together, from a peak guerrilla membership of 5,000 in 1975, the military slashed their numbers to between 1,000 and 1,300 by 1979.[52] Such catastrophic losses of up to 80 per cent were due in large part to the persistence of guerrillas in mounting frontal attacks on high-profile targets, including military installations, in which fighters were either killed or, worse, captured and tortured to reveal their comrades. The usual revolutionary cell structure, in which each fighter knows only a few comrades by name, did not protect the Argentine guerrillas from compromising their organizations under torture, because they had been recruited along with friends and because the movement provided an alternate social community. Therefore, although the press reported the deaths of most guerrillas as having been killed in shoot-outs with the military, "A significant number of these combatants probably were not killed in action but disappeared, that is to say, they were kidnapped, taken to clandestine detention centers, and eventually executed."[53] In short, up to 4,000 guerrillas lost their lives to this losing strategy. The implication for human rights analysis must be faced—that a significant minority of the disappeared in Argentina were guerrillas.

Why did the guerrillas make this blunder and persist in it to the end? Moyano cites a cluster of factors, including a mistaken belief derived from the Cuban Revolution that military action alone could create the conditions for revolution, the blind obedience of rank-and-file guerrillas due to their youth and emotional bonds to fallen comrades, and the isolation of the guerrillas from a public opinion that had turned against them. But the fundamental point is that a catastrophic failure of political judgment by the guerrilla leadership made them continuously vulnerable to military repression.

Among the accounts of repression in Argentina, Margaret Keck and Kathryn Sikkink make the strongest case that the human rights network achieved its goal of reducing the disappearances. In their view, the dictatorship did respond to international—particularly U.S. government—pressure and began to reduce disappearances after fall 1978, when the military leadership shifted and it accepted a visit by the Inter-American Commission on Human Rights, which occurred a year later.[54]

In my view, the persistence of guerrilla military operations after the 1976 coup suggests another explanation.

Although acts of government violence, including disappearances, declined each year of the dictatorship from a high point in 1976, they continued at a low level right through 1983, the last year of the Proceso.[55] I would argue that these data are more consistent with an explanation that attributes the decline but persistence of repressive violence to factors internal to the military government, rather than to domestic and international pressures from the human rights network.

From the data, it appears that the Argentine military did not reduce its use of repressive violence to very low levels (fewer than 100 acts per year) until 1980, after incidents of guerrilla military operations approached zero. Even by late 1979, when rebel numbers were already severely reduced, the Montoneros launched the "Popular Counteroffensive," which led to the deaths of many leaders and bitter splits among those that remained alive.[56] The Argentine military maintained severe levels of repression and conducted disappearances just as long as the guerrillas showed they could still strike back.

I conclude that the human rights network exposed the disappearances, but failed to end or restrain them.

If the Dirty War was indeed a war, it was not fought exclusively between the military and the guerrillas. The military, following the misleading logic of counterterror, kidnapped and killed perhaps tens of thousands of civilians, many targeted at random, in order to dry up the "sea" of sympathizers from which the guerrilla "fish" might recruit new members. This over-reliance on violence to respond to a political threat was the crucial blunder in the strategy of the military dictatorship.

It can be seen as a blunder because there was an alternative strategy available and because it failed to achieve the dictatorship's political goals. The military could have countered the guerrillas at much lower levels of violence. As Moyano suggests, "By the time of the coup the guerrillas had suffered a political, not a military defeat. This could have been exploited by the military through an active propaganda campaign aimed at the general population and through infiltration of the guerrilla movement, thus making the dirty war unnecessary."[57] This alternate strategy would have spared untold damage to the civilian victims, the country, and the military as an institution. Therefore, the disappearances and killings were misdirected—the wrong weapons aimed at the wrong targets. Human rights activists, and scholars who share their mindset, tend to misread the Dirty War as a kind of political insanity unconnected to any policy rather than as a consistent, ruthless commitment to a perverse policy.

This was a strategic blunder, not only because it was excessive, but even more because it could not have achieved the political goal of pacifying Argentine society. While counterterror appeared to work in Argentina (as it had not worked for the French in Indochina and Algeria or for the United States in Vietnam) by annihilating the guerrillas and terrorizing their sympathizers, this could not have been a lasting victory.

The Proceso leaders would have exalted their extreme violence as the historic solution to Argentina's problems, reinforcing the penchant for violence in civil society, which sooner or later would have generated another violent movement with its own messianic program. The Dirty War was a fundamentally flawed strategy because the lasting pacification of Argentine society, which the military claimed to seek, could not be obtained by the violent means of disappearances. In other words, Argentina could not make the transition to non-violent political disputation in the 1980s, and cannot continue to sustain democratic institutions, without the moral and political delegitimation of the Dirty War in the eyes of Argentine civil society.

Ironically, the culture of violence in Argentine society encouraged leaders of both the guerrillas and the military to make similar strategic blunders. Moyano assigns partial responsibility for the Dirty War to Argentina's "radicalized civil society, which first glorified violence as an agent of social change and then justified a ruthless repression as the only means of returning to the status quo ante."[58]

The delegitimation of the Dirty War, and the implicit delegitimation of the Cuban line, turned out to be the historic task of the human rights network, which served to prepare Argentina for a flawed but enduring democratization. The wave of democratization that Argentina helped to spread to the rest of Latin America was urgently needed as an alternative to the shooting war between left and right that permeated the region.

REGIONAL WAR IN LATIN AMERICA

From its inception in 1976, the Proceso military regime of Argentina viewed its military role as regional. When the Carter administration began to withdraw the United States from the role of military enforcer for the region in early 1977, the generals of Argentina took it upon themselves to fill the gap. Argentina provided military counterinsurgency training and arms sales, first to the Somoza government of Nicaragua before it fell in 1979, and later to El Salvador, Guatemala, and Honduras. With the prestige of its victories over the guerrillas at home, the Argentine military transferred its techniques and ideology of counterterror to Central America. The long arm of Argentine intelligence reached throughout Latin America and even Europe. Argentina provided military assistance to a violent military coup in Bolivia in 1980, against the opposition of the Carter administration. Hit squads targeted political opponents in eleven countries on two continents. According to Armony:

From 1977 on, Argentine paramilitary groups stalked, kidnapped, and assassinated Argentine political refugees throughout Latin America and Europe. Hit teams were sent from Argentina to track down exiled dissidents in Brazil, Uruguay, Paraguay, Bolivia, Peru, Venezuela, Mexico, Spain, Italy, Switzerland, and Belgium.[59]

Argentine intelligence, anti-communist governments in the region, and the American CIA at times were all part of a broad, regional network—a counter-network working against the human rights network. The armed portion of that network, partnered with independent criminal and military elements, "served as a conduit for drug and arms trafficking, money laundering, and terrorist activities, well beyond the original purpose of rolling back the Communist threat in the Western Hemisphere."[60]

As new caches of documents become available, more and more of this regional network emerges from the shadows. The latest research by John Dinges details Operation Condor, in which Argentina worked with the dictatorships of Chile, Brazil, Uruguay, Paraguay, and Bolivia to kidnap and assassinate hundreds of opposition leaders exiled throughout Latin America, Europe, and even the United States.[61]

After the Sandinistas overthrew the Somoza regime in Nicaragua in 1979, Argentine intelligence worked with remnants of Somoza's National Guard and other opponents of the Sandinistas to form the germ of what became the Nicaraguan Contras. Though the CIA sponsored the Contras under the Reagan administration after 1981, the Contras were not created by the United States. Argentine intelligence took its own initiative to create the Contras in 1979.[62]

In the conventional human rights account of the Argentina case, all the members of the network—NGOs, foundations, parts of governments, and parts of intergovernmental organizations—are unified by their shared commitment to the same universal norms, shared solidarity with the victims created by the violation of those norms, and shared opposition to the violators. Recent research shows that the loyalties of the most powerful network member—the U.S. government—were more deeply divided than was previously known.

The Carter presidency burnished the reputation for an "absolute" commitment to human rights, as Carter promised in his inaugural speech.[63] When Ronald Reagan became president in 1981 he made a point to renounce Carter's human rights rhetoric and directed the

CIA to work with Argentine intelligence to fight communist forces in Central America.

However, according to Congressional testimony given secretly in 1987 and declassified in the 1990s, the CIA had established links to the regional operations of Argentine intelligence *even during the Carter administration*. In 1978, CIA agents directly assisted a special unit of Argentine intelligence to establish a covert business in Fort Lauderdale, Florida whose function was to direct and finance Argentine military and intelligence activities in Central America.[64] CIA assistance continued through Carter's term. Whatever Carter's knowledge of, or responsibility for, these activities, the loyalties of the U.S. government vis-à-vis Argentina were deeply divided during precisely the period when its reputation for a strong commitment to human rights was at its peak.

The view that the Argentine military was not tamed or rendered timid by the international human rights network is reinforced by evidence from the regional hot war in Latin America. While disappearances were declining at home, Argentina's foreign military activity only escalated. There is no sign in this record of Argentine extraterritorial military action of a regime that is cowed by the opposition of the U.S. Congress or the Carter administration, or in any way responsive to the international human rights network.

Nor did the Argentine military increase disappearances at home when the U.S. government relieved its human rights pressure. By early 1980 Carter was already seeking allies for a tougher stance toward the Soviet Union and Patricia Derian resigned from the State Department, protesting the administration's plan to end official criticism of the Argentine regime.[65] After 1981 the Reagan administration worked to circumvent remaining congressional restrictions on military and intelligence cooperation with Argentina. Indeed, as reported by Ariel Armony, the election of Reagan triggered a wave of massive repression by anti-communist governments in Central America.[66] However, the Argentine dictatorship did not escalate disappearances at home after 1981. If the Argentine military had reduced its repression in response to international pressure and against internal considerations such as its perception of threat from the guerrillas, then we might expect an increase in repression when the external pressure was relieved. Instead, the Argentine military followed its own lights, not human rights pressure.

How did this picture of regional warfare between right and left transform into the wave of democratization that displaced military dictatorships and pacified armed guerrillas?

THE DEMOCRACY LINE AND LATIN AMERICA

If the Argentina human rights network fell short of achieving its own human rights goals, it contributed to an achievement that was not part of its official goals—the transition to democracy and the removal from executive power of the Proceso military regime. As Alison Brysk appraises the record: "The Argentine human rights movement achieved both more and less than it intended—less human rights reform and more democratization."[67]

The human rights NGOs contributed inadvertently and indirectly to the democratization of Argentina. First, they helped to fuel a legitimacy crisis for the military regime. This was accomplished not only by the detailed reporting of human rights violations, but also by the symbolic protests of groups like Las Madres de Plaza de Mayo.

The Argentine military had failed to fix the economy as it had promised in 1976, and by defeating the guerrillas had lost its other claim to legitimacy. In this context, the human rights movement exacerbated the military government's growing legitimacy crisis. The military's desperate attempt in 1982 to wrest the Falkland/Malvinas Islands from the British, and so to fight and win a real war, was itself the result of the legitimacy crisis and the best evidence of its reality.

After the Falklands defeat, the military was thoroughly delegitimated and sought a way out of power. The human rights movement had set the stage, without intending to, for democracy to be the most promising road to the future.

The Argentine democratization in 1983 was one of the first in what became the "Third Wave" of democratizations to sweep Latin America and parts of Asia and Africa, extending to Central Europe and some former Soviet republics after 1991.[68] Democratization in Argentina, and the broader human rights movement that contributed to it, fed the Third Wave in Latin America. Electoral democracy became almost universal in Latin America, with Cuba, and for a while Haiti and Peru, as the only exceptions. For many analysts this is sufficient evidence of the existence of a hemispheric norm of democracy.[69] I would agree, but expand the analysis.

A surprising and ironic convergence of perceived interests between two powerful political forces reinforced the spread of electoral democracy in the region during the 1980s. First, the Reagan administration shifted away from its initial complete rebuff to the discourse and practice of human rights and moved toward an ambiguous embrace of human rights subsumed under democratization. Second, beginning in the 1980s, but reaching completion only after the demise of the Soviet Union in 1991, the political left in Latin America abandoned its commitment to armed struggle following the Cuban line and accepted democracy as the framework for future political competition. The convergence of these two historic transformations formed the foundation of the norm of democracy in Latin America. This apparently universal norm is rooted in particular historical shifts and loyalties. The Argentina human rights network fueled the regional human rights movement, which contributed powerfully, but inadvertently, to the embrace of democracy by both the Reagan administration and the Latin American left.

Although human rights activists claim credit for transforming the Reagan administration policy, the reality was a more complex process of mutual cooptation and political illusion.[70] Before his election, Reagan was consistent in denouncing the Carter human rights policy across the board, as applied to both American allies and adversaries in the Cold War. After his election, however, Reagan continued Carter's treatment of the Soviet Union and Eastern Europe under the Conference on Security and Cooperation in Europe (CSCE), which was created by the 1975 Helsinki Accords. The strategy to use the CSCE review meetings to pressure the Soviet Union and its Warsaw Pact allies for their repression of dissidents had begun with successive Carter appointees, Arthur Goldberg and Max Kampelman. Reagan kept on Kampelman as head of the U.S. delegation to the CSCE review meeting—the only high-level Democratic appointee that Reagan did not replace.[71]

Reagan's policy toward American allies in the Third World did undergo a significant transformation. The early Reagan position was identified with the ideas of Jeane Kirkpatrick, expressed in a pair of 1979 articles in *Commentary*. In "Dictatorships and Double Standards," Kirkpatrick defended U.S. support for "authoritarian" governments that might become democracies, in contrast to communist "totalitarian" states that aspired to control every aspect of thought and society and were unlikely to change to democracies.[72]

Ironically, Kirkpatrick—no friend of human rights in U.S. foreign policy—shared a crucial premise with Amnesty International. Both expected communist governments to remain in power indefinitely. Amnesty embodied the approach that takes all governments as holding power with equal legitimacy, but holds them all to the same standards of human rights. The later Reagan policy, in contrast to both Kirkpatrick and Amnesty, saw communist governments as vulnerable to concerted pressure from within and without.

The shift in Reagan administration human rights policy can be dated from Reagan's speech before the British Parliament on June 8, 1982, "Promoting Democracy and Peace." In this speech, Reagan cited the Universal Declaration of Human Rights for its support of elections. Significantly, he made a prediction that was ignored or ridiculed at the time, by articulating "a plan and a hope for the long term—the march of freedom and democracy which will leave Marxism-Leninism on the ash heap of history."[73] George P. Shultz became Reagan's Secretary of State at the end of June 1982, replacing Alexander Haig, and Shultz played a key role in implementing the new direction.

Reagan's shift on human rights included several hidden implications. First, in his speech before the British Parliament he not only articulated the new policy rhetorically, he also proposed a new quasi-NGO (or QUANGO), to be sponsored and funded by the U.S. Congress. The National Endowment for Democracy was created in 1983 and still exits.[74] Its significance was not in any of its activities; what mattered was that it existed at all. NED occupied the civil society turf. By its very existence it asserted the NGO claim of possessing a global moral compass for applying democracy anywhere in the world. It also avowed a representative claim—that all people desire and deserve democracy as a matter of right. Oddly enough, by 1990 the United Nations was saying much the same thing.[75]

In the second implication, the new Reagan human rights policy redefined the normative center. Reagan recast human rights neutrality away from the Amnesty International stance rooted in the 1960s which took government regimes as given but demanded of them protection for the life and freedoms of their citizens. The Amnesty line, as I have described, concentrated on a narrow range of rights. The Reagan approach, in sharp contrast, targeted the overthrow of selected regimes, rulers, and political institutions (particularly communist parties), while maintaining tactical "flexibility" on specific human rights protections.

The third implication of the Reagan shift on human rights and democracy was the surprising political utility of the approach. On grand strategy, Reagan put the Soviet Union in a three-pronged pincer of military pressure, economic pressure, and normative and dissident pressure. Tactically, the administration could be relatively honest in admitting and publicly criticizing the human rights violations of its allies, while easing them toward elections and democracy on a highly selective basis.[76] The principle of selection was not, however, the need or opportunity to improve the government's human rights record, at least as an end in itself. It turned out that democratization, if carefully handled, could solve a set of problems that beset authoritarian governments and their international sponsors. Democratization can contribute to peacefully resolving succession crises, co-opt popular movements and their leaders, protect military institutions from the corrosive effects of holding power, and provide a political solution for insurgencies and internal wars.

The turn toward democracy by the left in Latin America coincided broadly with the Reagan shift. Many advocates of "Cuban line" armed struggle had been killed by the ruthless repression of military governments. Those who survived reassessed the value of even modest protections of civil and political rights. Juan Linz and Alfred Stepan observe that in the 1980s the left began to view "procedural democracy" as "a valuable norm in itself and as a political arrangement that offers both protection against state terrorism and some hope of electoral progress toward social and economic democracy."[77]

More than self-protection motivated this historic shift. In the wake of the collapse of the Soviet Union in 1991, the Latin American left had lost its sense of historic mission. The new commitment to democracy represented a profound reorientation of the social identity of the left—a conversion. According to Kamrava and Mora:

> the contagiousness of the horizontal relations of civil society within itself and the successful democratisation of Latin America would not have been possible without the overwhelming majority of the Left undergoing a deep ideological reassessment, the upshot of which was a "revalorisation" of democracy not just as a temporary tactic but as a permanent value.[78]

How was the conversion of the Latin American left to democracy related to human rights NGOs? There were three links. First, as the Argentine case shows, it was from human rights NGOs and their networks that individuals on the left, often in the midst of violent repression, learned the value of rights protections and NGO allies to keep themselves alive and intact. Second, the ideological power of human rights ideas appealed to the idealism of the left, encouraged by transnational alliances with like-minded groups in a new, "longitudinal" nationalism of the left.[79] Finally, the more that political grievances and hopes are expressed and channeled through NGOs, the less they are conceptualized and expressed in class terms. NGOs express and reinforce a pluralist/individualist structure of popular politics rather than a class structure of popular politics. As Jorge Castañeda observes, "the 'new' social protest was not class-based."[80]

Therefore, the most important influence of the Argentina human rights network was inadvertent—to act as a catalyst for the transition to democracy in Argentina and to contribute to a regional transformation of political culture and institutions by which both the Reagan administration and the Latin American left converged in supporting democratization. The Amnesty line seduced the Latin American left away from the Cuban line so that it could accept the democracy line.

The Argentina human rights network called forth a fascinating panoply of inspiring individuals and groups. Although it failed to stop the disappearances, and its successes are not easily transferable to other causes or countries, it was nevertheless a brilliant set of responses tailored to a unique historical moment, and it transformed a country and a continent for the better.

5
Dancing in the Dark:
NGOs and States in Former Yugoslavia

The 1990s were heady days for international NGOs, which expanded their numbers, increased their budgets, and extended their mandates into hitherto untouched areas. NGOs seemed to be rising in status and influence, taking a "place at the table" with states in international decision-making, and gaining leverage over states to make them embrace new norms.

There was some basis in reality for this enormous investment of trust in the promise of NGOs as the prime engines of global progress. Part of the credit for the global wave of democratization in the 1980s and 1990s went to "civil society" organizations and NGOs.[1] The end of the Cold War raised hopes for a "New World Order" in which international relations would be governed by universal norms more than interstate rivalries, and norm-governed behavior would emanate from the United Nations in New York down to NGOs on the ground in every Third World country. In a series of international conferences, NGOs met in sessions parallel to the meetings of official government representatives. Some participants believed they were pioneering a new global legislative arena in which governments would form the upper house and NGOs the lower house of an emerging world parliament.

The changes and ambitions that filled the minds of NGO innovators in the 1990s distracted attention from a more profound reality—as NGOs collectively shifted their institutional shape there was a parallel shift in the institutional shape of states. New states were born, powerful states retreated from roles and responsibilities, and some weak states collapsed altogether. Moreover, these patterns of state transformation were entangled with parallel transformations of NGO roles and activities.

In the imaginations of their boosters, not only were NGOs dancing solo, but they were also calling the tune for states. In reality, NGOs were dancing in the dark—with hidden political partners. As a case study of this phenomenon, this chapter documents the pervasive role of NGOs in the conflicts that accompanied the breakup of Yugoslavia from 1992 to 2001. The NGO network absorbed and institutionalized the conflicts in ways that profoundly shaped the successor states of Yugoslavia. There is no previous study on the roles of NGOs across all issue-areas in the wars of the former Yugoslavia.

NGOs IN YUGOSLAVIA

The U.S. State Department circulated the following wanted poster in Yugoslavia after the International Criminal Tribunal for the Former Yugoslavia indicted Slobodan Milosevic on May 22, 1999:

Up to $5 million reward

Wanted

For crimes against humanity

Slobodan Milosevic

President of the Federal Republic of Yugoslavia[2]

The crimes of Milosevic—committed during a series of wars that accompanied the breakup of Yugoslavia—were first exposed by NGOs in the early 1990s. NGOs delivered relief to victims of the wars, reported on violence against civilians, and advocated military action by governments and international organizations. At the same time, the warring parties incorporated the NGO presence into their tactics of war. NGOs advocated the creation of the International Criminal Tribunal for the Former Yugoslavia, and NGOs kept it alive when the governments that created it tried to starve it of resources. NGOs pushed for the Tribunal's indictment of Milosevic while he was still head of state—the first such attempt in history. NGOs exposed the fraudulent elections that drove Milosevic from power, and ultimately into the custody of the Tribunal. Finally, NGOs sought to generalize their impact in Yugoslavia by advocating the creation of a Permanent International Criminal Court. From April 1992, when ethnic cleansing in Bosnia began, to June 2001, when Milosevic was transferred to the custody of the International Criminal Tribunal in The Hague, NGOs mediated and catalyzed every step of the international response to the wars of Yugoslavia's demise.

The NGO response to Argentina's "Dirty War" of disappearances from 1976 to 1983 (addressed in chapter 4) was relatively straightforward compared to the NGO response to the wars in Yugoslavia during the

1990s. In the most obvious difference, human rights alone defined the principled, transnational response to the Argentine conflict. In Yugoslavia, by contrast, NGOs and other actors addressed an array of issues including refugees, internally displaced persons, human rights, genocide and crimes of war, disaster relief, Red Cross action for victims of war, and conflict resolution.[3] This observation points to a broad transformation of international humanitarianism that took place between these two cases. In the "new humanitarianism" that emerged in the 1990s, NGOs and the humanitarian network as a whole came to respond routinely with multi-mandate operations on all sides of internal wars.[4] In the same small wars, the attention of both U.S. intelligence agencies and humanitarian NGOs converged on the nexus between warfare and humanitarian suffering.[5]

When whole, the country of Yugoslavia was an ethnic patchwork of Orthodox Serbs, Roman Catholic Croatians and Slovenes, and Muslims spread among six republics. Before the creation of Yugoslavia after World War I, the Balkans had been an arena of struggle between the Ottoman Empire and the Austro-Hungarian Empire for a millennium. Nevertheless, the wars of the 1990s were not inevitable. They were planned, acquiesced in, or blundered into by Yugoslav and international leaders through a long series of political choices.[6]

Josif Broz Tito, the autocrat who had held Yugoslavia together since World War II, died in 1980. After Tito, a decade of economic crisis set the stage for opportunistic politicians to whip up nationalistic conflicts between ethnic groups.[7] With the general collapse of communism in the region, the Yugoslav Communist Party dissolved in early 1990. The United States, preoccupied with war in Iraq and instability in the Soviet Union, accepted the Western European move to take the lead on Yugoslavia.

The world watched in 1991 as the Soviet Union broke up, with unexpected ease, into 15 countries which had been its constituent republics. Although Yugoslavia had a similar federal structure, the European Community (EC) was initially determined to preserve its unity. As individual republics declared their independence—Slovenia and Croatia in June 1991 and Bosnia in February 1992—fighting broke out between ethnic groups in each of the new states. The Yugoslav National Army, once an institution for national unity, was now dominated by ethnic Serbs and commanded by Slobodan Milosevic, who used the army to aid Serb minorities in breakaway republics seeking to create a "Greater Serbia." The EC, under pressure from Germany and the rapid flow of events, abruptly shifted policy to recognize the independence of Slovenia and Croatia in January 1992 and Bosnia-Herzegovina in April 1992.

Bosnia became the arena for the longest conflict and the largest scale of violence because its population had no ethnic majority, only a Muslim plurality (44 per cent) and large minorities of Serbs (31 per cent) and Croats (17 per cent). This "new war" was fought with the objective to carve out territories of exclusive ethnic occupancy.[8] Violence was directed almost entirely against civilians, using tactics of "ethnic cleansing" that included killing, rape, torture, house burning, and the destruction of religious and cultural landmarks, all designed to force the migration of the targeted group and to make the survivors never want to return. While all three groups practiced ethnic cleansing, most—perhaps 90 per cent—was conducted by Serbs against Bosnian Muslims as part of a strategy to create an ethnically pure Greater Serbia.[9] This was genocide by any definition, but the governments in a position to stop it were determined not to call it genocide until after it was completed. NGOs and journalists, in contrast, did call genocide by name.

HUMAN RIGHTS INFORMATION AND U.S. INTELLIGENCE

The flow of information from war and disaster zones has followed a consistent pattern since the 1970s—particularly in Africa, but also Asia and Central America—in which NGOs act as the primary sources of information for international journalists and governments.[10] In Africa, according to Alex de Waal:

> Journalists are usually dependent upon relief workers for many or all of the following: access to the country, local transport, access to feeding centers, accommodation, telecommunication, electricity, translators, recreation and social support, information, understanding of the situation and storyline, sound bites, and medical care.[11]

Many of the same NGOs, newspapers, and individual relief workers and journalists transfer their experience from one humanitarian crisis to the next.

In apparent violation of this pattern, journalists and national intelligence sources appeared to supplant NGOs as the primary conduits for information during the wars of former Yugoslavia. Did Yugoslavia break the pattern of NGO primacy in the flow of information from war zones?

Bosnian Serbs, with direction and resources from Milosevic in Serbia, began the "ethnic cleansing" of Bosnian Muslims in April 1992, immediately after the European Community recognized the new state. High-profile press coverage began only in July, led by Roy Gutman in *Newsday* during the week beginning July 19. Gutman broke the story of Omarska concentration camp on August 2. Ed Villiamy of the *Guardian* and two reporters from British Independent Television News reached Omarska and Keraterm camps on August 5. Their stories, read and viewed the next day, portrayed emaciated Bosnian Muslims behind barbed wire—images whose parallels to Nazi concentration cample were unmistakable.[12] In the public clamor for American action that followed these stories, and under criticism from rival candidate Bill Clinton in the presidential election campaign, President Bush made his first public statement deploring the camps on August 7. Bush promised only, "And we will not rest until the international community has gained access to any and all detention camps."[13]

The most important obstacle to well-informed intelligence in this case was that President Bush, with the agreement of all his top advisors, had already decided that the United States would not undertake military intervention in Bosnia. Secretary of State James Baker declared, "We don't have a dog in this fight." Given the low demand from policymakers for intelligence on atrocities, the intelligence bureaucracies devoted few resources to producing it. Nevertheless, Jon Western, an analyst in the Bureau of Intelligence and Research of the State Department, spent three days over the Fourth of July weekend in 1992 working with a CIA colleague to analyze a large volume of both classified and unclassified information. They made the first analytical connection between the pattern of Serb military action and the pattern of ethnic cleansing, concluding that the two phenomena were coordinated to provoke a massive flight of Bosnian Muslims. But Western's July 4 analysis was neither invited nor welcomed by his superiors.[14]

After his August 7 statement President Bush mandated a well-staffed analysis of the Bosnian camps, but this took weeks to prepare. "By the third week in September," according to a State Department official, "we had a very large, comprehensive list of camps, with descriptions, places, information on inmates, conditions, maps."[15] However, U.S. intelligence agencies were not specifically assigned to compile evidence of crimes against humanity until October.[16] After Clinton took office in 1993, the CIA, under its new Director

James Woolsey, sent agents to interview Bosnian camp survivors in Europe. Finally—in December 1994—the U.S. intelligence community assembled a relatively complete picture of ethnic cleansing committed against Bosnian Muslims during 1992, and assigned responsibility for 90 per cent of it to the Bosnian Serbs.[17]

The evidence justifies two apparently contradictory conclusions. First, had the Bush administration been willing to discover genocide in Bosnia and take action to halt it, it could have found the intelligence to justify such action early in 1992. Second, there is some truth to the official claims that the United States possessed no direct intelligence to verify accounts of specific atrocities. The gap between these two conclusions is explained only in part by the Bush administration's disinterest in the matter. The other crucial factor is, of course, NGOs.

U.S. intelligence understood Serb strategic intentions in Bosnia within a few days of the beginning of ethnic cleansing in April 1992.[18] The details of specific atrocities, however, were known to NGOs before they were known to U.S. intelligence and international journalists. Indeed, NGOs were the main suppliers of this information to intelligence and journalistic consumers. The pattern held. NGOs— either by collecting the information themselves, or by leading journalists and CIA agents to the refugees to be interviewed—were the primary conduit of information on genocide in Bosnia to the outside world.

Both relief NGOs and human rights NGOs were active in the former Yugoslavia during the 1990s. One count put the number of relief NGOs for the entire former Yugoslavia at 91 international agencies and 35 local agencies.[19] The relief role of NGOs, some of which performed remarkable and heroic service, deserves attention for its own sake, aside from its contribution to the flow of information. NGOs kept alive at least tens of thousands of people in Bosnia by getting food aid through—even on pack mules—when the UN could not.[20] George Soros, the financier-turned-philanthropist, donated $50 million for Bosnia aid during 1993, outspending the U.S. government.[21] Soros channeled much of his funding to tailored NGO programs such as those designed by Fred Cuny for the besieged city of Sarajevo. Working through International Rescue Committee, Cuny brought in seeds for household vegetable gardens, pallets of books for psychological and cultural relief, and special gas-powered combination stove/heaters. To power the stoves, he brought in 15 miles of plastic piping and mobilized 15,000 citizens to dig trenches for the gas lines. In his most ingenious project, Cuny rebuilt the city's water system to save Sarajevans from constant sniper fire while fetching water.[22]

The role of relief NGOs in providing access for international journalists and human rights activists to interview victims and witnesses of atrocities is often "outside the frame," and not directly acknowledged in the resulting published stories and reports. Nevertheless, since most such reports relied on the testimony of Bosnian displaced persons who were gathered in humanitarian camps and attended by NGOs, it is reasonable to infer that NGO relief personnel played a central role in providing interviewer access.

The role of human rights NGOs is easier to trace. Helsinki Watch maintained "at least one or more staffers present in Bosnia and other parts of former Yugoslavia throughout all of 1992 and 1993."[23] In addition to its regular presence, Helsinki Watch sent two investigative missions to the region from March 19 to April 28, and May 29 to June 19, 1992. They were on the ground in Bosnia, therefore, when the war of genocide and ethnic cleansing began in April. Their book-length report, released in August 1992, directly acknowledged its primary sources of information. Concerning violence in Bosnia, "Much of the testimony was taken from displaced persons within Bosnia-Hercegovina and from refugees who fled to Yugoslavia, Croatia and Slovenia." The report concluded, "The findings in this report, and the reports from Bosnia-Hercegovina by independent news media, provide at the very least *prima facie* evidence that genocide is taking place."[24] It called upon the UN Security Council to take effective action to suppress the genocide in Bosnia-Hercegovina and to hold legally accountable those responsible for war crimes.

Journalists, intelligence agencies, and humanitarian NGOs were all poking around in former Yugoslavia during the summer of 1992. But who told what to whom? The evidence indicates that Helsinki Watch investigators and NGO relief workers in Bosnia and its environs knew the details of specific attacks and acts of ethnic cleansing before international journalists reported them and before the U.S. intelligence community knew them.

Roy Gutman got his first concentration camp story, published on July 19, by accompanying representatives of the International Committee of the Red Cross (ICRC) in their inspections of the camps.[25] For some of his reports in late July, Gutman interviewed refugees from Muslim villages that had been taken by Serb forces;

Helsinki Watch investigators had previously interviewed refugees from these same villages.[26]

U.S. intelligence relied heavily on "open source" information from humanitarians and journalists to know what was happening in Bosnia. From the start of the war Jon Western, the analyst in the State Department Bureau of Intelligence and Research, "was tasked with sifting through some 1,000 documents on Bosnia a day—open source reports from foreign and American journalists and international human rights groups, local press translations, classified cables from the field, satellite intelligence, refugee testimony, and telephone and radio intercepts."[27] Among his sources, the journalists, human rights groups, and even classified intelligence cables from the field all relied, directly or indirectly, on refugee testimony. His only sources exclusive to intelligence collection were satellite images and communications intercepts. But these provided precious little value added. Satellite photos of prisoners assembled in a field, or of "disturbed earth" in that field a few days later, can only tell the story of a mass execution and mass graves when the storyline is previously supplied by other sources—which in Bosnia inevitably meant refugee testimony mediated by humanitarian relief and human rights NGOs. Electronic communications intercepts by intelligence organizations could establish which paramilitary groups were operating in an area, but precisely what they were doing could be learned in more detail, again, only from refugee testimony.

In August 1992, when President Bush was trying to avoid the Bosnia issue, and before U.S. intelligence had paid serious attention to atrocities there, "According to a senior intelligence official, what little the Central Intelligence Agency did know at the time was coming from *Newsday* and other papers, and from television." Yet in December 1994, more than two years later, in the CIA's exhaustive report on ethnic cleansing in Bosnia, "the main achievement of this work by the CIA, creative and comprehensive as it was, was merely to confirm officially, and to amplify modestly, a story that had already been documented in detail by the press, by relief agencies, and by independent human rights organizations, whose information the CIA itself acknowledged."[28] After the vaunted agencies of the American intelligence community turned their full powers to the question of Bosnian atrocities they could only manage to "amplify modestly" the story told by refugees through NGOs.

The Africa pattern held—all outside investigators depended directly or indirectly on NGOs for access to the victims and their testimony. The pattern held, yet it assumed a modified form. The former Yugoslavia was more densely populated than the typical African disaster arena with members of the "global class"—those who spoke English, spent dollars or deutschmarks, and had passports and plane tickets to enter and leave when they wished.[29] Members of the global class in former Yugoslavia included relief workers, UN bureaucrats, journalists, and embassy representatives. In addition, the former Yugoslavia had its own group of competent, honest, and brave local journalists with one foot in the global class and the other rooted in local realities.[30] Members of the global class shared tips and information with each other; NGOs were at the head of this line, but they did not have exclusive access to human rights information.

MAKING THE TRIBUNAL

The United States and European major powers all demurred from accepting the responsibility to halt the genocide and war crimes occurring in the former Yugoslavia. Instead, they promised to prosecute and punish in an International Criminal Tribunal the individuals who had committed the genocide and war crimes.

Gary Jonathan Bass, in his comparative study, *Stay the Hand of Vengeance: The Politics of War Crimes Tribunals*, acknowledges limited NGO support for the Yugoslavia Tribunal. Nevertheless, he argues, "Pressure from NGOs is not a necessary condition for the establishment of a war crimes tribunal. The courts at Leipzig, Constantinople, Nuremberg, and Tokyo were set up without the benefit of today's human rights NGOs."[31] The perennially crucial factors, according to Bass, are that liberal states with legalist domestic norms are most likely to pursue war crimes tribunals, but within narrow limits of self-interest, and only when public opinion is outraged over the war crimes in question.

Bass's argument is sound, as far as it goes. What he misses, however, is that for this particular tribunal, created largely by this liberal American nation in the 1990s, NGOs were a necessary condition and constitutive factor.[32] No NGOs, no Tribunal. Without NGOs, the International Criminal Tribunal for the Former Yugoslavia would not have been established, would not have survived in any effective form, and would not have caught its big fish—Slobodan Milosevic—indicted, in custody, and on trial at The Hague.

No prominent human rights NGO had ever called on the UN Security Council to establish an international war crimes tribunal when Aryeh Neier, Executive Director of Human Rights Watch, decided to include such a proposal in the organization's August 1992 report, *War Crimes in Bosnia-Hercegovina*.[33] The report cited the relevant provisions of international law, provided evidence of genocide and war crimes, and suggested the names of ten key Serb and Bosnian Serb leaders who should be prosecuted. The idea caught on quickly among governments and other NGOs. It progressed through the UN in late 1992, pushed by U.S. Secretary of State Lawrence Eagleburger in the waning months of the Bush administration. The United States introduced a resolution, which passed the UN Security Council on October 6, 1992, to form a Commission of Experts to collect evidence on war crimes in former Yugoslavia. After Bush lost the November presidential election, Eagleburger made a speech in December endorsing the proposal for an International Tribunal and naming his own list of ten Serbs to be prosecuted.[34]

The Tribunal was also spurred into life by the appearance of vivid press and television reports on concentration camps in Bosnia at precisely the moment in August 1992 when Helsinki Watch released its report of genocide and called for a Tribunal. Aryeh Neier calls this timing "crucial" for the emergence of the Tribunal, though a "coincidence."[35] It may not have been entirely a coincidence. Evidence suggests possible hidden links between journalists, the International Committee of the Red Cross, and Helsinki Watch.

In addition to the Red Cross "assistance" mission in the former Yugoslavia, which provided food relief using 24 warehouses and 300 vehicles, the ICRC dedicated more than 100 expatriate delegates to a "protection" mission for detainees.[36] Normally, the ICRC engages in a form of discreet protection—visiting detainees on all sides of a conflict and appealing to authorities for the proper treatment of detainees while maintaining strict neutrality among the warring parties. Discreet protection contrasts sharply with the standard approach of human rights NGOs, which protect victims by publicizing violations in a strategy of shaming the perpetrators. The ICRC was so profoundly challenged by the realities of Bosnia that it acted—quite uncharacteristically—much like a human rights NGO, even bending its own strategic commitment to discretion.

The ICRC pulled its delegates out of Bosnia in late May after unknown assailants ambushed a relief convoy to Sarajevo, killing senior delegate Frederic Maurice. Patrick Gasser, one of the first delegates to return at the end of June, discovered the Manjaca concentration camp in northern Bosnia where 2,300 Muslim men were held sweltering in metal livestock sheds. Gasser reported this to his ICRC superiors in Geneva, who debated for two weeks the dilemma of whether to publicize the findings and risk losing visitation access to these and other detainees, or to keep silent and perhaps become morally complicit in genocide. They chose the risky compromise that Red Cross delegates would lead other investigators to discover and publicize the prisoners' conditions.

This was how Gasser came to collaborate with Gutman and other journalists to get the story out. "Without divulging details of the I.C.R.C.'s findings," Michael Ignatieff reports, "Gasser provided the corroboration necessary for *Newsday* to run its stories."[37] Nicholas Berry goes further, arguing that the ICRC drew the attention of journalists and governments to concentration camps in Bosnia as part of its "unspoken mission" of undermining war as an effective tool of policy.[38]

Helsinki Watch gained powerful moral and political leverage in its case for an International Tribunal by exposing a United Nations cover-up of genocide in Bosnia. Helsinki Watch somehow obtained a copy of a memorandum dated July 3, 1992 in which an officer of the UN Protection Force (UNPROFOR) reported to the UN Secretariat in New York the existence of several Serb-run "concentration camps" inside the Bosnian border with Croatia. Helsinki Watch charged in its August 1992 report that "high-ranking UN officials withheld this information from the press and the public and apparently did little, if anything, to stop abuses in these camps."[39]

Who leaked the memo to Helsinki Watch? It could have been mid-level staff in UNPROFOR or UNHCR in the field, or someone at a U.S. embassy, or even UN staff in New York. But my bet is that Red Cross delegates were involved in the equation, and that the ICRC helped to point both Gutman and Helsinki Watch investigators to the story of the death camps.

The evidence is incomplete, but it suggests that the ICRC, behaving much like a human rights NGO, may have been the link that led both Helsinki Watch and international journalists to break the story of the Serb camps at the same moment. These not altogether coincidental events in turn helped fuel the momentum for an International Criminal Tribunal at precisely the time in August 1992 when Helsinki Watch issued the call for it.

To understand the development of the Tribunal from the time it was authorized by the UN Security Council, it is essential to understand the international political context. In the words of Gary Jonathan

Bass: "The tribunal was built to flounder ... the establishment of the Hague tribunal was an act of tokenism by the world community, which was largely unwilling to intervene in ex-Yugoslavia but did not mind creating an institution that would give the *appearance* of moral concern. The world would prosecute the crimes that it would not prevent."[40] This political use of the Tribunal by the governments that created it—as a gesture that appeared more emphatic and effective than it actually was—made the Tribunal highly compatible with NGOs. NGOs normally operate in a similarly ambiguous political environment in which partners attach contradictory latent agendas to NGO operations.

The United Nations Commission of Experts, established in October 1992 to gather evidence of war crimes in the former Yugoslavia, was sandbagged from the start by the appointment of an elderly chairman, an inadequate budget, and active obstructionism from France, Britain, and the Office of Legal Affairs in the UN bureaucracy. The Commission was saved from oblivion only because its vice-chairman, Cherif Bassiouni, effectively took over operations and quickly raised $1.4 million from American foundations to more than double the budget.[41] The UN Secretariat in New York abruptly closed the Commission in April 1994, without consulting the Security Council, and months before the Tribunal prosecutor's office could take over its responsibilities. Bassiouni simply continued the work of the Commission on his own until Richard Goldstone took office as Chief Prosecutor in August 1994.[42] This would have been impossible without NGO support.

Under the umbrella of the Commission, Bassiouni and his network of NGO collaborators had managed to compile an enormous volume of documentation, including refugee testimony on torture and mass murder at 900 prison camps, and the existence of 150 mass graves. In 1993, members of the Commission had been permitted to inspect, but not to publicize or copy, U.S. satellite photos of Brcko prison camp. In 1994, U.S. intelligence denied Bassiouni's request to declassify satellite photos and communications intercepts so they could be included as part of the Commission's evidence. Yet, when the CIA completed its own comprehensive study of ethnic cleansing in December 1994, it managed only to "confirm officially, and to amplify modestly" on the Commission's report.[43]

American intelligence officials often engaged in a tantalizing information tease with the Commission of Experts, and later the Tribunal itself. In the information tease, it was never clear whether

U.S. intelligence was holding back its really good information to protect "sources and methods," or whether U.S. intelligence actually had very little to add to the "open source" intelligence it gathered from human rights NGOs.

Bassiouni was able to breathe life into the Commission in part because his support network included many American law schools. Bassiouni himself worked out of the International Human Rights Law Institute at DePaul University College of Law, where he taught.[44] In 1995 American University, Washington, DC, established an office for technical assistance to the Tribunal prosecutor, with funding from George Soros's Open Society Institute.[45] The Human Rights Center at SUNY-Buffalo School of Law organized Tribunal Watch, also in 1995.[46] Such advocacy institutes within American law schools, and the foundations that support them, are all part of the NGO world.

Most striking about the Commission of Experts was not merely that it relied on NGO support, but that the Commission itself acted like an NGO with respect to entrepreneurial fundraising, working through a network, and functioning in partnership with governments that simultaneously mandated and undercut its work. The Commission itself was "NGO-ized."

Helsinki Watch, which originally conceived the Tribunal, not surprisingly took a leadership role in supporting it. Beginning in early 1993, the NGO collected testimony from victims and witnesses in former Yugoslavia and compiled it as legal evidence for the Tribunal, rather than as material for a public campaign of pressure. This required that data on the names of interviewees and time and place of the interviews not be released in public reports, but be kept in secure files away from Helsinki Watch offices until it was passed on to the Tribunal. Helsinki Watch sent 30 file boxes of documents to the Tribunal Prosecutor after the office was established in 1994. It also sent Ivana Nizich, one of its key investigators and authors on the former Yugoslavia, to work directly in the Prosecutor's office starting in January 1996.[47] Helsinki Watch continued to feed information to the Prosecutor throughout the 1990s.

Physicians for Human Rights provided a unique form of support by exhuming mass graves in former Yugoslavia. Treating a grave as a crime scene, and using techniques of forensic medicine and forensic archeology, PHR provided critical supporting evidence to the prosecutor. The first exhumation at Vukovar began 18 October 1992—less than two weeks after the UN Security Council resolution to establish the Commission of Experts.[48] During the 1980s, a handful of individuals had pioneered the application of forensic techniques to human rights cases in many countries, including Argentina and Iraq.[49] These individuals, including Robert Kirschner, William Haglund, Eric Stover, and Clyde Snow, congregated at PHR in the 1990s, making it the acknowledged leader in the field. PHR was the driving force behind years of exhumations in Bosnia, including mass graves from the 1995 Srebrenica massacre. Sometimes exhumations were carried out directly by PHR, and sometimes by PHR staff working for the Tribunal.[50]

A comprehensive assessment of the role of NGOs in the Tribunal, only hinted at here, would account for the people, expertise, information, political influence, and amount and sources of funding brought to bear by NGOs. But we do have statements by Tribunal principals. Richard Goldstone, the first Chief Prosecutor, credited NGOs as essential for both the founding and continuance of the Tribunal: "I have absolutely no doubt that without the push from non-governmental organizations in many countries, we would not have either of the international criminal tribunals at all. If we're to rely solely on the goodwill of politicians, we would not be in existence very long."[51] Both Goldstone and Antonio Cassese, President of the Tribunal (somewhat like a chief justice), came to New York to consult directly with Human Rights Watch activists at their offices during 1995. Cassese's briefing highlighted the importance of American NGOs. In William Korey's account of the meeting, Cassese

> referred to a conversation he had had with Tadeusz Mazowiecki, the former Polish Prime Minister and later the UN's Special Rapporteur on Yugoslavia. Mazowiecki had advised him that the Tribunal must rely upon the American government for its very existence and sustenance and, therefore, American public opinion was central to its survival. It was for that reason that NGOs in America had particular "clout."[52]

Cassese well understood that not all NGOs are created equal; those based in American society have more influence because they can reach the U.S. government, and because Americans tend to have greater resources and longer experience to bring to bear in the NGO game.

Goldstone and Cassese provide the best response to Gary Jonathan Bass' argument that NGOs are not a necessary condition for the establishment of a war crimes tribunal. Bass points to mass and elite public opinion as one of the crucial factors that sometimes push liberal states to support the establishment of war crimes tribunals. The U.S.

government acted as the chief patron of the Yugoslavia Tribunal in his account, with idealists such as Richard Holbrooke and Madeleine Albright playing crucial roles in the Clinton administration. Bass does not illuminate the NGO side of this story.

American idealists in general during recent decades, and Holbrooke and Albright in particular, have tended to locate themselves within NGO professional and social networks. Richard Holbrooke made his first trip to Bosnia in August 1992 on a fact-finding mission as a board member of the International Rescue Committee. After assisting Bill Clinton in his presidential campaign in the fall and recommending to Clinton the successful tactic of criticizing Bush's policy on Bosnia, Holbrooke visited Sarajevo in December 1992. He traveled with Lionel Rosenblatt of Refugees International. After serving in the Clinton State Department from 1993 to 1995, and engineering the Dayton Peace Accords for the former Yugoslavia, Holbrooke left government and became chairman of the board of Refugees International.[53] When Madeleine Albright, as U.S. Ambassador to the UN in 1995, sought to bolster the fledgling Tribunal that she had helped to create, she asked a branch of the American Bar Association to create a coalition of supportive NGOs. As a result of her initiative, the Coalition for International Justice was inaugurated in September 1995 with 30–40 NGO members to advocate for the Tribunal to the U.S. government and public, and directly to the UN bureaucracy.[54]

The evidence suggests, therefore, that NGOs were essential to the origins and operations of the Tribunal, and to the degree of success it achieved. But there is yet another layer to the story. How did more powerful actors, including the U.S. government, pursue their foreign policies in a landscape so crowded with NGOs?

U.S. FOREIGN POLICY IN A SEA OF NGOs

To understand the constitutive politics of the Yugoslavia Tribunal, it is best to examine the timing and context of its indictments of the three big fish: Rodovan Karadic, president of the Bosnia Serb Republic, Ratko Mladic, commander of the Bosnian Serb Army, and Slobodan Milosevic.

On July 25, 1995 Goldstone indicted Karadic and Mladic for genocide and crimes against humanity, including killings in the camps of Manjaca, Omarska, and Keraterm during 1992. Goldstone's timing was either very shrewd or very lucky. Only two weeks earlier Mladic had begun the sack of the United Nations' "safe haven" of

Srebrenica, eventually killing more than 7,000 Bosnian Muslim men who had taken refuge there. News accounts based on refugee testimony poured out for weeks.[55] Four days before the indictment, NATO members had agreed to launch air strikes if the Serbs continued to attack safe havens. The day after the indictment the UN safe haven of Zepa fell to the Serbs. On July 31, a coalition of 27 NGOs, at the initiation of Human Rights Watch, issued a statement calling for "multilateral military action" with "American leadership" to stop the genocide in Bosnia.[56]

Wittingly or unwittingly, the timing of the Tribunal's indictment of Karadic and Mladic played into a campaign of information— emanating from journalists, human rights NGOs, and U.S. intelligence—condemning the Bosnian Serbs and legitimating the use of military force against them.

American intelligence officials later said that they did not foresee the 1995 Serb attack on Srebrenica and that their "best information came from human rights groups, the United Nations and the press, not from spies, satellites or eavesdropping."[57] In an unusual move, American intelligence was marshaled to corroborate publicly the information from human rights NGOs and the press. On August 8, Ambassador Albright presented to the UN Security Council satellite photos of "possible mass graves" near Srebrenica. She also released U-2 spy plane photos to the press. A CIA official told a Senate hearing that "American intelligence has found a clear pattern of 'ethnic cleansing' by the Bosnian Serbs since 1992."[58]

The military force legitimated by this information campaign took two forms. First, in early August Croatia recaptured its Krajina region from Serb dominance in "Operation Storm," driving out more than 100,000 Croatian Serbs in the largest single act of ethnic cleansing in the war.[59] This was the first military setback for the Serbs in four years of fighting and was welcomed by Holbrooke and others in the U.S. government to pressure the Serbs to make a peace deal.[60] Human rights criticism of "Operation Storm" in Europe and the U.S. was muted by general outrage over the ongoing Serb attacks on UN safe havens in Bosnia. The second form of military force came from the air. On August 29, following a particularly brutal Serb shelling of civilians in Sarajevo, NATO launched several weeks of intensive bombing against Bosnian Serb military targets.

Were Croatia's "Operation Storm" and NATO's bombing campaign coordinated to bring the Serbs to the negotiating table? Under the UN arms embargo of former Yugoslavia, the U.S. could not give military aid to Croatia. Instead, the Pentagon referred Croatia's defense minister to a private American military training company, Military Professional Resources, Inc. (MPRI), whose retired U.S. officers trained the Croatian military in tactics developed during the Gulf War. MPRI denies that any of its staff participated in planning or carrying out "Operation Storm," but suspicion remains that some part of the U.S. government—acting through MPRI—gave Croatia the means and the green light to retake Krajina.[61]

Was the Tribunal's indictment of Karadic and Mladic timed and coordinated with U.S. diplomatic and military policy? There is no direct evidence that the U.S. government influenced the timing of the indictment. However, in this indictment, as well as the 1999 indictment of Milosevic, Serb leaders were indicted for earlier crimes only when they launched a new and dramatic escalation in military aggression. Appearance suggests the indictments may have been first threatened to deter new Serb military actions, and later delivered when the Serbs launched new attacks.

The Karadic and Mladic indictments meshed well with American diplomacy in other respects. They fit the "Milosevic strategy" pursued successfully by Holbrooke to exclude the Bosnian Serbs from any direct role in peace talks, and to deal solely with Milosevic who would be expected to control and deliver other Serb groups.[62] The isolation of Karadic and Mladic by the July indictment was not planned, according to one State Department official, but had "accidentally served a political purpose."[63] On November 16, during the Dayton negotiations, the Tribunal issued a second indictment of Karadic and Mladic, this time for genocide and war crimes at Srebrenica only three months earlier. Goldstone's deputy prosecutor argued that this new indictment was timed to influence negotiators at Dayton to respect the prerogatives of the Tribunal. But Goldstone was in Washington on November 15 and 16 to discuss intelligence cooperation with the heads of the Defense Department, the National Security Council, and the CIA. He wanted communications intercepts from during the Srebrenica massacre, and later said that he received everything that he wanted.[64] For the second indictment of Karadic and Mladic in November, if not the first one in July, U.S. intelligence-sharing may well have provided the crucial corroboration and determined the timing.

Before and during the Dayton negotiations in November 1995, the U.S. negotiating team missed few opportunities to remind Milosevic that he too could be tied to the war crimes of the Bosnian Serbs. The

CIA drew up a memo, shown to Milosevic, linking his government to the brutal Serb warlord known as Arkan.[65] The November indictment of Karadic and Mladic became part of this threat aimed at Milosevic. Secretary of State Warren Christopher would raise the subject of human rights at Dayton, "reminding Milosevic that his good reputation was by no means assured."[66]

The Dayton Agreement, signed November 21, 1995, brought four years of peace to former Yugoslavia. When war returned in 1999, it arrived in the Kosovo region of Serbia, where the Serb military "ethnically cleansed" more than a million Albanian-speaking Muslims from their homes.[67] On May 27, 1999, during the three-month NATO bombing campaign against Serbia, the new Tribunal prosecutor, Louise Arbour, announced the indictment of Slobodon Milosevic for crimes against humanity in Kosovo. This time the NGO role in gathering evidence for the Tribunal was larger and more institutionalized than ever before. For example, International Crisis Group carried out field documentation of war crimes using a methodology of its own design. The mission involved 46 international and 123 local staff, operated in Albania and Kosovo from May to December 1999, and forwarded 4,700 witness reports directly to the Tribunal in The Hague.[68] And this time the fingerprints of U.S. intelligence were more clearly manifest than ever before. Although other NATO countries had promised and delivered intelligence to the Tribunal, the U.S. information, including imagery and electronic intercepts, was provided the day before the indictment was signed.[69] The American threat of indictment at Dayton was fulfilled.

Because Milosevic was a sitting head of state at the time of his indictment, the prospects for him to stand trial at the Tribunal appeared to be even more remote than for Karadic and Mladic. Nevertheless, he reached The Hague first, in June 2001, and his trial began in February 2002. After the Tribunal had him in custody, it issued additional indictments for his earlier crimes in the 1991 war in Croatia and the 1992–95 war in Bosnia.[70]

Before he was sent to the Tribunal, Milosevic lost power, and how he did so provided the culminating role for NGOs in the wars of the former Yugoslavia. The political opposition to Milosevic took a new turn in October 1998 when a few student veterans of earlier protests founded Otpor ("Resistance"). Playing to their strengths and the government's weaknesses, Otpor emphasized humor and non-violence. After the Kosovo bombing their organizing took hold. Belatedly, the U.S. government began to offer training and assistance to Otpor through NGO channels. Freedom House in Washington funded Civic Initiatives in Belgrade to print and distribute thousands of copies of materials offering nonviolent tactics to overthrow the dictatorship. Retired U.S. Army colonel Robert Helvey provided intensive seminars in nonviolent strategy for political revolution in March and April, 2000. Funding for the Serb opposition flowed from the U.S. Agency for International Development through a series of GONGOs (government-organized NGOs), including the National Endowment for Democracy, the U.S. Institute of Peace, and the International Republican Institute. Milosevic attempted to steal the September 2000 election, but the opposition had mobilized broad popular support in both urban and the rural areas. In the campaign of civil disobedience that followed, the police and military refused to fire on the civilian nonviolent demonstrators, depriving Milosevic of his crucial pillars of support.[71] Once Milosevic lost power, the democratic government moved within a year, though somewhat reluctantly, to arrest and send him to The Hague.[72]

In a sea of NGOs flowing in different directions, the U.S. government has greater capacity than any other single actor in the world to keep track of them, channel them, thwart them, or ride them in a chosen direction. By the same token, a relatively small number of NGOs can create a new current or push together in a particular direction in hopes of influencing the U.S. government, which is known to be permeable to the flow of NGOs.

NGO-IZATION OF THE WAR[73]

In the former Yugoslavia during the 1990s, NGOs were everywhere—on the ground in every region, linked to every major actor, and involved with every major issue. In addition to the situations where NGOs were directly involved, the conflicts were thoroughly NGO-ized, in two different respects.

NGOs were not the only kind of international actor involved in Yugoslavia's conflicts, they were also saturated with inter-governmental organizations (IGOs) from both Europe and the United Nations system. Indeed, the wars of Yugoslavia's demise were perhaps the most multilateralized conflicts before or since. The United Nations was engaged through the UN Secretariat and UN Security Council in New York; through humanitarian agencies such as the UN High Commissioner for Refugees, the UN Commission on Human Rights, UNICEF, and the World Food Program; and through peacekeeping troops under UN Protection Force (UNPROFOR) I and II. Europe responded through the European Community, the Conference on Security and Cooperation in Europe, the Western European Union, and NATO.[74]

In the first form of NGO-ization, these other, more powerful international actors inserted into the former Yugoslavia tended to act very much like NGOs. The UN High Commissioner for Refugees was designated the lead agency for aid to refugees and internally displaced persons, and it was backed by UNPROFOR troops from France, Britain, and Belgium. However, UN troops withheld military force to deliver humanitarian assistance, and instead *negotiated* humanitarian access with the various warring parties in much the same manner that relief NGOs have done in dozens of internal wars. Like NGOs, UN relief workers and peacekeeping troops sometimes revealed and sometimes concealed information on atrocities.[75]

Even following the 1995 Dayton Peace Accords, more heavily armed IFOR troops have consistently declined to arrest indicted war criminals Karadic and Mladic. Armed actors become NGO-ized when they act as if they are not armed. Unarmed, but highly prestigious institutions such as the UNHCR, the European Community, and the Conference on Security and Cooperation in Europe failed to decisively shape the conflicts.[76] Instead, in classic NGO style, they opportunistically filled the interstices of the conflict and bowed to the political agendas of the adversaries and the sponsors.

In the second form of NGO-ization, the warring parties and major external states all incorporated the presence and operations of NGOs into their military-political strategies. Milosevic and other champions of Greater Serbia realized quickly that major power governments would acquiesce in very high levels of violence and forced displacement if only most refugees could be contained within the old boundaries of the former Yugoslavia.[77] This put the aid NGOs as well as UNHCR and the ICRC in the difficult moral position of saving lives while facilitating ethnic cleansing.[78]

It is less generally recognized that the Muslim leaders of Bosnia-Herzegovina also incorporated the humanitarian NGO presence into their political strategy. They understood their military weakness vis-à-vis Milosevic and the Bosnian Serbs. Nevertheless, when they declared independence in 1992 they hoped that the deaths of thousands of their citizens would draw in the international community on their side of the war and against the Serbs.[79] By monitoring this violence, portraying it to the world, and advocating military action, aid NGOs, human rights NGOs, and journalists were all essential to this strategy.[80]

Both the Serbs and the Bosnian Muslims accomplished some, but not all, of their goals through their NGO strategies. The Serbs successfully removed most Muslims from the areas they claimed in Bosnia (though not in Kosovo), but they failed to annex these areas officially to Serbia proper. The Bosnians belatedly, in 1995 and again in 1999, managed to use the humanitarian victimization of Muslims to draw the U.S. and NATO into the war on their side, and they successfully maintained the official borders of Bosnia-Herzegovina.

It is ironic that the same NGO network that was rendered useful to U.S. foreign policy was also utilized by opposing sides in the war.

The International Tribunal for the Former Yugoslavia is a special case of an NGO-ized multilateral institution that has thrived precisely by making itself useful to and compatible with U.S. foreign policy. Just as the U.S. has selectively activated the Tribunal by sharing U.S. intelligence information to corroborate certain Tribunal initiatives, it has occasionally deactivated the Tribunal by threats and pressure. In an example of deactivation, the U.S. reacted strongly when a task force within the Tribunal Prosecutor's office conducted a study of whether NATO violated laws of war in its bombing of Kosovo and Serbia in 1999.[81] The study was not pursued. In some cases the United States has worked through the Tribunal without taking public responsibility for the outcome—doing the deed without leaving fingerprints. However, in supporting the creation of the Tribunal, the U.S. sought the pretense of acting decisively in the face of genocide without undertaking the costs of actually doing so: it left fingerprints without doing the deed.

More broadly, the Tribunal's effectiveness at every step has depended radically on its capacity to catch the wind blown by the current agenda of U.S. foreign policy. This very NGO-like dependent symbiosis with a state is not an impurity in an otherwise politically pristine Tribunal. Instead, it represents the constitutive and energizing politics of the Tribunal, without which it would neither exist nor be effective.

In drawing some overall conclusion about the effects of NGOs in the conflicts of the former Yugoslavia it is important to guard against deterministic or rigid interpretations of causality. NGOs are international organizations that institutionalize world politics, but they are also wild cards whose consequences in a particular situation are indeterminate.

Yugoslavia broke apart in the context of a dense international network of NGOs and other actors pursuing an array of humanitarian mandates on all sides of the wars. The presence of the network created a set of indeterminate obstacles and opportunities for all the powerful actors. In the event, the same NGOs and the same network became incorporated into the strategies of all the warring parties and all the external states. In this sense NGOs were indeed dancing in the dark with hidden political partners. The NGO network, by its very existence, "absorbed" and institutionalized the conflicts in the former Yugoslavia in an indeterminate manner that influenced the outcome of the wars and shaped the successor states.

POSTSCRIPT: A PERMANENT INTERNATIONAL CRIMINAL COURT

The Rome Statute for the International Criminal Court (ICC) was adopted on July 17, 1998 and came into force on July 1, 2002. By 2004, the International Criminal Court had appointed judges and a prosecutor, but had yet to issue an indictment or try a case. NGOs played an enormous role in the gestation and formation of the ICC.[82] The Coalition for an International Criminal Court, founded in 1995, boasted more than 1,000 NGO members in 2004.[83] Ironically, given its NGO paternity, the ICC itself may well fail because it is insufficiently NGO-ized, particularly vis-à-vis the United States.

President Clinton signed the treaty shortly before leaving office, but never brought it to the U.S. Senate for ratification, and then recommended to his successor that it not be brought to the Senate without some crucial modifications. President Bush subsequently "unsigned" it, declared that the U.S. government would not recognize the Court's jurisdiction over American citizens, and has demanded "status of force" agreements granting immunity for U.S. military forces from each country where they are stationed.[84] In spite of the Bush administration's approach, I would argue that the real problem with the ICC is not the need for American immunity, but the absence of instrumentalities for American political control. Resentful of American power, the ICC's European and NGO creators may have made it too strong and independent to succeed. They may have deprived it of the ability to catch the winds of American foreign policy priorities ... like an NGO.

David Rieff, a seasoned observer of war and humanitarian action, points to a split within the liberal left coalition that supports the ICC. One group seeks to institutionalize the human rights approach to war in a powerful international court. "The problem with the human rights approach," he argues, "is less that it is wrong than that it is unsustainable in the absence of a world government, or, at the very least, of a United Nations system with far more money, autonomy, and power than it is ever likely to be granted by member states."[85] Short of a world government, the only actor capable of asserting human rights norms against well-armed violators is the U.S. military. Rieff understands the implications, which point toward a new imperialism, led by the United States, to suppress the worst human rights catastrophes. Here he is challenged by the other sector of the left, which is defined by a powerful animus against any extension of American global power.

The vision of a new imperialism against human rights violators appears more remote than ever after September 11, 2001, particularly with unpopular American occupations of Iraq and Afghanistan. But the political problem for supporters of the ICC remains the same.

The court is supported by an unstable coalition on the liberal left. There are those who seek to harness U.S. power to enforce global human rights through the court (but without submitting the court to U.S. political control), and those who hope the court will restrain and confine American power.[86] It is unlikely that both groups will get their way. In order to succeed, the ICC must NGO-ize itself, incorporating either an anti-American agenda and finding little legal success, or a pro-American agenda and selective legal success. If either of these outcomes occurs, one of the liberal left factions that supported the idea of the court will be alienated by the court as a political reality.

6
Engineering Fertility

No sector of global NGOs has shaped the lives and bodies of women more than the population control network. Population NGOs have forged powerful alliances with NGOs in the fields of women's rights and environmentalism to create a "network-of-networks" that has defined the meaning of progress for poor women and the developing world as a whole. Much of this work of alliance-building culminated in the International Conference on Population and Development held in Cairo during September 1994.

This chapter describes the "Cairo consensus" on women, environment, and population, as well as dissension from both feminist and religious viewpoints. It explores the historical emergence of the three NGO sectors that formed the Cairo consensus, and how they were engineered into alliance by governments and foundations. NGO wars between rival networks became more intense "after Cairo," and this chapter focuses on one of these NGO wars, fought in the halls of the United Nations. The chapter also probes crucial ideological premises for engineering fertility and controlling population.

THE CAIRO CONSENSUS AND DISSENT

The "Cairo consensus," which was sealed and celebrated at the 1994 International Conference on Population and Development, included two significant components.[1] In the first, the consensus endorsed a set of policy tools. Foreign aid from rich countries in the global North to poor countries in the global South would be redirected toward a combination of education for girls and women, availability of contraceptive technologies, and support for women working in gainful employment, and much of this foreign aid would be channeled through NGOs. This combination of policies constitutes a *modular technique* in the sense discussed in chapter 1—a set of easily replicated practices that can be used by NGOs anywhere in the world to create a similar, predictable effect.

The second component of the Cairo consensus was a simple causal theory linking those policy tools to global problems in the three fields of women's rights, environmental protection, and population control.

In the theory, empowering women through education, contraception, and paid work would lead them to delay marriage and pregnancy and so have fewer children over their reproductive lifetimes, which would reduce population growth and thereby ease pressure on the environment. This theory has several advantages for acting as a guide for policy—it is simple, plausible, can be funded cheaply, and promises to reconcile any conflict between the individual freedom of poor women and the collective goals of population control and environmental protection.

The Cairo conference itself consisted of a meeting of 3,500 members of 183 governmental delegations, who together formulated the United Nations Programme of Action on population and development.[2] Following customary practice at such international meetings, 5,000 NGO representatives met in parallel with the official conference. One group of delegations in the government conference, led by the Vatican and joined by several Islamic and Catholic countries, opposed any endorsement of abortion in the Program for Action. Their dissent, while forceful and prominent, made a limited impact on the consensus, except to rule out any attempt to designate access to abortion as a universal women's right. Although standing as a significant bloc in the governmental conference, the anti-abortion coalition was quite feeble in the parallel NGO meeting, where the claim to represent people at the grassroots was verified by most observers.[3]

The prominence of the religious dissenters in news coverage and scholarship has distracted attention from the *feminist dissenters* who called into question the Cairo consensus at a much more fundamental level. Betsy Hartmann is an activist and scholar who believes firmly in the "inviolability of individual reproductive rights," including the availability of contraception and abortion, but who is critical of the Cairo consensus on at least three grounds.[4]

First, Hartmann points out that the foreign aid targets set by the Cairo process were heavily skewed toward funding for contraceptives, with relatively little aid targeted for the broader goals of reproductive health supported by women's groups. Hartmann explains the array of services under a reproductive and sexual health approach:

These include pregnancy care (prenatal and postnatal care, safe delivery, nutrition, and child health), STD [sexually transmitted disease] prevention and treatment, basic gynecological care (screening for breast and cervical cancer), sexuality and gender education, and referral systems for other health problems.[5]

Women's groups were drawn into the Cairo consensus with the promise of foreign aid for the broad agenda of reproductive health services, then the actual aid was skewed to the narrow agenda of contraceptives. This is the classic political ploy of bait and switch.

Second, Hartmann critiques the causal theory behind the Cairo consensus. According to the theory, the laudable goal of empowering women is reduced almost entirely to the single tactic of educating girls. To effectively empower women in the Third World would require a much more comprehensive economic and social agenda. According to Hartmann, real women's empowerment would require encouraging women to create independent trade unions in free trade areas, reversing World Bank structural adjustment programs that strip government social services, and empowering poor men by creating jobs that allow them to meet their family economic obligations.[6] In this second aspect of her critique, Hartmann exposes the false assumption of *magic bullet causality* in the Cairo consensus. This is the assumption that NGOs can use their modular technique to achieve its intended impact regardless of the local economic, social, and political context (see chapter 1).

Third, the Cairo consensus strongly encourages NGOs to play the lead role in implementing future population programs. But Hartmann understands that "NGOs have frequently been used as a weak substitute for public services eroded under structural adjustment."[7] Indeed, the turn toward NGOs in foreign aid is part of a wider pattern by which governments in both the North and South withdraw from their responsibility to provide basic welfare services to poor people. As Hartmann points out, "The larger—and often unspoken—issue is how a broad sexual and reproductive health approach can be achieved in the context of deteriorating health conditions and services."[8] The reality in much of the Third World, particularly sub-Saharan Africa, is that the economic and political context has been moving for two decades in the opposite direction from empowering poor women or men.

I would take Hartmann's insight another step, and argue that it is no coincidence that the Cairo consensus emerged when it did. Its latent agenda is precisely to legitimize the withdrawal from responsibility for the poor by governments in both the South and North. It does this by assigning responsibility for providing basic services to NGOs, which will never be able to do so at any comprehensive level but which can be used to deflect blame for failures away from governments in the South. In addition, the consensus reduces "empowerment of women" to the magic bullet technique of educating girls, which governments in the North can fund at low levels while cutting their total international development aid and still claim to have met their responsibilities.

Therefore, the Cairo consensus is reductionistic in three respects: in theory by reducing empowerment of women to educating girls; in practice by reducing foreign aid to shipping contraceptives; and in politics by shifting the responsibility for the failure of the whole program from governments to NGOs.

BEFORE CAIRO—FORGING NGO ALLIANCES

In addition to its substantive claims, the Cairo consensus was, and remains, a political coalition. It is an alliance, or network-of-networks, among NGOs in the fields of women, environment, and population. It is also an alliance between NGOs in those three fields and more powerful actors including certain governments, foundations, and UN agencies. Since international conferences have played a key role in the forging of these alliances, it is important to understand the complexity of politics within such conferences.

In the diplomacy of international conferences such as Cairo 1994, the government delegation and the NGO delegation from the same country are often not entirely independent of each other, but instead closely linked. There are at least three distinct patterns in how governments and NGOs manipulate each other's representative claims at such conferences. The most clumsy and obvious is the practice by some authoritarian governments of creating GONGOs (government-organized NGOs) and sending them to pose as independent voices at UN meetings. According to a study of NGO participation at world conferences:

> Countries such as China have either declared party organs (such as the All China Women's Federation) to be NGOs or established new organizations (such as the Human Rights Society of China) in order to participate in the NGO forums at international UN conferences.[9]

Such obvious GONGOs tend to be recognized by other conference participants and hence wield little influence.

In a second pattern, U.S. presidential administrations since the early 1980s have appointed leaders of ideologically harmonious NGOs to join the U.S. government delegation to international conferences, and have funded other friendly NGOs to attend the parallel NGO forums. On women's issues, this favored treatment has fallen to different sets of NGOs as control of the presidency has oscillated between the two major political parties. The pattern originated with President Ronald Reagan, who aligned the Republican Party firmly with "social conservatives." Since Reagan came to power in 1981, most interested American NGOs have polarized along party lines, with those opposing abortion and defending the traditional family aligning with Republicans, and those supporting a broad agenda of reproductive rights linked to the Democrats.[10]

The third pattern may be the most surprising. Several Latin America governments send delegates to UN meetings whose positions, particularly on the abortion issue, contradict their official government policies at home. In order to get by with this, there must be a degree of inattention by the national press and the public of such countries. In the cases of Peru, Chile, and Argentina this contradiction has been explained as a ploy by coalition governments, which hand over control of international conferences to their socialist party partners.[11]

If the politics of representation at international conferences includes—along with reasoned persuasion—a measure of rivalry, horse-trading, manipulation, and prevarication, that is evidence, after all, that such meetings are a form of politics. At such international conferences NGOs are wild cards whose influence is not easily predictable. Like wild cards, NGOs can be traded, buried, or played by other actors in a variety of ways, and their value can change in the course of the game. With this inherent political variability of international NGOs kept in mind, the recent history of NGOs in the fields of population, environment, and women will be more intelligible.

In the genealogy of population management during the twentieth century, technologies of fertility control were first deployed by governments for purposes of *eugenics*—to ensure that the "unfit" (whether defined in mental, criminal, or racial categories) produced fewer children than the "fit." Eugenics arose in the early twentieth century by stages (see chapter 3). First, a few foundations and NGOs promoted the discourse of "scientific" eugenics at a series of international conferences during the 1910s and 1920s. Then, governments accepted the consensus of "race hygiene" and began implementing it as policy. By 1940, a dozen countries had implemented some mandatory sterilization and another dozen were considering doing so. The German Nazi regime carried the assumptions of eugenics to their logical conclusion—to eliminate rather than merely sterilize those designated as "unfit."

After World War II, following the thorough political and scientific discrediting of eugenics ideology, population policies took a new direction under *neo-Malthusian* theories which recommend managing population growth to harmonize with national economic development. Under neo-Malthusianism, a "subordinate discourse" of *individual choice* has also flourished. The discourse of individual choice urges maximizing reproductive freedom, especially for women, through the availability of contraceptive and abortive technologies.[12]

The discourse of individual choice provides the ideological link between the women's movement and the population control movement. Neo-Malthusianism and individual choice agree on making contraceptive and abortion options available to women. However, neo-Malthusianism can allow only a limited scope for women's freedom of choice. As Linda Gordon observes, "There is, of course, no hidden hand that guarantees that population size will be appropriately regulated by individual desires alone."[13] Within a neo-Malthusian vision, to achieve government population targets it may be necessary to regulate reproductive choice. Who enforces this regulation of women's choice and fertility, by what means, and with what results? As part of an answer to such questions, Gordon looks behind the NGOs to the powerful individuals and foundations who have leveraged financial and scientific resources to create and redirect NGOs toward new purposes.

During the 1950s, when the Rockefeller Foundation was laying the groundwork for the "green revolution" of high-yield wheat and rice that would later make the Indian subcontinent self-sufficient in food (see chapter 1), John D. Rockefeller III wanted to modify this agenda. He advocated a dual foundation strategy of green revolution plus population control. When the Rockefeller Foundation rejected his full recommendations, he founded the Population Council to pursue this agenda independently.[14] Gordon traces the lineage of the population control establishment back to the earlier eugenics movement:

> Both organizationally and individually, eugenists became population controllers between 1930 and 1950. In the late 1940s the Milbank Memorial Fund, one of the main backers of eugenic and birth-control research, began to support research and writing about overpopulation in underdeveloped countries.

In 1952 Frederick Osborn, a leading eugenist, organized the Population Council. Osborn later set up the Population Association of America, and his cousin Fairfield Osborn later became a leader of Planned Parenthood-World Population. The Rockefeller Foundation, key funder of eugenic work, joined Milbank in 1936 in giving Princeton (Henry Fairfield Osborn's and John D. Rockefeller III's alma mater) an Office of Population Research. In the 1940s OPR became a kind of sanctuary for eugenist demographers. Kingsley David, Clyde Kiser, Frank Notestein, Dudley Kirk, and Frank Lorimer all worked there. When Rockefeller formed the Population Council, these five men moved to it immediately.[15]

For Gordon, the neo-Malthusian agenda of population control is really a covert form of eugenics.

Her analysis also illustrates that those who create and shape crucial NGOs can sometimes forge a global policy consensus that redirects the most powerful nations. Wielding structural power, NGOs can occupy the "commanding heights" of the political-cultural landscape to define the meaning of progress for people and governments (see chapter 2). The right NGO at the right time can be a small rudder that turns an enormous ship of state.

NGOs had led the way in bringing about the dominance of eugenics policy in many countries before World War II. After the war, NGOs again led the way in establishing the neo-Malthusian and individual choice agendas of population control. NGOs sponsored most international population control conferences held through the 1960s. The International Planned Parenthood Federation (IPPF) and the International Union for the Scientific Study of Population were particularly prominent in this role.[16] After 1967, when the United Nations established the UN Fund for Population Activities (UNFPA), the sponsorship of most international conferences shifted to governments acting through the UN. Again, as in the eugenics wave, government policy followed the consensus of international discourse which was first formed in international conferences by a few determined NGOs. In 1950, no country had a policy to reduce population; by 1990, 71 countries did.[17]

The alliance of the three NGO sectors of population, environment, and women in the Cairo consensus came about not long after the proliferation of NGOs in sheer numbers within each sector, which dates from about 1970. Foundings of new environmental NGOs surged around the 1972 UN Conference on the Human Environment, and again around the 1992 UN Conference on Environment and

Development (Rio Summit), where more than 1,400 NGOs were officially represented.[18] In the population field, local affiliates of the International Planned Parenthood Federation were located in 50 countries in 1967, almost 90 countries in 1977, and more than 120 countries in 1987.[19] More than a third of all women's NGOs that existed in 1999 had been formed during the United Nations Decade for Women (1975 to 1985).[20] Why parallel increases in the number of NGO actors would lead to a convergence of substantive agendas is not entirely clear. One might expect an increase in the number of actors to lead to a divergence of their agendas. Part of the explanation may be a pattern found in all three sectors—NGOs were founded in large numbers only after, and to a large extent in response to, an agenda and a UN forum for legitimation, funding, and networking that had already been established by an earlier wave of pioneer NGOs.

In the event, many leading environmental NGOs, particularly in the United States, have adopted a population control agenda. This dates back to 1968, when Paul Ehrlich's *The Population Bomb* was originally published by the Sierra Club. In the early 1980s the National Audubon Society launched the Global Tomorrow Coalition of more than 100 environmental and population NGOs. In the 1990s more mainstream environmental NGOs—including the National Wildlife Federation, National Resources Defense Council, Cousteau Society, and Worldwatch Institute—embraced Malthusian population agendas.[21]

Alongside these mainstream groups, Hartmann identifies two other streams of environmental NGOs. On the left she finds a non-Malthusian movement for "social justice ecology," including NGO coalitions such as Development Alternatives with Women for a New Era (DAWN).[22] On the right is a "fascistic wing" of population environmentalism, represented by NGOs such as the Carrying Capacity Network, some of which advocate mandatory contraception for poor women and a crackdown on immigration.[23]

Today's women's groups can claim a lineage to the mass movements that fought for women's suffrage in the late nineteenth and early twentieth centuries. Nevertheless, the contemporary NGO organizational form can exist either with, or more often without, a mass movement membership under it. In contemporary UN diplomacy, *women's NGOs* are accepted as complete surrogates for, and representative voices of, *women's movements*. Most observers simply count NGOs; no one asks how many members a particular NGO has back home or who funds it. By this measure, NGO participation multiplied over the three international conferences held during the UN Decade for Women: 4,000 people participated in the NGO forum in Mexico City (1975), 7,000 in Copenhagen (1980), and 14,000 in Nairobi (1985).[24] At these meetings many of the same women met repeatedly and entered into broad-based dialogue and experimentation to find a "frame of meaning" that could capture a wide range of concerns of women, especially across the North–South divide. The issue frame of "violence against women" emerged from this process, and became the basis for a global network and campaign that resonated with a broad public and also linked the diverse problems of domestic violence, sex-selective abortion, sexual slavery, and female genital mutilation. The campaign relied on creative innovation by individual NGO entrepreneurs such as Charlotte Bunch, head of the Center for Women's Global Leadership.[25]

FUNDING CONSENSUS

The creation of a transnational network and campaign demands substantial material resources as well as rich relational and ideational contributions. The requirements for a basic NGO office in a Third World capital (rent, phone, fax, computer with Internet, salary for an English-speaking professional), as well as plane tickets and accommodations for networking at international conferences, all cost money. This may seem obvious—so obvious, perhaps, that many studies of NGO international conferencing simply ignore this dimension entirely. In so doing they have accepted uncritically the claim that the NGO forum at a particular international conference somehow represents "global civil society." Much research remains to be done on the material dimension—the political economy—of international NGO networking. So far, a few studies have begun to draw back the veil.

Several key foundations facilitated the growth of the global NGO network on women's human rights. In the United States the Ford Foundation, the Shaler Adams Fund, and the MacArthur Foundation played leading roles. Significant foundation support did not precede, but followed, the explosion of women's NGOs in the 1980s. Foundation support grew slowly during the Decade for Women from 1975 to 1985 and peaked during the first half of the 1990s. Most important for this analysis, foundations ensured that representatives of certain women's NGOs showed up at international conferences dealing with women's issues, and also meetings on population and human rights issues. According to Keck and Sikkink, "Foundations were key supporters of the organizing efforts that made women's groups a powerful presence at the Vienna World Conference on Human Rights [1993], as well as the Cairo Population Conference [1994] and the Beijing Women's Conference [1995]."[26] And on the particular question of plane tickets for the Vienna conference, "Grants from European and North American governments and foundations provided travel and accommodation funds for many NGO participants, especially from the south."[27] From these hints it is clear that the donors—primarily foundations and governments in North America and Western Europe—were in a position to select which Third World NGO activists would represent "global civil society" at major international conferences.

Turning to population NGOs, their biggest funding sources are the United States, Japan, Western European governments, and several key foundations. The Ford and MacArthur Foundations are at the top of this list, both supporting progressive programs in reproductive health. The Hewlett, Mellon and Rockefeller Foundations concentrate more resources in the population field.[28]

Ford and MacArthur appear to be two strategic, crossover foundations with extensive links to NGOs and activists in both the global women's movement and the global population movement. Ford is alone among global foundations in maintaining a network of 13 regional offices throughout the world, whose staffs select and develop local NGOs and tailor grants with a degree of subtlety and attention to detail that is unsurpassed by any other global grant maker.[29]

In the NGO world, the Population Council is unique in its hybrid structure and global influence.[30] The Population Council is both a foundation and an NGO. Like a foundation, it possesses internal sources of funding. The Rockefeller Foundation provided the Population Council with its own endowment at its founding, which continues to produce a reliable base income. In addition, the Population Council maintains a for-profit wing that markets certain contraceptives in the United States. As an NGO, the primary activity of the Population Council is research. It maintains a Center for Biomedical Research in New York to design new contraceptive technologies, and also supports sophisticated social scientific research on promoting contraceptive use in the Third World.

The key to the Population Council's influence lies in its network of 18 field offices throughout the Third World. In this respect it most resembles the Ford Foundation. Population Council research *in* the Third World is conducted as much as possible by scholars *from* the Third World. In this way the result is not merely the research publications themselves, but—more importantly—career support for Third World intellectuals and policy influence by shaping consensus and grooming future government experts. Seven Third World cities whose intellectual and political elites will be crucial to shaping the future of world population are host to field offices of both the Ford Foundation and the Population Council: New Delhi, India; Jakarta, Indonesia; Hanoi, Vietnam; Cairo, Egypt; Nairobi, Kenya; Johannesburg, South Africa; and Mexico City.

What is the effect on Southern NGOs of this steady diet of funding from Northern foundations, governments and NGOs? In a 1993 article, Rajni Kothari described how critical Third World activists are corrupted and co-opted:

> Leading activists and intellectuals who have gained influence in the thinking of many people are being "bought up," not just in the sense of collecting hefty per diems, project grants, travel budgets, and foreign trips (which can be corrupting, and even intoxicating), but in the far more basic sense of being provided with more and more avenues of recognition and praise. ... Most of the great dissenters against Western Civilization strike their mortal blows to the West in seminars they attend in the West; how many of them have fought the West from the real grass roots of their own societies?[31]

Betsy Hartmann makes similar observations focused specifically on the population industry:

> Money helps to lubricate the relationship between the population establishment and Third World elites—it is probably no exaggeration to say that foreign support for population control has largely been bought at Western taxpayers' expense. ... Third World members of the Old Boy population network (for they continue to be mainly upper-class men, though more women are now joining the ranks) are constantly rewarded with scholarships and travel grants, funding for pet projects, prizes, and renown in the international press.
>
> Although these material rewards help to cement the alliance, the identity of interests between foreign agencies and Third World elites goes far beyond the perks. Both are part of the new class of world managers, which has begun to transcend differences in culture.[32]

This kind of slow socialization over years and decades, with its selective empowerment of carefully groomed Third World elites, is a powerful instrument for shaping a manageable voice of global civil society. Nevertheless, in the run-up to Cairo 1994 the consensus-builders were particularly active.

The 1992 "Earth Summit" (Conference on Environment and Development) held in Rio de Janeiro served as a dress rehearsal for Cairo, though the population consensus did not fare well in Rio. In the United States, five top NGOs had formed the Campaign on Population and Development (COPE) in 1990 to educate the public on links between population growth and environmental degradation. *People*, the magazine of the International Planned Parenthood Federation, was re-titled *People and the Planet* and made a joint venture with a network of population and environmental NGOs. *People and the Planet* articulated what would later become the Cairo consensus on population, environment, and women. Rio, however, produced dissent rather than consent, both from Third World governments who wanted Northern governments to accept more responsibility for environmental destruction, and also from feminists. Before the conference, 1,500 activists from around the world had formed Women's Action Agenda 21 to condemn the idea that women's fertility was to blame for environmental destruction.[33] While women's NGOs were divided over whether to align with the population control agenda at Rio, they were united in opposition to the Vatican and its allies that sought to avoid any mention of abortion or contraception in conference deliberations.

Defeated in Rio, the population/environment coalition regrouped for Cairo. They renegotiated the consensus, giving more weight to the feminist agenda of reproductive freedom. At the same time, the American public was treated to a massive public relations blitz orchestrated by a team of elite opinion shapers: Timothy Wirth, President Clinton's Undersecretary of State for Global Affairs, Ted Turner and Jane Fonda of CNN and the Turner Foundation, the Pew Charitable Trust's Global Stewardship Initiative, and the UN Fund for Population Activities.[34]

In evaluating the construction of a network-of-networks and the formation of the Cairo consensus prior to the 1994 conference, two conclusions are warranted. First, more research is needed on the *incentive power* of foundation and government grant-making in encouraging the creation of certain kinds of NGOs with preferred ideological orientations, and on the *selective power* of foundation and government travel funding in choosing which NGO representatives speak for global civil society at a particular international conference. Nevertheless, available evidence supports a second conclusion that foundations and governments from the United States and Western Europe played a crucial role in shaping the convergence of agendas between women's NGOs and population NGOs during the 1990s. Foundations and governments engineered the consensus on how governments and NGOs would engineer the fertility of women.

AFTER CAIRO—FIGHTING NGO WARS

Of the many NGO wars over population and fertility, one particular skirmish deserves attention for what it reveals about contested claims of grassroots representation and global moral authority. These claims are the coin of the realm in the NGO world—battles over them are serious and hard fought.

Diplomatic representatives of Pope John Paul II participated in the 1994 Cairo population conference as a *government* delegation, not as an NGO in the parallel forum. The "Holy See" (legally distinct from Vatican City) has the legal status of a "non-member state permanent observer" in the United Nations. This status creates a problem in principle and a problem in practice for NGOs that disagree with the Holy See on fundamental policy questions.

The moral authority claimed by the Holy See is inseparable from its juridical status. And its juridical status is accepted by about 170 states with which it maintains diplomatic relations. Those states grant legal recognition to, and exchange ambassadors with, a sovereign subject of international law which is neither the Vatican micro-state nor the Roman Catholic religious community, but claims to be "*the Holy See*, namely, the Pope and Roman Curia, universal and spiritual authority, unique center of communion."[35] In principle, therefore, the Holy See claims to possess universal spiritual and moral authority above any particular state, above all states together, and even above—this is truly shocking for the NGO mindset—all states and thousands of NGOs meeting together in an international conference.

The Holy See claims to occupy the same moral space that NGOs occupy—that moral space above governments from which universal norms emanate. Whether NGOs view the moral authority claims of the Holy See as grandiose, anachronistic, and positively medieval depends on whether they are fighting on the same side. When NGOs and the Holy See agree, as they sometimes do on issues of peace and human rights, both are happy. However, on issues of reproductive health their relationship has been the NGO equivalent of war.[36]

Advocates of the wide availability of contraception and abortion, and of their use in population control, have taken the moral authority of the Catholic Church very seriously for a long time. Dr John Rock, one of the co-inventors of the birth control pill in 1960 at Harvard Medical School, was himself a Catholic. He understood that there was no medical reason why the pill could not be designed to induce a menstrual period in women only once every three or four months (as some versions now do). Nevertheless, he insisted that the design of oral contraceptives, and their regimen for use, be built around a four-week cycle ending with menstruation. Rock did this precisely in an attempt to make the birth control pill acceptable to Catholic leaders as a "natural" form of fertility regulation. According to Malcolm Gladwell,

> Today, the Pill is still often sold in dial packs and taken in twenty-eight day cycles. It remains, in other words, a drug shaped by the dictates of the Catholic Church—by John Rock's desire to make this new method of birth control seem as natural as possible.[37]

During the early 1960s, John Rock worked with top officials of Planned Parenthood and other advocates of contraception to cultivate Catholic leaders in meetings at the Vatican and the University of Notre Dame. They were disappointed when Pope Paul VI condemned all "artificial" means of contraception in his 1968 encyclical, *Humanae Vitae.*

Oddly enough, for more than two decades after *Humanae Vitae* neither Paul VI nor his successor John Paul II used the diplomatic authority of the Holy See to reinforce their religious authority. From 1968 to 1990 the Catholic Church put little serious effort into influencing family planning policy, either nationally or in multilateral organizations.[38] Only in the 1990s did the Vatican problem in principle also become a problem in practice for population control NGOs.

When the Holy See did begin to assert its diplomatic voice in the international conferences of the 1990s, NGOs that opposed it fought back. The most effective method was simply to overwhelm the parallel NGO meetings at international conferences with thousands of NGOs that collectively spoke with the presumptive moral authority of global civil society. Finally, in a move as obvious as it was surprising, one NGO thought to challenge the Holy See's platform for projecting its diplomatic voice—that is, the Holy See's sovereign status and membership in governmental forums at the United Nations and international meetings.

Catholics For a Free Choice (CFFC) was formed in the United States in 1973, following a U.S. Supreme Court decision that legalized abortion. The mission of CFFC has always been to encourage and legitimize Catholic dissent from official church teaching on abortion and contraception. When the Holy See became more assertive in global reproductive politics during the 1990s, CFFC also expanded its international operations. The two entities, both of which claim to represent Catholics and to wield the symbolic moral authority of Catholicism, clashed strongly in the 1994 Cairo meeting on population. According to Frances Kissling, the president of CFFC since 1982, "The Vatican tried unsuccessfully to prevent CFFC from participating in the Beijing conference [in 1995]."[39] Also in 1995, Kissling retaliated by circulating a petition asking the United Nations to reconsider the status of the Holy See in the UN system.

The NGO war between the Holy See and CFFC reached a peak in March 1999 when CFFC launched the "See Change" campaign to downgrade the legal status of the Holy See at the UN. The NGO argued that the Holy See fails to meet the international legal criteria for statehood, and is merely the government of a religious community:

No other religion is granted this elevated status. Other religions participate in the UN like most other non-state entities—as nongovernmental organizations. Because UN conferences operate on consensus, the ability to disagree with the majority consensus has significant power.[40]

Were the campaign to succeed, the grandeur of the Holy See would be reduced to the status of merely one more NGO among thousands of others at international meetings. Were it to succeed, this would be a powerful move.

CFFC publicized the campaign in 1999 and 2000 at a series of international meetings built around the implementation of previous international conferences or the preparation for conferences yet to come. Kissling prepared a "shadow report" on the Holy See and circulated it to government delegations and the UN Secretariat. In addition to considerable positive coverage in the international press, CFFC gained 450 endorsements for the campaign from other NGOs.

Then came another surprise. An explicitly Catholic NGO, with a "pro-family" agenda compatible with the positions of the Holy See, launched a counter-campaign. In March 2000, Austin Ruse of the Catholic Family and Human Rights Institute (C-FAM) produced a "Declaration of Support of the Holy See at the UN" signed by 1,015 NGOs from 44 countries.[41] This development was surprising because the existence of the Catholic hierarchy with its traditional claim of moral authority had left the niche of Catholic NGOs relatively undeveloped. In fact, C-FAM was a fledgling NGO established in 1997.

The NGO war had become a battle for endorsements. No one knew (or even cared) how many real people were represented by the NGOs on either list, or what larger movements or causes they represented, or which foundations or governments or direct mail contributors funded them. Getting a longer list of NGOs than the other side became an end in itself, a presumptively legitimate surrogate for the voice of "global civil society." Of course, this is the same assumption behind the politics of NGO forums at international conferences.

To date, no state has withdrawn diplomatic recognition from the Holy See. Yet the war continues on the websites of the two NGOs with "Catholic" in their names.[42]

In this rather mild NGO fracas, the real story is to be found in the multiple permutations of moral authority claimed in international politics, from the grassroots of NGO representation below states to the commanding heights of universal norms above states.

PREMISES OF POPULATION CONTROL

Eugenics is a body of ideas and policies that once bore the cachet of enlightened science and progressive politics; today, it draws almost universal opprobrium. We might wish that people in the 1920s had examined more critically the premises and implications of the accepted population ideology.

What are the premises of neo-Malthusian theory?

Paul Ehrlich has been the leading American popularizer of population control for several decades. Central to his influence is the idea of "carrying capacity"—the notion that there is an identifiable maximum density of human population that the world, or any region thereof, can sustain without doing permanent damage to the natural environment. Betsy Hartmann examines this idea, which is at the heart of Malthusian thought, and finds that the aura of cool, scientific theory conceals a severe political program:

Thus, his latest book (co-authored with Anne Ehrlich) *The Population Explosion*, compares the exponential growth of human populations to that of pond weed, and warns us that nature may end the population explosion "in very unpleasant ways," such as famine and AIDS, if people do not act immediately.

The pond weed view of the species reinforces racism and sexism. The white middle-class elite, to which the Ehrlichs and many other population control advocates belong, is unlikely to view itself in these terms; instead the metaphor extends primarily to the dark-skinned poor. In *The Population Explosion* the Ehrlichs refer to babies born in Bangladesh and the Philippines as "mouths"—a common Malthusian slur. Implicitly, it is women's fertility which is out of control; it is as if women have never consciously exercised control over reproduction, except in modern family planning programs.[43]

In Hartmann's analysis, neo-Malthusianism is really a disguised form of eugenics by class, race, and gender. They (dark-skinned, poor, women) are to be targeted for fertility control so that we (white-skinned, rich and middle class, men and women) may avoid the projected future horrors of population regulation imposed by a vengeful "nature." Therefore, the coercive tendency of population control policy is no accident. The legitimacy of coercion follows directly—though covertly—from the premises of neo-Malthusian theory.

As we have seen, Linda Gordon traces the career paths of key leaders from the eugenics establishment of the 1920s and 1930s directly to the new population control organizations of the 1940s and 1950s. Hartmann traces the eugenics roots of population control through their shared theoretical premises. Gordon and Hartmann make the feminist case against a political alliance between women's groups and the population establishment. In doing so, however, Gordon and Hartmann assume that the individual choice agenda of complete reproductive freedom for women is entirely distinct from the Malthusian population control agenda at every level.

What are the premises of individual choice?

Deborah Barrett and David John Frank suggest that the premises of the individual choice discourse and the neo-Malthusian discourse are quite closely linked:

In the postwar world polity, individual rights not only became compatible with but definitionally linked to neo-Malthusianism. The shift to individual choice and neo-Malthusian thinking stems from the crystallization of the definitive model of a national society based on individuals and personhood, managed by an active central authority structure, and devoted to progress. The individual choice and neo-Malthusian models are really two sides of the same coin, especially since economic development was itself individualized at that time (per capita measures replacing the corporate measures of earlier times, such as total population, total industrial production, miles of railroad track). The expansion and sacralization of citizenship—the conjunction of the individual and the nation—have legitimated these development-centered models of population control.[44]

The argument is nuanced, but can be stated more simply. In a society whose highest value is individual choice, social and political progress will be measured by growth (or at least stability) in per capita income, as the necessary though not sufficient condition for enlarging individual choice. A government whose success is judged by its ability to maintain the conditions for such growth must attempt to control the rate of population growth to hold it below the rate of economic growth. (This is the case because per capita income is the total gross domestic product divided by the population.) Therefore, an individual choice society must be a neo-Malthusian society.

Barrett and Frank neither deplore nor celebrate the bond they discover between the premises of individual choice and Malthusian discourses. However, implications of their insight may call into question the viability of Gordon's and Hartmann's project of individual reproductive freedom without neo-Malthusian population control.

The obvious syllogism is simplistic and unconvincing. If individual choice is really Malthusianism (Barrett and Frank), and if Malthusianism is really eugenics against the weak (Hartmann), then individual choice must be linked to eugenics as well. A slightly longer chain of reasoning may be more illuminating. The premise of individual freedom, defined as expanding per capita income and universalized to an entire society, requires in principle that the society control the fertility of at least some citizens whenever the rate of economic growth falls below the rate of population growth. If we acknowledge that economic growth will not always accommodate the freely chosen rate of fertility, it follows that there will be times when the reproductive freedom of some women will be sacrificed for the economic freedom of others in the society. If the entire world is viewed as a single society—and this is the premise of all NGO and foundation operations conducted under putatively global norms—it is not hard to see that the burden of sacrifice is likely to fall on those who lack wealth, power, or status; that is, poor, dark-skinned, women in the Third World.

In short, a society whose highest value is individual choice for everyone will sacrifice the weak for the sake of the powerful. Paradoxically, the non-substitutable dignity of each human person, and the human rights that derive from that dignity, are lost when individual freedom is the highest social value. On which chief premise other than individual freedom might a global society be based to avoid this crisis and contradiction of values? The question is beyond the scope of this study. But it is part of the challenge facing NGOs in the fields of women and the environment, and indeed anyone who cares about those causes.

7
Changing Partners, Shaping Progress: The Future of NGOs

NGOs are wild cards in world politics; their form and influence are highly variable. The most important impact of NGOs and transnational networks is often an inadvertent consequence rather than either success or failure in achieving official NGO goals. Nevertheless, the plasticity of NGOs can be mapped. Each NGO is an amalgam of its transnational social and political partners. In the future, NGOs will continue to create networks by forming partnerships across nations. But which nations? And which partners? NGOs will continue to carry the latent agendas of their social and political partners. But which agendas? NGOs will continue to promote simplistic, universal causal theories to support their magic bullet solutions to global problems. But which problems? And which theories?

This concluding chapter identifies continuities and emerging trends in the future of NGOs. The continuities may be more obvious. Old NGOs live on, new ones mimic classic NGO names, and NGOs continue to serve as the favored response to insoluble problems. However, the changes are more important. NGOs accustomed to working in partnership with governments are operating where there is no government. And NGOs increasingly embrace profitmaking corporations and wealthy entrepreneurs among their societal partners. The future direction of global progress is at stake in the war between Al Qaeda and the United States, both of which seek to instrumentalize NGOs in the struggle. And NGOs, having emerged out of a religious culture in the eighteenth and nineteenth centuries, and having secularized in the twentieth century, find themselves navigating a strange world of post-humanist mandates and religious resurgence in the early twenty-first century.

CONTINUITIES

Old NGOs live on.

The Infant Formula Action Coalition (INFACT) promoted a global boycott of Nestlé products from 1977 to 1984 in order to stop Nestlé's promotion of infant formula to poor mothers in the Third World whose children would be healthier with breast milk. INFACT never went out of business as an NGO, but apparently has split into two. One successor INFACT is based in Boston and retains the acronym but no name, perhaps to indicate that it has gone beyond infant formula. This INFACT campaigned against General Electric from 1984 to 1993 to persuade it to abandon the manufacture of nuclear weapons, and since 1993 has turned to boycotting corporations linked to the tobacco industry.[1] Another INFACT, the Infant *Feeding* Action Coalition based in Toronto, Canada, continues the boycott of Nestlé. This INFACT is the official North American representative of IBFAN—the global network of 150 NGOs under the International Baby Food Action Network.[2]

Several Argentine human rights NGOs that emerged during the Dirty War from 1976 to 1983 continue to work. Centro de Estudios Legales y Sociales (CELS), originally founded in 1979, now co-sponsors a website with the National Security Archive out of Washington, DC to make available thousands of recently released documents from the U.S. Department of State for judicial proceedings and identification of victims.[3] Both the Mothers and the Grandmothers of the Plaza de Mayo continue to pressure the Argentine military and government to fully account for those who are still missing and to punish individual military officers who were responsible for the disappearances. The grandmothers use genetic testing to identify children who were abducted or born in captivity and adopted by military families, and then to reunite these grown children with their biological families.[4]

There appears to be no let-up in the proliferation of new NGOs in world politics. Many new NGOs signal their global moral compass and their claim to supranational moral authority by choosing an evocative name. Among the most popular "surnames" for new NGOs are "International" (after Amnesty International) and "Watch" (after the WorldWatch Institute and Human Rights Watch). There are many wonderful variations on these two themes:

Aide Médicale Internationale; Air Serv International; Benevolence International; Children International; Grassroots International; Handicap International; HealthNet International; Media Action International; Mental Disability International; Nomad International; Nonviolence International; Solidaridad Internacional; Traffic International; Transparency International; Women's Campaign International.

Amazon Watch; British Irish Rights Watch; Burma Watch; Caspian Revenue Watch; Children's Rights Watch; Corp Watch; Global Forest Watch; Global Trade Watch; Group Watch (publiceye.org); Indonesian Corruption Watch; Iraq Democracy Watch; Iraq Occupation Watch; Iraq Revenue Watch; NGO Watch; ODA Watch; OECD Watch; Pacific Media Watch; Palestinian Media Watch; Peace Watch; Peace Negotiation Watch; Philippine Migrant Watch; PR Watch; Refugee Watch; Security Watch; Sinks Watch; Sweatshop Watch; Women Acting Together for Change (WATCH).

NGOs will continue to do some things very well, such as forming links with relatively closed societies. Three days after a severe earthquake hit Bam, in Iran on December 26, 2003, 71 international relief NGOs were already on the scene. These included 30 American and 11 British NGOs, despite the U.S. designation of Iran as a member of the "Axis of Evil," and despite the presence of American and British soldiers occupying neighboring Iraq. Seven of the 71 NGOs were identifiably Islamic or based in Muslim countries, including Islamic Aid and Islamic Relief from Britain.[5] The point is not simply that the NGOs responded quickly, but also that this new network of societal and political partnerships is available for being mobilized for a wide range of possible purposes. In another example, North Korea is perhaps the most closed society in the world, and the government continues to exclude all but a few NGO and UN observers while accepting their food aid. Yet a few NGOs interviewing North Korean refugees in China managed to confirm what the North Korean government was denying—that a major famine in the mid-1990s killed at least 1 million North Koreans.[6]

More interesting than the continuities are the new ways NGOs are acting as wild cards in world politics.

WHERE THERE IS NO GOVERNMENT

It is largely true that NGOs are operating everywhere in the world. However, there are a few exceptions. North Korea has managed to largely fend off an NGO incursion. The other large and significant "NGO-free zone" has been the Democratic Republic of Congo (former Zaire) since 1998. Ironically, these two countries exclude NGOs for precisely the opposite reasons. The isolation of North Korea stems from the severe, Stalinist totalitarianism of Kim Jong Il. In contrast, NGOs avoid much of the Congo due to the near-complete collapse of the government and the regional war that has raged within its boundaries since 1998.

Too much coercive government or too little government would seem to exclude NGOs. The common feature of both conditions is the absence of *protection* for free, non-violent, social interaction—the much-abused concept of civil society. For civil society to thrive, the imperative is not to dismantle all government, but to build the kind of government that actively protects rather than intrudes upon civil sociality.

Large areas of Central Africa—including much of the Congo and parts of neighboring countries—have for several years lacked protection for civil society. NGOs and international organizations generally avoid leaving equipment, large caches of supplies, and expatriate staff on the ground in such areas for extended periods. But there are several different levels of insecurity. In areas of intermediate instability expatriates may not stay overnight, but they do not necessarily keep out entirely. At the peak of the violence and forced migration during 1999 and 2000, Nairobi served as a base for international access to stateless areas of the Congo.[7] NGO staff, UN officials, foreign embassy personnel, and religious leaders would fly into less unstable areas of the Congo for a day visit, sometimes leaving behind food or medical supplies. Arms smugglers and other transnational criminals also relied on Nairobi as a base for access to many of the same stateless areas.

The International Rescue Committee devised an innovative means to highlight the plight of millions of civilians living in the Congo. IRC hired an epidemiologist, Les Roberts, to estimate how many people had died as a result of the conflict. Roberts and his team conducted large-scale mortality surveys each year starting in 2000, using statistical inference from interviews with several hundred households randomly selected within designated health zones. The results have been startling. The IRC estimates that during four years from August 1998 and August 2002 about 3.3 million people died from the ongoing conflict.[8] Of these, perhaps 20 per cent died from direct violence and the rest from preventable disease and starvation. The death rate from direct violence has declined since the 2001 peace accord between Rwanda and the Democratic Republic of the Congo, and the later arrival of UN observers. But the death rate from disease has remained high.

As the warfare has subsided, the IRC and other humanitarian organizations have increased their presence on the ground. By mid-

2003 the IRC had established a headquarters in the capital, Kinshasa, and field offices in six other cities. Nevertheless, in its latest mortality survey, pilots refused to fly to certain unstable areas which were originally to be included in the study.[9]

The point is that large areas of Congo remain beyond the reach of government or international organizations. Yet NGOs like IRC manage to devise an array of tactics for maintaining whatever level of engagement the security situation, and donor generosity, will allow. The act of counting the dead, almost regardless of the accuracy of the information, asserts one of the prerogatives and duties of sovereign government. By counting the dead, the IRC undertook a rudimentary protection role. The IRC asserted a quasi-governmental role for itself in a region where there was no government.

The Central African Republic (CAR) has not yet been deeply affected by the war in its neighbor Congo to the south. But like Congo, the CAR includes enormous expanses of territory that the writ of the central government does not reach. Here the issue is a combination of security and the environment. The audacity of this NGO initiative is conveyed by the opening paragraph from a 2002 article in *National Geographic News:*

> In an effort to save the last large piece of pristine savanna in Africa, a band of Wyoming conservationists have received permission from the president of the Central African Republic (CAR) to raise an anti-poaching militia to patrol the eastern fourth of the Texas-size country. Led by Bruce Hayse, a family practitioner from Jackson, the group intends to drive out marauding gangs of Sudanese poachers who are rapidly decimating the region's wildlife and terrorizing villagers. The conservationists have been given shoot-on-sight authority.

Bruce Hayse doesn't wear a cowboy hat, but he does seem to evoke the Wyoming heritage of bringing law and order to the Wild West. "Unfortunately, the poachers weren't going to leave just because we told them to," he said. "If we were going to save this place people would have to be killed." Backing up these fighting words, Hayse created an NGO, Africa Rainforest and River Conservation, which hired a former mercenary from South Africa to recruit and train an anti-poaching force of 400 men from the local area.[10]

The NGO mission of "counter-poaching" is a serious one where there is no government, and the ARRC is working in partnership or consultation with several leading environmental NGOs, including the World Wildlife Fund, the Wildlife Conservation Society, the International Union for the Conservation of Nature, and the Bushmeat Crisis Task Force.[11]

NEW CORPORATE PARTNERS

NGO campaigns *against* particular multinational corporations are not new.

In addition to the Nestlé boycott, labor unions launched boycotts of U.S. textile companies Farah and J. P. Stevens in the 1970s. Corporate campaigns initiated by unions have tended to be limited to a single country, while non-union NGO campaigns have tended to be transnational, at least through the 1980s. The campaign against Nike sweatshops in Asia was initiated in 1989 by a coalition of union and non-union NGOs.[12] Jarol Manheim has documented 34 distinct corporate campaigns launched by nonlabor groups from 1989 to 1999, most of which fit the pattern of transnational networks led by NGOs.[13] On the environmental front, eight of these campaigns involved the Rainforest Action Network and six involved Greenpeace.

In the 1990s campaigns against corporations burgeoned, but the corporations themselves also counterattacked. Sometimes acting with guidance from sophisticated international public relations firms, corporations learned to sponsor their own NGOs to articulate a pro-business message with the presumptive authority of civil society. Critics of these groups respond by discrediting them with the "greenwash" label.[14]

With this long record of confrontation between NGOs and corporations, it is surprising to see a strong new trend toward partnership. In the year 2000 UN Secretary General Kofi Annan sponsored the "Global Compact" and invited greater cooperation among corporations, the United Nations, and NGOs. The Global Compact encourages corporations to voluntarily identify and promote best practices based on principles of human rights, worker rights, and environmental protection.[15] It quickly attracted criticism from TRAC (Transnational Resource and Action Center, now named CorpWatch). TRAC argues that the UN allows known abusers of human rights and the environment to join the Global Compact, that the initiative involves no monitoring or enforcement, and that "companies get a chance to 'bluewash' their image by wrapping themselves in the flag of the United Nations."[16] A more positive assessment can be found in the research produced by SustainAbility, which describes itself as "a hybrid organization: part strategic management consultancy, part world-class think-tank and part energetic public interest group."[17] With astonishing audacity, this organization wants to be accepted as both an international corporate public relations firm and also something like an NGO committed to the principles of sustainable development. Its critics might view this as greenwash taken to a whole new level. However, SustainAbility's research achieves a degree of sophistication that will not be easily dismissed, particularly since the organization appears to welcome the kind of monitoring that NGOs like CorpWatch are undertaking.[18]

In the proliferation of corporate–NGO–UN partnerships, one stands out as a startling new departure. In June 2000 the Exxon-Mobil oil company, the World Bank, and several environmental NGOs reached an agreement that opened the way for World Bank financing of an oil pipeline—completed in 2003—from Chad to the coast of Cameroon.[19] According to the agreement, revenue from the pipeline goes into a monitored escrow account and must be spent for designated purposes such as health, education, and national parks. Marina Ottaway criticizes such tripartite negotiations as "global corporatism," and argues that the pipeline agreement "pushes the concept of corporate representation to a new extreme, giving foreign NGOs the right to speak for a population that has not been consulted in any meaningful way."[20]

Many actors claim to speak for the people in this dance of representation, which may or may not contribute to citizens' welfare and generate enduring political participation. The UN, NGOs, corporations, and very often the governments themselves, are unelected and unrepresentative. The quality of the political consequences will not be universal or global, but local. The results depend on how institutions of democratic representation deepen within each country.

Corporations and NGOs can develop links in quite another way—through individual entrepreneurs who devote their personal fortunes to philanthropy. In contrast to Carnegie, Ford, and Rockefeller of an earlier age, donors of the "new philanthropy" take a more direct hand in giving away the money they have accumulated, some while still quite young and continuing to make money.[21] Bill Gates, George Soros, and Ted Turner are the most prominent of the new billionaire philanthropists. These men are motivated by a cultural competition for reputations of great generosity and public-spiritedness, as well as by the desire to leave a personal imprint on the world. From dramatic business success they carry a level of personal confidence that "allows them to believe that what in most cases would take a social movement to achieve, they can achieve single-handedly," says sociologist Paul Schervish.[22] Indeed, a single billionaire philanthropist can leverage social investment to change international norms, create new physical and social technologies, and attract donations from other foundations, governments, and individuals to a pet cause.

Turner concentrates heavily on the linked issues of environmental protection and population control, giving about $50 million a year through the Turner Foundation, and also using the United Nations Foundation which he created in 1998 through his own pledge of $1 billion.[23]

The Bill and Melinda Gates Foundation has given away more than $6 billion since 1994. Since 2000, Gates' grants have accelerated to about $1 billion each year and their focus has turned resolutely international. Gates has given more than $3 billion to Global Health programs, including AIDS treatment, prevention and control of global infectious diseases such as malaria and polio, and reproductive health.[24]

Soros gives away $400 million a year through the Open Society Institute and Soros Foundations Network. Most of his past giving aimed to promote political liberties in the new republics of the former Soviet Union and former Yugoslavia. However, according to his allocations in recent years, the United States is the country with the greatest need for a more "open society."[25] In contrast to Gates, Soros has shifted from an almost exclusive international focus toward reforming American society. Soros devoted $90 million in 2002—almost a quarter of his annual giving—to an array of programs promoting social and civil liberties in America. These included urban education reform, abolishing the death penalty, protecting civil liberties in the War on Terror, providing palliative care for the dying, controlling guns, legalizing drugs, and promoting the availability of emergency contraception.[26]

These three billionaire NGO Titans may be accused of many things—seeking to make the world safe for wealthy Americans, or safe for healthy Americans, or safe for wildlife. They illustrate once again the variability and magnetism of the NGO organizational form for those who want to make a difference.

POST-HUMANIST NGOs

Since the 1787 founding of the Society for the Abolition of the Slave Trade, NGOs have been counted on to defend human dignity. They might have offered a simplistic analysis or an ineffective remedy, but their intentions were humanistic. Today, little more than two centuries later, not a few NGOs aim to transform or abolish humanity. These are the post-humanist NGOs.

In December 2002, at a news conference in Hollywood, Dr Brigitte Boisselier announced the birth of the first cloned human baby. However, she presented no baby, no baby pictures, and no evidence of human cloning. While many dismissed Boisselier's claims as fraudulent, she did succeed in planting the dream of easily available human cloning in the global media and consciousness.

Boisselier is director of Clonaid, a profit-making company located in an unidentified country. Clonaid makes no claim to be non-profit, yet it presents an ambiguous organizational face that resonates in several respects with the conventional image of an NGO. The most direct evidence of this is the name. While Clonaid is not the only for-profit corporation to use the "aid" suffix, the trope is perhaps more associated with NGOs (Christian Aid, ActionAid, NetAid). "Clonaid" echoes NGO discourse, implicitly claiming the presumptive legitimacy that many people give to NGOs. Another reproductive technology company mines the same vein of NGO legitimacy by calling itself "Repromed International."[27] The Reproductive Cloning Network, which sponsors a website to provide free cloning information, explicitly identifies itself as a non-profit organization, as does the affiliated Human Cloning Foundation.[28]

A powerful utopian longing permeates the Clonaid literature. For the individuals and families who may seek its services, Clonaid makes astounding promises. The organization claims to have found living cells in the bone marrow of a child who had been dead and buried for four months, and plans to work with the parents to clone the child. (Will he or she be a copy of the first child, or a new, distinct person?) The implied promise of resurrection or reincarnation is pervasive: "The main goal of CLONAID™ is to offer reproductive human cloning on a worldwide basis to infertile couples, homosexual couples, people infected with the HIV virus *as well as to families who have lost a beloved family member.*"[29]

For those who want to venture deeper into utopia, Clonaid proudly proclaims its links to the Raëlian religious movement, in which Dr

Brigitte Boisselier is a bishop. Raël, the movement's founder and leader, teaches that "today's cloning technology is the first step in the quest for eternal life. Once we can clone exact replicas of ourselves, the next step will be to transfer our memories and personality into our newly cloned brains, which will allow us to truly live forever."[30]

Clonaid could be merely a scam. Yet it is taken surprisingly seriously, with Boisselier meriting an interview with Sir David Frost.[31] In addition, several other NGOs closer to the plausible mainstream tap into the same broad vein of public sentiment. The World Transhumanist Association was founded in 2000 and is led by a group of philosophers, science fiction writers, biologists, and entrepreneurs.[32] In 2002 WTA crafted "The Transhumanist Declaration" which begins:

> (1) Humanity will be radically changed by technology in the future. We foresee the feasibility of redesigning the human condition, including such parameters as the inevitability of aging, limitations of human and artificial intellects, unchosen psychology, suffering, and our confinement to the planet earth.[33]

The declaration conveys a measured tone of technical authority, and everything it foresees has already begun with the advent of antibiotics, computers, psychoactive drugs, and space travel. Yet, at the same time it promises a utopia without limits, in which aging, physical and mental suffering, and stupidity are merely "parameters" to be pushed back indefinitely by technology. The ancient longing to overcome suffering and death and human limitation used to be the stuff of religion. These promises are made explicit by WTA's affiliated organizations such as the Immortality Institute, whose mission is "conquering the blight of involuntary death,"[34] and BLTC Research, founded in 1995 for "paradise engineering" to "abolish the biological substrates of suffering. Not just in humans, but in all sentient life."[35]

Even mainstream commentators envision utopian outcomes for all society from the reproductive revolution. Richard Cohen has argued in *The Washington Post* against regulation of cloning technologies. He directly asserts post-humanist, utopian philosophical premises for the coming reproductive revolution: "This is the bravest of new worlds. And it will require some brave, new thinking. Terms like 'ethical' or 'human dignity' simply cloud the debate."[36] The unbounded plasticity of the human body to genetic engineering is the crux of this revolution, as it was for the dystopia portrayed in Huxley's *Brave New World*, to which Cohen alludes without irony.

But Cohen is correct in one respect: if reengineering the human body is accepted as progressive, then ideas such as human dignity, and perhaps even humanity, are indeed outdated and regressive. The ambiguous, pseudo-NGO Clonaid; incorporated nonprofits like the Reproductive Cloning Network, the World Transhumanist Association, and the Immortality Institute; and for-profit corporations like Repromed International and BLTC Research—all promote a post-human future.

The tendency toward post-humanist notions of universal welfare and justice is not limited to the lunatic fringe of NGOs. Sectors of the environmental movement are deeply imbued with post-humanist ideas, even if only a few environmental NGOs attempt to translate the most radical ideas into equally radical tactics.

The leading radical environmental NGO of the 1980s, EarthFirst!, was conceived on a camping trip in the remote Pinacate desert of Mexico. Dave Foreman and four other men, disgruntled with the mainstream environmental movement, retreated into nature to plot the future of environmentalism. The group consciously enacted a story-line drawn from the writings of Edward Abbey. They chose the stage setting of the Pinacate desert based on one of Abbey's essays, and while in the desert they committed themselves to carrying out the vision of radical environmentalism portrayed in Abbey's novel, *The Monkey Wrench Gang*.[37] Following Abbey, the signature tactic of EarthFirst! became monkeywrenching—spiking trees to damage the heavy equipment used to cut them down.

These founders of EarthFirst! acted less from an elaborate philosophy and more from passion for the wilderness and frustration with the political compromises of mainstream environmentalism. Nevertheless, as EarthFirst! gained support through the 1980s, its radical agenda of direct action converged with radical environmental philosophies. In 1985, the same year that Dave Foreman published his how-to book, *Ecodefense: A Field Guide to Monkeywrenching*, Bill Devall and George Sessions also published *Deep Ecology*.[38] Devall and Sessions featured the thought of Arne Naess, a Norwegian mountaineer, activist, and philosopher who coined the term "deep ecology" in 1973.

Two of Naess's philosophical ideas found wide resonance in the ranks of radical environmentalists. The first idea, *biocentrism* or biocentric equality, is based on an intuition "that all things in the biosphere have an equal right to live and blossom and to reach their own individual forms of unfolding and self-realization within the larger self-realization."[39] The second of Naess's lead ideas is an expansive, even mystical, concept of *self-realization* in which the "self" embraces not only the narrow individual ego, and not only other humans, but all life in the biosphere.

Dave Foreman decided in 1987 that EarthFirst! needed a stronger philosophical foundation, and publicly affirmed the ideas of deep ecology in speeches and articles.[40] Consciously emulating Martin Luther King, Foreman and other radical environmentalists in the 1980s saw themselves as extending the civil rights movement to non-human species. If monkeywrenching and other "direct action" tactics necessarily involved damage to property, at the same time EarthFirst! embraced an ethic of nonviolence toward humans.

Ironically, some of the ideas of deep ecology might have been used to justify tactics of much greater violence, and might be so used in the future. If all species have equal rights, and if human activity is causing the extinction of around 20,000 species each year,[41] then humans are clearly the aggressors. Within this interpretation of biocentrism, the use of violence against the single aggressor species on behalf of the many victim species would be justified as self-defense. What sort of violence might achieve a drastic reduction in the human population without damaging other species? This question had already entered the minds of EarthFirst! leaders during the 1980s, as did the dream of a drastic, involuntary reduction of human population. Foreman himself, commenting to an Australian magazine in 1986 on the ongoing Ethiopian famine, argued that:

> the worst thing we could do in Ethiopia is to give aid—the best thing would be to just let nature seek its own balance, to let the people there just starve … The alternative is that you go in and save these half-dead children who never will live a whole life. Their development will be stunted. And what's going to happen in ten years' time is that twice as many people will suffer and die.[42]

This was not an entirely isolated sentiment within the movement. Writing in the *EarthFirst! Journal*, an author using the pseudonym Miss Ann Thropy pointed to the benefits of the AIDS epidemic. The writer opined, "If radical environmentalists were to invent a disease to bring human population back to ecological sanity, it would probably be something like AIDS," adding that as "radical environmentalists, we can see AIDS not as a problem, but a necessary solution."[43] AIDS is perfect, of course, because it targets only humans without hurting other species. The misanthropy implicit in the radical environmental movement is made explicit in this piece of heavy-handed humor.

In the event, the deep ecology movement of the 1980s did not produce violence directed against humans, in spite of some strands of its ideology of deep ecology. Perhaps the gentle mysticism of Naess's idea of self-realization somehow restrained the green rage against humanity implicit in his idea of biocentrism. However, violence against humans has emerged from another cluster of environmental NGOs with the deceptively cute acronyms of ELF and ALF, some of whose members adhere to another environmental philosophy concerned with animal rights.

The Animal Liberation Front (ALF) originated in England in 1976, part of the historically more militant British animal rights movement that also produced the Band of Mercy, the Hunt Retribution Squad, the Animal Rights Militia, and the Justice Department.[44] The radical environmentalist scenes in the U.K. and U.S. converged somewhat in the 1990s. A younger generation of American activists became impatient with EarthFirst! and split off to form the more radical Earth Liberation Front (ELF), which they consciously modeled on ALF. ALF itself also developed a significant North American following in the 1990s. In contrast to deep ecology, the animal rights movement sympathizes not only with species as a whole, but also with the rights and sufferings of individual animals.

Both ELF and ALF have taken the tactics of sabotage and arson far beyond anything attempted by EarthFirst! at its most militant. The scale and frequency of these attacks have mushroomed since 1999. The largest single act of environmental sabotage to date took place on August 1, 2003—a $50 million arson fire that destroyed an unfinished condominium complex in a San Diego development adjacent to Rose Canyon, which is rich in wildlife. The ELF later accepted responsibility for setting the fire. Between ELF's attacks on housing developments, ski lifts, and gas-guzzling sport utility vehicles, and ALF's attacks on furriers, meat companies, and universities and corporations that use animal testing, the FBI estimates that the two groups have carried out 600 criminal acts in the U.S. since 1996.[45]

Although the FBI has identified ecoterrorism as a top priority for homeland security, ELF and ALF are elusive targets. They are less organizations than extremely decentralized movements. They function with no hierarchy, no membership list, and no meetings.

Sympathizers are encouraged not to identify themselves to one another or to neighbors. At first glance there is nothing overt about either entity except a website and a press office to receive reports of attacks from news sources or anonymous communications and to give interviews to the media.[46] Until recently, ELF and ALF had publicly identified spokespersons, but in late 2003 both press offices were accepting only encoded or indirect electronic communications.[47]

ELF and ALF straddle a wide contradiction between their increasingly radical and destructive tactics on the one hand, and the mainstream animal rights and welfare movement on the other. The ALF is more explicitly bellicose in its rhetoric, especially in Britain. In the words of Robin Webb, identified as the ALF Press Officer,

> Animal liberation is not a campaign, not just a hobby to put aside when it becomes tiresome or a new interest catches your eye. It's a war. A long, hard, bloody war in which all the countless millions of its victims have been on one side only, have been defenseless and innocent, whose one tragedy was to be born nonhuman.[48]

In apparent contradiction, the websites of both ELF and ALF affirm the principle, "To take all necessary precautions against harming any animal, human or non-human."[49]

While neither group has yet killed a person in the United States, there are indications of a militant trend in their actions and rhetoric away from the model of nonviolent protest exemplified by Martin Luther King, whose example could still inspire Foreman in the 1980s. According to Bron Taylor of the University of Florida,

> I think many people in the ELF would probably say … that the idea of classic civil disobedience to arouse the conscience of the wider community just isn't a high priority because it can't be aroused. It's too mired in the corporate juggernaut.[50]

More ominously, after the destruction of a U.S. Forest Service laboratory in August 2002 an e-mail message from ELF's press office in Portland, Oregon explicitly renounced the principle that had forbade harming any animal, human or nonhuman:

> In pursuance of justice, freedom, and equal consideration for all innocent life across the board, segments of this global revolutionary movement are no longer limiting their revolutionary potential by adhering to a flawed,

inconsistent, non-violent ideology. While innocent life will never be harmed in any action we undertake, where it is necessary, we will no longer hesitate to pick up the gun to implement justice, and provide the needed protection for our planet that decades of legal battles, pleading protest, and economic sabotage have failed so drastically to achieve.[51]

The distinction between property and life is giving way to a distinction between guilty life and innocent life.

Ironically, the extremists of ELF and ALF are not so far out of the mainstream. People for the Ethical Treatment of Animals (PETA) is considered a mainstream environmental NGO and claims more than 700,000 members. PETA uses humor, endorsements from actors and supermodels ("Pamela Anderson Speaks out for Chickens," "Alicia Silverstone Talks Turkey"), and massive educational and media blitzes to promote its message of animal rights.[52]

Despite the veneer of moderation, PETA is both openly and covertly sympathetic to the goals and actions of the Animal Liberation Front. One of the "Frequently Asked Questions" on the PETA website queries, "How can you justify the millions of dollars' worth of property damage by the Animal Liberation Front (ALF)?" PETA responds that "The animal rights movement is nonviolent," yet at the same time, "any large movement is going to have factions that believe in the use of force." PETA compares ALF to the Underground Railroad for freeing American slaves and the French Resistance against the Nazis, thereby implicitly justifying either nonviolent or violent resistance to evil. PETA cites the exposure and condemnation of animal cruelty that has followed ALF attacks.[53] In short, without explicitly saying so, PETA accepts a division of labor modeled on many Third World liberation movements, casting ALF as the military wing taking up the armed struggle in the same movement for which PETA is the nonviolent political wing.

Less openly, PETA helps fund an animal rights conference in the Washington, DC area every year during the week of July 4. ALF and ELF activists are invited to speak or staff tables to promote their activities. At the 2001 conference Bruce Friedrich of PETA told a panel:

If we really believe that animals have the same right to be free from pain and suffering at our hands, then of course we're going to be blowing things up and smashing windows. ... I think it's a great way to bring about animal liberation, considering the level of suffering, the atrocities. I think it would be great if all of the fast-food outlets, slaughterhouses, these laboratories, and banks that fund them, exploded tomorrow.[54]

This incriminating quote and the information on PETA funding of the conference are reported by another liberal American NGO that has lined up four square against the new ecoterrorists. The Southern Poverty Law Center, with roots in the civil rights movement, has monitored and condemned neo-Nazis, the Ku Klux Klan, and white supremacist groups in the United States for more than three decades. The Southern Poverty Law Center condemns ELF, ALF, and PETA in the same category as these fascist organizations.

The animal rights movement has received a tremendous and ongoing boost from the philosophy articulated by Peter Singer in his 1975 book, *Animal Liberation*. On the basis of the principle of equality, Singer argues that all sentient animals have interests based on their ability to suffer pain, interests whose ethical weight must be factored into decisions about using animals to benefit humans. Singer erases the sharp line of distinction between humans and other animals. While it may be ethical to kill animals to ensure the survival of humans, in this view, not every use of animals is justifiable. As PETA literature puts it, "animals are not ours to use for food, clothing, entertainment, or experimentation." From the same principles, Singer can imagine that euthanasia or infanticide may constitute ethical means to minimize human suffering.

Singer's approach seems benign and resonates ever more strongly in contemporary culture.[55] If not Singer's ideas, then what other ethical principles might be used to limit the brutal treatment of animals? However, this approach represents the sharp edge of Arne Naess's principle of biocentrism without the moderate mysticism of his principle of self-realization through unity with all life. The claim that "speciesism" is as bad as racism is a battle-cry; it can be used to justify violence on a growing scale. The most radical activists of ELF and ALF are only beginning to explore the frontiers of violence that these universal principles might be used to justify.

The radical environmental organizations and the clownish Clonaid are both examples of a post-humanist trend among NGOs—the contemporary custodians of civilization's universal moral principles. In one respect they seem to be polar opposites: Clonaid looks to science as the savior of humanity from the scourge of death; ALF wants to blow up the scientific laboratories that experiment on animals. However, at a more profound level, they have the same point of departure. The human person is no longer at the center of their moral universe. Clonaid wants to improve the human person out of existence, while ALF wants to roll back the human race to make room for the animals. Both share a deep hostility to human nature as given.

In certain academic and activist circles it is considered shameful to find oneself accused of anthropocentrism, or speciesism, or of taking too seriously human needs and concerns while neglecting the wider web of life. There is no broadly intelligible response in the face of such accusations. Contemporary culture and philosophy are mute and passive in the face of the eclipse of the human person. Consider how archaic, intellectually narrow, and politically regressive Martin Luther King's justification of civil disobedience reads today, only 40 years after his famous "Letter From Birmingham Jail":

> How does one determine whether a law is just or unjust? A just law is a man-made code that squares with the moral law or the law of God. An unjust law is a code that is out of harmony with the moral law. To put it in the terms of St. Thomas Aquinas: An unjust law is a human law that is not rooted in eternal law and natural law. Any law that uplifts human personality is just. Any law that degrades human personality is unjust.[56]

Eternal law? Natural law? Human personality? Ideas that so recently energized the civil rights movement today evoke little more than a shudder or a blush.

NGOs and the movements they express and promote have come a long way. It is a profound irony that animal rights thinking is rooted philosophically in the late eighteenth century—the same period that produced the Anti-Slavery Society. Peter Singer quotes, for inspiration and authority, a famous passage from Jeremy Bentham. Reflecting on the early successes of slave liberation evident in 1789, Bentham wrote, "The day *may* come when the rest of the animal creation may acquire those rights." And Bentham also articulated the utilitarian ethical calculus that is the basis for the contemporary eclipse of the human person: "The question is not, Can they *reason*? nor Can they *talk*? but Can they *suffer*?"[57]

Note that suffering, whether human or animal, is intolerable in this view. Suffering must be eliminated. It is not a great leap to the logical implication that if any sentient being cannot be cured of its suffering or defect, it must be emancipated from it by death. In an odd twist, mercy, understood as the intolerance of suffering, becomes an imperative for death.

I believe there may be grounds for resisting such a post-humanist, and post-human, future. However, whether one supports or opposes it, the diverse and prominent roles played by NGOs in enacting this agenda illustrate vividly the structural power of NGOs to occupy the commanding heights of world culture and from there to shape actors—not only states but also persons. This structural power of NGOs to shape persons is why the religious historical roots of NGOs, and the participation of NGOs in the troubling resurgence of religion, are so important.

RESURGENCE OF RELIGION

A global resurgence of religion in both culture and politics erupted at the end of the twentieth century.[58] NGOs have participated in several dimensions of this phenomenon, some perhaps welcome and others disturbing.

Before this global revival became evident, the second half of the twentieth century had appeared to many as the culmination of a long history of modernization and secularization. The central global conflict between communism and capitalism had pitted two secular ideologies against each other, and the emerging Third World embraced variations of secular nationalism. Some viewed the end of the Cold War in around 1990 as the final triumph of secular democracy over all other models of legitimate government.[59]

International NGOs contributed to the secular trend. Most nineteenth-century global reform movements had emerged out of particular religious communities, especially liberal Protestant, and had evinced a peculiarly religious faith in collective moral progress (see chapter 3). After 1945, however, international NGOs overwhelmingly expressed their mandates in terms of universal secular principles. NGOs rooted in faith communities muted their religious identities, particularly in former colonial countries where many NGOs embraced the development agenda.[60]

From the vantage point of the early twenty-first century, it seems quite possible that the secularization of public purposes during the second half of the twentieth century did not represent the end of history, but instead a passing moment in a much longer story. In earlier centuries, transnational civil society had been permeated by religious actors spreading religious models of the relationships among person, society, and state. If the definition of "transnational civil society" is broadened beyond conventional NGOs to include other movements, organizations, and communities, then religious actors assume a much more central place, even today. Susanne Hoeber Rudolph argued in 1997:

> Religious communities are among the oldest of the transnationals: Sufi orders, Catholic missionaries, and Buddhist monks carried word and praxis across vast spaces before those places became nation-states or even states. Such religious peripatetics *were* versions of civil society. In today's post-modern era, religious communities have become vigorous creators of an emergent transnational civil society.[61]

Such transnational religious expressions take many forms: preachers and missionaries, political modernizers, charities and humanitarian agencies, prayer groups and charismatic movements, official religious leaders, and even NGOs. They may be autonomous from the state, subordinate to the state, or spread by one state in the societies of others.[62] There are myriad variations and hybrids. Paul Gifford comments on the broad "NGO-ization" of Christian communities in Africa, as African clergy depend on international relief NGOs for communication, transportation, and general support.[63] In many Middle East countries, liberal elements of civil society who favor greater freedom of speech and association find themselves allied with authoritarian governments as their only protection against radical Islamist sectors of civil society who would severely curtail such freedoms if they gained political power.[64]

Christian evangelicals have exercised a growing influence in U.S. foreign policy on human rights since the late 1990s, putting on the table new issues such as international religious freedom, genocide in Sudan, AIDS treatment and prevention, and international sex trafficking. But this was not a grassroots upwelling from evangelical believers. Instead, several non-evangelical NGO entrepreneurs brought the evangelicals into U.S. human rights policy.

International religious freedom became the catalyst issue. Nina Shea had directed the conservative, Catholic, Puebla Institute during the 1980s, criticizing the Sandinista government of Nicaragua for violations of religious freedom and other human rights.[65] Michael J. Horowitz had been a labor lawyer and law professor, and worked in the Reagan administration in the early 1980s. By 1995 the Puebla Institute had been absorbed by Freedom House, where Shea directed the Center for Religious Freedom, and Horowitz was ensconced at the Hudson Institute.[66] Together they organized a conference on January 23, 1996 under the theme, "Global Persecution of Christians," which attracted predominantly evangelical religious leaders.

This was how a Catholic and a Jew mobilized American evangelical Protestants in favor of international religious freedom, and in the process reshaped the global human rights movement. But individual visions require institutional support and must generate institutional realignment to succeed. Freedom House, founded in 1941, had defined itself in opposition to totalitarianism through World War II and the Cold War. As the conservative pillar of American human rights NGOs, Freedom House threw its reputation and resources behind Nina Shea's initiative on religious freedom in 1995, despite deep misgivings among more liberal human rights NGOs. As the U.S. Congress considered major legislation in 1997, leaders of other American human rights NGOs weighed in as supporters of religious freedom while also shaping the bill toward a more universalistic stance. In this way Nina Shea at Freedom House managed to draw into dialogue and consensus on religious freedom Kenneth Roth of Human Rights Watch, William Schulz of Amnesty International USA, Felice Gaer of the Blaustein Institute for the Advancement of Human Rights, and Leonard Rubenstein of Physicians for Human Rights, among many others.[67]

The U.S. Congress passed the International Religious Freedom Act in 1998. The law created two new institutions: an Office of International Religious Freedom at the U.S. Department of State to issue an annual report on religious freedom and persecution in all foreign countries, and also the U.S. Commission on International Religious Freedom with members appointed by the president and congressional leaders from both parties.[68] These institutions are broadly analogous to the State Department Office on Human Rights and Humanitarian Affairs created in 1976 and the National Endowment for Democracy created in 1983 (see chapter 4). By amplifying selected international norms, by creating an institutional locus for potential influence on U.S. foreign policy, and by generating a network of new and old transnational NGOs, such institutions can transform the debate on human rights.

The pattern set by the NGO network on international religious freedom in 1998 was followed with variations by NGO networks that mobilized around the Trafficking Victims Protection Act of 2000, the Sudan Peace Act of 2002, and the Emergency Plan for AIDS

Relief of 2003. In each case, conservative Christian NGOs mobilized American public attention toward a long neglected human rights issue, and established NGOs welcomed the injection of political will while shaping and joining the resulting consensus.[69] Of course, on international "family" issues, conservative and liberal NGOs have found considerably less common ground.[70]

NGOs AFTER SEPTEMBER 11

An organization that resides in transnational, if not civil, society initiated a new world-historical juncture on September 11, 2001. Nothing evokes the most appalling dimensions of the global resurgence of religion than suicide pilots who believe their faith calls them to fly airplanes into large buildings.

Al Qaeda's attacks on New York and Washington, and the ensuing American wars in Afghanistan, Iraq and the global War on Terror, have switched global politics and society onto new rails, leading to destinations unknown. How will 9/11 transform transnational civil society? There is much more going on here than meets the eye. Simplistic responses will not serve.[71] I would suggest three points of entry into the question, explored here in a preliminary way.

At a first take, two competing power centers—the U.S. government and Al Qaeda—are working to instrumentalize global civil society to serve their rival goals and visions.

The global impact of September 11 stems not only from the massive scale of casualties, but also from the capacity of the attackers to change the skyline of New York City. No entity—state, revolutionary group, corporation, or NGO—has ever used global media so effectively to implant an image in the minds of people throughout the world. Much of the world tends to exaggerate the power and invincibility of America, and this is particularly true for people living under authoritarian governments in the global periphery. This preconception only amplifies the message of the falling towers—that America is vulnerable and that the power of the global Muslim *umma* unified under Osama bin Laden's vision is unlimited.

Al Qaeda is not the first violent liberation group to utilize transnational charities as conduits for cash and people across borders. The Provisional Irish Republican Army raised money among Irish Americans in the United States for more than 30 years through Irish Northern Aid (NORAID) and did so with the effective acquiescence of the U.S. government.[72] At the peak of Al Qaeda's transnational network it had infiltrated or created several Islamic charities, particularly in Saudi Arabia, the Balkans, Southeast Asia, and even North America.[73] By forging links to charitable NGOs, radical Islamists gain sources of funding and an audience for propaganda and potential recruitment. The tactic has long been practiced by Hezbollah in southern Lebanon and Hamas among the Palestinians. Ironically, during the 1980s the United States encouraged Saudi Arabia to finance the mujahedin resistance against Soviet forces in Afghanistan, using both governmental and charitable channels.[74] Some of these same channels funded the rise of the Taliban and Al Qaeda in the 1990s.

Al Qaeda has weathered an onslaught of military, legal, and financial pressure since September 2001. To the extent that it has been operationally decapitated, it has reverted to a loose network of like-minded but largely autonomous organizations—similar to the organizational form of NGO networks.[75]

When world politics takes a new direction, many NGOs reshape themselves, whether in response to financial or legal incentives, or in spontaneous response to the changing normative environment. After the United States overthrew the governments of Afghanistan in 2002 and Iraq in 2003, international NGOs contributed to the tasks of reconstruction, humanitarian assistance, and democratization in both countries. Then, in the simmering insurgencies that followed the initial American victories, NGOs became targets in both countries as well.[76] Next, human rights NGOs condemned these attacks on NGOs as human rights violations and war crimes.[77] During 2004, insurgents in Iraq effectively drove out of the country almost all expatriate staff of international NGOs and UN humanitarian agencies, leaving the U.S. military largely stripped of the legitimacy associated with international civil society.

The new environment created by the U.S. "War on Terror" has generated another wave of NGO shape-shifting that is less directly involved in the military front-line states of Iraq and Afghanistan. The Coalition for International Justice, established in 1995, promotes international criminal prosecution of war crimes committed in former Yugoslavia, Rwanda, East Timor, Cambodia, and Sierra Leone.[78] While the Coalition is a relatively young NGO that leans toward the liberal-left of the American political spectrum, Freedom House is a venerable 60-year-old NGO with a center-right profile. Neither NGO officially endorses specific American military interventions, but prominent Board members of both organizations have done so.[79] The

1990s brought out the interventionism in American human rights NGOs. In the case of the Coalition, Advisory Board member Aryeh Neier promoted U.S. military intervention in Somalia and Bosnia during the early 1990s through his leadership of Human Rights Watch (see chapter 5). The Balkan Action Committee—formed in 1999 to promote NATO's humanitarian war in the Kosovo region of Yugoslavia—drew a relatively broad cross-section of endorsements, including Morton Abramovitz and Bianca Jagger from the Coalition board and Zbigniew Brzezinski and Jeane Kirkpatrick from the Freedom House board.[80] The Committee for the Liberation of Iraq, formed in 2002, had a more hard-right profile, sharing only Jeane Kirkpatrick and Richard Perle with the Freedom House board, and no one from the Coalition board.[81] Immediately before the war in Iraq in early 2003, Freedom House made two moves to align itself, indirectly yet clearly, with Bush administration foreign policy. From the Committee for the Liberation of Iraq, Freedom House drew Ruth Wedgewood as a new member of its Board of Trustees, and R. James Woolsey as its new Chairman.[82]

These examples show how American human rights NGOs, from center-left to center-right, have realigned themselves to some degree with Bush administration foreign policy. However, such realignment is not limited to the American NGO establishment. Spanish Judge Baltasar Garzon became internationally known for the 1998 indictment of former dictator Augusto Pinochet of Chile. Pinochet was grounded in London for almost two years while Britain considered Garzon's request to extradite him to Spain (see Introduction). Garzon cited the legal doctrine of "universal jurisdiction" to bring charges against anyone for crimes against humanity. In September 2003 Judge Garzon turned this doctrine against Al Qaeda, issuing an international arrest warrant for Osama bin Laden and 34 other terrorism suspects and claiming that Al Qaeda operatives in Spain played a crucial role in planning the attacks of September 11, 2001.[83] This was the first legal indictment of Osama bin Laden for the September 11 attacks.

Universal jurisdiction has generated other indictments in the War on Terror. The American-led Coalition Provisional Authority in Iraq offered a U.S. $25 million reward and circulated a wanted poster for Saddam Hussein, while leaving the details of an indictment for after he was captured.[84] A 1993 law gave Belgian courts the power to try war crimes cases regardless of the nationalities of the perpetrators and victims or the locations of the crimes. One lawsuit accused President

Bush of war crimes in the 2003 invasion of Iraq. A higher court later threw out the case, and the Belgian parliament restricted the law.[85] But for a while Saddam Hussein was wanted in Baghdad and George W. Bush was wanted in Brussels. (As of this writing, Saddam is in custody, but Bush is still at large.)

The most singular and visible NGO in the world may be the Norwegian Nobel Committee. When the Committee awarded the 2002 Nobel Peace Prize to former U.S. President James Earl Carter, many observers saw this as an oblique jab at the more bellicose policies of President George W. Bush as he prepared to invade Iraq. Nevertheless, it came as a surprise when Nobel Committee Chairman Gunnar Berge broke tradition by making the censure public and explicit. "The prize," Berge said, "must be interpreted as a criticism of the present U.S. administration."[86] Berge's breach of custom created a rift in the Norwegian Nobel Committee, which was publicly aired as well.

In 2003 the Committee awarded the Nobel Peace Prize—without political commentary—to Shirin Ebadi of Iran. Ebadi, a woman, a Muslim, and a human rights lawyer, lost no time in calling for the release of political reformers and journalists from prison in Iran.[87]

Subtly, in this case, the Norwegian Nobel Committee has applied a tested tactic to a new arena of conflict. Ebadi's award marked the ninth time since 1975 that the Nobel Peace Prize had gone to a pro-democracy activist working in the non-violent opposition to an authoritarian government.[88] Of those nine cases, six countries have since made a transition to democracy. The successful transitions, and their Nobel laureates, are the Soviet Union (Andrei Sakharov, 1975); Argentina (Adolfo Perez Esquivel, 1980); Poland (Lech Walesa, 1983); South Africa (Desmond Tutu, 1984); Guatemala (Rigoberta Menchu, 1992); and East Timor (Carlos Belo and Jose Ramos-Horta, 1996). Along with Ebadi's Iran, two other cases still await a transition: Tibet (the Dalai Lama, 1989); and Burma (Aung San Suu Kyi, 1991).

The causal links between the Nobel Peace Prize and the democratic transition are not simple or automatic. Nevertheless, it is reasonable to infer that the Norwegian Nobel Committee has been prescient and wise in many of its past selections, discerning inchoate movements toward human rights or democracy and adding the diffuse though significant force of its international normative authority to existing forces.

What is remarkable in the 2003 award is that Iran is a member of Bush's "Axis of Evil," the small club of states, including also Iraq and

North Korea, that are pursuing nuclear weapons while maintaining ties to transnational terrorists. Were Ebadi's democracy movement to succeed in Iran, the courts, police, and the entire foreign policy bureaucracy of the Iranian government would come under the control of democratically elected leaders. Such leaders might reasonably be expected to give up the expensive and risky pursuit of nuclear weapons in compliance with Iran's own obligations in the Nuclear Non-Proliferation Treaty. This scenario would allow Iran to peacefully exit the Axis of Evil.

Having directly deplored American military methods in 2002, the Norwegian Nobel Committee indirectly supported American political goals in 2003. This move is all the more likely to succeed for having been made obliquely and ambiguously.

This dualistic picture of Bush and bin Laden each bending rival sectors of transnational society to his own will is incomplete and, by itself, simplistic. At a second take, neither "Islam" nor "the West" is a monolithic social entity; instead, a multitude of competing and countervailing trends complicate the picture.

Muslims worldwide express their faith in a wide variety of ways. According to Seyyed Hossein Nasr, radical Islamists employ a discourse of tradition, but their real aim is a political project that renounces the social reality of "traditional Islam" as it exists in Muslim neighborhoods and nations.[89] Other Muslim scholars propose that Islam can be compatible with a liberal political order and a post-imperial international system.[90] The Muslim tradition of nonviolence is often overlooked, but is documented in the extensive bibliography, "Islam, Peace and Nonviolence" compiled by Karim Douglas Crow under the auspices of the peace NGO, Nonviolence International.[91] As a direct response to the events of September 11, a group of young American Muslims founded Muslims Against Terrorism, recast in 2003 as Muslim Voices for Peace.[92]

Civil society in "the West" is also full of cross-cutting forces. Major NGOs report and critique human rights violations by the U.S. government in the War on Terror and in Iraq, while also documenting three decades of abuses by Saddam Hussein.[93] At least two new NGOs monitor the American-led occupation and reconstruction of Iraq, Iraq Occupation Watch and Iraq Revenue Watch, the latter funded by billionaire George Soros through his Open Society Institute.[94]

The diffuse anti-globalization movement that arose in the late 1990s was briefly stunned by the events of September 11, but regained its equilibrium and reconstituted itself on a much grander scale, at least outside the United States, as the global opposition to President Bush's War on Terror. During the buildup to the U.S. war to overthrow the government of Iraq in early 2003, protestors mobilized a transnational movement of unprecedented scale. As reported by Indymedia—a non-commercial, volunteer, Internet media network—an estimated 12–20 million people demonstrated against the war in more than 800 cities on a single day—February 15, 2003. The day of protest was called by another diffuse network entity, the European Social Forum.[95] The Stop the War Coalition in Britain has kept its sense of humor while protesting war—it toppled a statue of Bush during his visit to London in November 2003, a satiric reference to the toppling of Saddam Hussein's statue in Baghdad earlier in the year. The Coalition has issued a deck of playing cards, "Regime Change Begins at Home," depicting "unwanted politicians," including George Bush and Tony Blair.[96] The Coalition has cooperated with the Muslim Association of Britain to mobilize demonstrations against American-led military action in Afghanistan and Iraq.[97] This illustrates a growing alliance between the anti-globalization movement and moderate Muslim organizations.

At a third take, the deepest stakes in this conflict may be lost in the pursuit of mere victory. Al Qaeda is a totalitarian movement that will Talibanize—that is, extinguish—civil society wherever it gains political power. On the other side is "the West" which seems increasingly polarized and in some danger of losing its collective "global moral compass" for the future of civil society. The growing links between NGOs and corporations are not entirely encouraging for the prospects of preserving a sphere of civil society that is autonomous from both the market and the state. Some post-humanist NGOs are defining what is progressive for humanity in ways that would abolish the human person.

Whoever wins the conflict that President Bush calls the "War on Terror," the loser could be global civil society. Therefore, in this new century the greatest challenge for NGOs—the self-appointed vanguard of global civil society—may be to deepen their commitment to humanism, to find new ways to advocate the freedom of the human person and the solidarity of the human community.

Appendix
Active NGOs Discussed in This Book

USE WITH CARE AND JUDGMENT—list includes QUANGOs, GONGOs, BONGOs, twins, frauds, foundations, dreamers, and a few terrorists, along with many generous and politically savvy professionals.

ActionAid
London
www.actionaid.org

Africa Rainforest and River
Conservation
Jackson, Wyoming
www.Africa-rainforest.org

African Rights
London
www.africanrights.org

Aide Médicale Internationale
Paris
www.amifrance.org

Air Serv International
Warrenton, Virginia
www.airserv.org

Amazon Watch
San Francisco, California
www.amazonwatch.org

American Friends Service
Committee
Philadelphia, Pennsylvania
www.afsc.org

Amnesty International
London
www.amnesty.org

Andrew W. Mellon Foundation
New York
www.mellon.org

Animal Liberation Front
London
www.animalliberationfront.com

Antislavery International
London
www.antislavery.org

Bill and Melinda Gates Foundation
Seattle, Washington
www.gatesfoundation.org

BLTC Research
Brighton, UK
www.bltc.com

British Irish Rights Watch
London
www.birw.org

Burma Watch
Edmonton, Alberta
www.burmawatch.org

Bushmeat Crisis Task Force
Washington, DC
www.bushmeat.org

CARE USA
Atlanta, Georgia
www.careusa.org

Carrying Capacity Network
Washington, DC
www.carryingcapacity.org

Carter Center
Atlanta, Georgia
www.cartercenter.org

Caspian Revenue Watch
New York
www.eurasianet.org/policy_forum/
crw.shtml

Catholic Family and Human Rights
Institute
New York
www.c-fam.org

Catholics For a Free Choice
Washington, DC
www.cath4choice.org

Center for Civil and Human Rights
University of Notre Dame Law
School
Notre Dame, Indiana
www.nd.edu/~cchr

Center for Human Rights and
Humanitarian Law
Washington College of Law at
American University
Washington, DC
www.wcl.american.edu/humright/
center

Center for International Maize and
Wheat Improvement
Mexico City
www.cimmyt.org

Center for International Media
Action
Brooklyn, New York
www.mediaactioncenter.org

Center for Public Integrity
Washington, DC
www.publicintegrity.org

Center for Women's Global
Leadership
Rutgers University

New Brunswick, New Jersey
www.cwgl.rutgers.edu

Center for Legal and Social Studies
or CELS (Centro de Estudios Legales
y Sociales)
Buenos Aires, Argentina
www.cels.org.ar

Children International
Kansas City, Missouri
www.children.org

Christian Aid
London
www.christian-aid.org.uk

Civic Initiatives
Belgrade, Serbia and Montenegro
www.gradjanske.org

Clonaid
undisclosed location
www.clonaid.com

Coalition for an International
Criminal Court
New York and The Hague
www.iccnow.org

Coalition for International Justice
Washington, DC
www.cij.org

CorpWatch
Oakland, California
www.corpwatch.org

Council for Hemispheric Affairs
Washington, DC
www.coha.org

Cousteau Society
Hampton, Virginia
www.cousteau.org

Crimes of War Project
Washington, DC
www.crimesofwar.org

Development Alternatives with
Women for a New Era (DAWN)
Suva, Fiji
www.dawn.org.fj

EarthFirst!
Tucson, Arizona
www.earthfirst.org

Earth Liberation Front
undisclosed location
www.earthliberationfront.com

Egyptian Organization for Human
Rights
Cairo, Egypt
www.eohr.org

European Social Forum
London
www.esf2004.net

Ford Foundation
New York
www.fordfound.org

Freedom House
Washington, DC
www.freedomhouse.org

Global Forest Watch
Washington, DC
www.globalforestwatch.org

Global Trade Watch
Washington, DC
www.citizen.org/trade

Grandmothers of the Disappeared
(Las Abuelas de Plaza de Mayo)
Buenos Aires, Argentina
www.abuelas.org.ar

Grassroots International
Boston, Massachusetts
www.grassrootsonline.org

Greenpeace International
Amsterdam, The Netherlands
www.greenpeace.org

GroupWatch
Silver City, New Mexico
www.namebase.org/sources/
TN.html

Handicap International
Lyons, France
www.handicap-international.org

HealthNet International
Amsterdam, The Netherlands
www.healthnetinternational.org

Hudson Institute
Washington, DC
www.hudson.org

Human Cloning Foundation
Atlanta, Georgia
www.humancloning.org

Human Rights Center
SUNY-Buffalo School of Law
Buffalo, New York
wings.buffalo.edu/law/bhrlc/

Human Rights Watch
New York
www.hrw.org

Ibn Khaldun Center for
Development Studies
Cairo, Egypt

Immortality Institute
Birmingham, Alabama
www.imminst.org

Indict
London
www.indict.org.uk/index.php

Indonesian Corruption Watch
Jakarta, Indonesia
www.antikorupsi.org

INFACT
Boston, Massachusetts
www.infact.org/aboutinf.html

Infant Feeding Action Coalition
(INFACT Canada)
Toronto, Ontario
www.infactcanada.ca/
InfactHomePage.htm

International Baby Food Action
Network
Toronto, Ontario
www.ibfan.org

International Campaign to Ban
Landmines
Washington, DC
www.icbl.org

International Commission of Jurists
Geneva, Switzerland
www.icj.org

International Committee of the Red
Cross
Geneva, Switzerland
www.icrc.org

International Crisis Group
Brussels, Belgium
www.crisisweb.org

International Fellowship of
Reconciliation
Alkmaar, The Netherlands
www.ifor.org

International Human Rights Law
Institute
DePaul University College of Law
Chicago, Illinois
www.law.depaul.edu/institutes_
centers/ihrli

International League for Human
Rights
New York
www.ilhr.org

International Peace Bureau
Geneva, Switzerland
www.ipb.org

International Physicians for the
Prevention of Nuclear War
Cambridge, Massachusetts
www.ippnw.org

International Planned Parenthood
Federation
London
www.ippf.org

International Republican Institute
Washington, DC
www.iri.org

International Rescue Committee
New York
www.theirc.org

International Save the Children
Alliance
London
www.savethechildren.net

International Union for the
Conservation of Nature
Gland, Switzerland
www.iucn.org

International Union for the
Scientific Study of Population
Paris
www.iussp.org

Iraq Occupation Watch
Baghdad, Iraq
www.occupationwatch.org

Iraq Revenue Watch
New York
www.iraqrevenuewatch.org

Irish Northern Aid (NORAID)
New York
www.inac.org

Islamic Aid
London
www.islamicaid.org.uk

Islamic Relief
Birmingham, UK
www.islamic-relief.com

MacArthur Foundation
Chicago, Illinois
www.macfound.org

Médecins Sans Frontières
Paris
www.msf.org

Mental Disability Rights
International
New York
www.mdri.org

Mothers of the Disappeared
(Asociación Madres de Plaza de
Mayo)
Buenos Aires, Argentina
www.madres.org

Mothers of the Disappeared (Madres
de Plaza de Mayo Linea Fundadora)
Buenos Aires, Argentina

Muslim Voices for Peace
New York
www.mvp-us.org/index.php

National Audubon Society
New York
www.audubon.org

National Endowment for
Democracy
Washington, DC
www.ned.org

National Resources Defense Council
New York
www.nrdc.org

National Security Archive
Washington, DC
www.gwu.edu/~nsarchiv

National Wildlife Federation
Reston, Virginia
www.nwf.org

NetAid
New York
www.netaid.org

NGO Watch
Washington, DC
www.ngowatch.org

Nomad International
Tokyo
www.nomad-int.org

Nonviolence International
Washington, DC
www.members.tripod.com/nviusa/
index2.htm

Norwegian Nobel Committee
Oslo, Norway
www.nobel.no/index.html

ODA Watch—Pacific Asia Resource
Center
Tokyo
www.parc-jp.org

Open Society Institute and Soros
Foundation Network
New York
www.soros.org

Otpor ("Resistance")
Belgrade, Yugoslavia
www.otpor.org.yu

Oxfam
Oxford, UK
www.oxfam.org.uk

Pacific Media Watch
Sydney, Australia
www.pmw.c2o.org

Palestine Media Watch
Dunn Loring, Virginia
www.pmwatch.org

Pax Christi International
Brussels, Belgium
www.paxchristi.net

Peace People
Belfast, Northern Ireland
www.peacepeople.com

People for the Ethical Treatment of
Animals (PETA)
Norfolk, Virginia
www.peta.org

Pew Charitable Trusts
Philadelphia, Pennsylvania
www.pewtrusts.com

Philippine Migrants Rights Watch
Manila, The Philippines
www.pmrw.org

Physicians for Human Rights
Boston, Massachusetts
www.phrusa.org

Population Association of America
Silver Spring, Maryland
www.popassoc.org

Population Council
New York
www.popcouncil.org

PR Watch
Center for Media and Democracy
Madison, Wisconsin
www.prwatch.org

Public Citizen
Washington, DC
www.citizen.org

Pugwash Conference on Science
and World Affairs
Rome, Italy
www.pugwash.org

Rainforest Action Network
San Francisco, California
www.ran.org

Refugee Watch
South Asia Forum for Human Rights

Kathmandu, Nepal
www.safhr.org/refugee_watch.htm

Refugees International
Washington, DC
www.refugeesinternational.org

Reproductive Cloning Network
New York
www.reproductivecloning.net

Repromed International
Limassol, Cyprus
www.repromedinternational.com

Research Triangle Institute
International (RTI)
Research Triangle Park, North
Carolina
www.rti.org

Rockefeller Foundation
New York
www.rockfound.org

Sasakawa Peace Foundation
Tokyo
www.spf.org/e

Security Watch
International Relations and Security
Network
Zurich, Switzerland
www.isn.ethz.ch

Service for Peace and Justice
(Servicio de Paz y Justicia, SERPAJ)
San Jose, Costa Rica
www.serpajamericalatina.org

Shaler Adams Fund
San Francisco, California
www.shaleradams.org

Sierra Club
San Francisco, California
www.sierraclub.org

Sinks Watch
Gloucestershire, UK
www.sinkswatch.org

Solidaridad Internacional
Madrid, Spain
www.solidaridad.org

Southern Poverty Law Center
Montgomery, Alabama
www.splcenter.org

Stop the War Coalition
London
www.stopwar.org.uk

SustainAbility
London
www.sustainability.com

Sweatshop Watch
Oakland, California
www.sweatshopwatch.org

Traffic International
Cambridge, UK
www.traffic.org

Transparency International
Berlin, Germany
www.transparency.org

Turner Foundation
Atlanta, Georgia
www.turnerfoundation.org

United Nations Foundation
Washington, DC
www.unfoundation.org

United States Institute of Peace
Washington, DC
www.usip.org

War Resisters League
New York
www.warresisters.org

Washington Office on Latin
America (WOLA)
Washington, DC
www.wola.org

Wildlife Conservation Society
Bronx, New York
www.wcs.org

William and Flora Hewlett
Foundation
Menlo Park, California
www.hewlett.org

Women's Campaign International
Washington, DC

World Transhumanist Association
Willington Connecticut
www.transhumanism.org

WorldWatch Institute
Washington, DC
www.worldwatch.org

World Wildlife Fund
Washington, DC
www.worldwildlife.org

Notes

INTRODUCTION

1. "Millions March Worldwide to Denounce Bush's War Plans," Independent Media Center, February 15, 2003, <www.indymedia.org/en/2003/02/107355.shtml>.
2. Warren Hoge, "Alleging Bias, Lawyers for Pinochet Appeal," *International Herald Tribune*, December 16, 1998; T. R. Reid, "For Pinochet, Hope for Home Rests outside Law," *International Herald Tribune*, November 27–28, 1999; Fiona McKay, "Universal Jurisdiction in Europe," June 30, 1999, <www.redress.org/publications/UJEurope.pdf>, London, Redress.
3. T. R. Reid, "Pinochet Setback Unlikely to Stop Spanish Judge," *International Herald Tribune*, January 17, 2000. See also Charles Trueheart, "Regardless of Outcome, Pinochet Case Sets Precedent," *International Herald Tribune*, January 19, 2000.
4. Jane Perlez, "Who Rules Foreign Policy's Roost?" *International Herald Tribune*, December 15, 1999.
5. Presentation by Alison Des Forges and Monique Mujawamariya, conference on Non-Governmental Organizations, Early Warning, and Preventive Diplomacy, Harvard University, April 8, 1995. See also Alison Des Forges, "Making Noise Effectively: Lessons from the Rwandan Catastrophe," in Robert I. Rotberg (ed.), *Vigilance and Vengeance: NGOs Preventing Ethnic Conflict in Divided Societies* (Washington, DC: Brookings, 1997); and Alison Des Forges, *Leave None to Tell the Story: Genocide in Rwanda* (New York: Human Rights Watch, 1999), pp. 624–44.
6. Charles William Maynes, "A New Strategy for Old Foes and New Friends," *World Policy Journal*, Vol. 17, No. 2 (2000), pp. 68–76.
7. Boutros Boutros-Ghali, Foreword to Thomas G. Weiss and Leon Gordenker (eds), *NGOs, the United Nations, and Global Governance* (Boulder, CO: Lynne Rienner, 1996), p. 10.
8. Barry James, "Crisis Group Aims to Fill Diplomatic Reporting Gap," *International Herald Tribune*, January 11, 2000; International Crisis Group, <www.crisisweb.org>.
9. Paul Gifford, "Some Recent Developments in African Christianity," *African Affairs*, Vol. 93 (1994), p. 521.
10. Steven Erlanger, "The Bad and the Beautiful Come to Honor Arkan," *International Herald Tribune*, January 21, 2000.
11. Laurie Goodstein, "Muslims Hesitating on Gifts as U.S. Scrutinizes Charities," *New York Times*, April 17, 2003; Jerry Guidera and Glenn R. Simpson, "U.S. Agents Raid Homes and Businesses Affiliated with Chairman of Islamic Fund," *Wall Street Journal*, March 21, 2002; Judith Miller, "Terrorists Rely on a Few Islamic Charities, U.S. Suspects," *International Herald Tribune*, February 21, 2000.
12. Lee Hockstader, "Barak Inquiry Focuses on Charities Linked to Briton," *International Herald Tribune*, January 31, 2000.

13. For early, critical views of the turn to NGOs in the 1990s, see Shirin Sinnar, "Mixed Blessing: The Growing Influence of NGOs," *Harvard International Review* (Winter 1995/96), pp. 54–7, 79; Laura MacDonald, "A Mixed Blessing: The NGO Boom in Latin America," *NACLA Report on the Americas*, Vol. 28, No. 5 (1995), pp. 30–5; and Alan Fowler, "Distant Obligations: Speculations on NGO Funding and the Global Market," *Review of African Political Economy*, No. 55 (1992), pp. 9–29.

CHAPTER 1

1. Tom Farer, "New Players in the Old Game: The De Facto Expansion of Standing to Participate in Global Security Negotiations," *American Behavioral Scientist*, Vol. 38, No. 6 (1995), pp. 842–66; Jessica T. Mathews, "Power Shift," *Foreign Affairs*, Vol. 76, No. 1 (1997), pp. 50–66.
2. See chapter 2 for a survey of NGO theory.
3. Hugh Dellios, "For Sponsors: Image and Reality Worlds Apart," and Graeme Zielinski and David Jackson, "'At times, I've wanted to turn it off too'," both in *Chicago Tribune*, March 15, 1998.
4. On feminism as "universalist faith," see Jean Bethke Elshtain, "Exporting Feminism," *Journal of International Affairs*, Vol. 48, No. 2 (Winter 1995), pp. 541–58.
5. On the self-authorization of international NGOs, see John Boli and George M. Thomas (eds), *Constructing World Culture: International Nongovernmental Organizations Since 1875* (Stanford, CA: Stanford University Press, 1999), p. 37.
6. William Korey, *NGOs and the Universal Declaration of Human Rights* (New York: St. Martin's Press, 1998), pp. 160–1.
7. Ibid., p. 167.
8. The Nobel Peace Prize was awarded to Seán MacBride, President of the International Peace Bureau (1974), Andrei Sakharov, human rights campaigner in the Soviet Union (1975), Betty Williams and Corrigan Mairead, co-founders of the Peace People in Northern Ireland (1976), Amnesty International (1977), Mother Teresa of Calcutta (1979), Adolfo Pérez Esquivel, Argentine human rights campaigner (1980), Lech Walesa, founder of Solidarity trade union and Polish human rights campaigner (1983), International Physicians for the Prevention of Nuclear War (1985), Aung San Suu Kyi, Burmese opposition leader and human rights advocate (1991), Rigoberta Menchú Tum, Guatemalan campaigner for indigenous peoples' rights (1992), the Pugwash Conference on Science and World Affairs (1995), the International Campaign to Ban Landmines (1997), and Médecins Sans Frontières (1999).
9. Gregg Easterbrook, "Forgotten Benefactor of Humanity," *Atlantic Monthly* (January 1997), pp. 75–82.
10. L. T. Evans, *Feeding the Ten Billion: Plants and Population Growth* (Cambridge: Cambridge University Press, 1998), pp. 133–50.
11. Ibid., p. 178.
12. Easterbrook, "Forgotten Benefactor of Humanity," p. 80.

13. For example, see Julie Fischer, *Nongovernments: NGOs and the Political Development of the Third World* (West Hartford, CT: Kumarian Press, 1998); and Ann M. Florini (ed.), *The Third Force: The Rise of Transnational Civil Society* (Washington, DC: Carnegie Endowment for International Peace, 2000).

14. On the related notion of "modular repertoires of contention" as applied to social movements, see Charles Tilly, *Popular Contention in Great Britain, 1758–1834* (Cambridge, MA: Harvard University Press, 1995); and Sidney Tarrow, *Power in Movement: Social Movements and Contentious Politics*, 2nd edn (Cambridge: Cambridge University Press, 1998), Chapter 2, "Modular Collective Action."

15. Margaret E. Keck and Kathryn Sikkink, *Activists Beyond Borders: Advocacy Networks in International Politics* (Ithaca, NY: Cornell University Press, 1998), p. 27.

16. Alex de Waal, *Famine Crimes: Politics and the Disaster Relief Industry in Africa* (Oxford: James Currey, 1997), p. 70, quoting Kenneth Hewit, "The Idea of Calamity in a Technocratic Age," in Kenneth Hewit (ed.), *Interpretations of Calamity, from the Viewpoint of Human Ecology* (Boston, MA: Allen and Unwin, 1983), p. 5.

17. For standard accounts, see Peter Gill, *A Year in the Death of Africa: Politics, Bureaucracy and the Famine* (London: Grafton Books, 1986); and Kurt Jansson, Michael Harris, and Angela Penrose, *The Ethiopian Famine*, 2nd edn (London: Zed Books, 1990).

18. Interviews by author with officials of the UN Food and Agricultural Organization and the World Food Program, Rome, May 14, 1991.

19. Interviews by author with staff of Save the Children UK, Addis Ababa, Ethiopia, September 2, 1991.

20. Helen Young and Susanne Jaspers, *Nutrition Matters: People, Food and Famine* (London: Intermediate Technology Publications, 1995), p. 133, quoted in de Waal, *Famine Crimes*, p. 71.

21. Alex de Waal, *Evil Days: 30 Years of War and Famine in Ethiopia*, An Africa Watch Report (New York: Human Rights Watch, 1991).

22. On the expulsion of Médecins sans Frontières from Ethiopia, see Fiona Terry, *Condemned to Repeat? The Paradox of Humanitarian Action* (Ithaca, NY: Cornell University Press, 2002), pp. 48–9, 238.

23. Allan Hoben, "The Cultural Construction of Environmental Policy: Paradigms and Politics in Ethiopia," in Melissa Leach and Robin Mearns (eds), *The Lie of the Land: Challenging Received Wisdom on the African Environment* (Oxford: James Currey, 1996).

24. Ibid., p. 186.

25. Mary Ann Glendon, *A World Made New: Eleanor Roosevelt and the Universal Declaration of Human Rights* (New York: Random House, 2001).

26. David P. Forsythe, "The United Nations and Human Rights, 1945–1985," *Political Science Quarterly*, Vol. 100, No. 1 (1985), pp. 249–69.

27. Robert O'Brien, Anne Marie Goetz, Jan Aart Scholte, and Marc Williams, *Contesting Global Governance: Multilateral Economic Institutions and Global Social Movements* (Cambridge: Cambridge University Press, 2000).

28. P. J. Simmons, "Learning to Live with NGOs," *Foreign Policy*, No. 112 (Fall 1998), pp. 82–96; Stephen J. Kobrin, "The MAI and the Clash of Globalizations," *Foreign Policy*, No. 112 (Fall 1998), pp. 97–109.
29. Moisés Naim, "Lori's War: The FP Interview," *Foreign Policy* (Spring 2000), pp. 29–55.
30. For a sophisticated presentation of this vision of globalization, see Richard Falk, *Predatory Globalization: A Critique* (Malden, MA: Polity Press, 1999).
31. James Petras, "NGOs: In Service of Imperialism," *Journal of Contemporary Asia*, Vol. 29, No. 4 (1999), pp. 429–40.
32. Ibid., p. 439.
33. Lucy Taylor, "Exploring Civil Society in Post Authoritarian Regimes," in Ian Hampsher-Monk and Jeffery Stanyer (eds), *Contemporary Political Studies 1996*, Vol. II (Glasgow: Proceedings of the Annual Conference of the Political Studies Association of the United Kingdom, 1996), cited in O'Brien et al., *Contesting Global Governance*, p. 58.
34. Mustapha Kamil al-Sayyid, "A Civil Society in Egypt?" in Augustus Richard Norton (ed.), *Civil Society in the Middle East*, Vol. 1 (Leiden: E. J. Brill, 1995).
35. John Waterbury, *The Egypt of Nasser and Sadat* (Princeton, NJ: Princeton University Press, 1983); Robert Springborg, *Mubarak's Egypt: Fragmentation of the Political Order* (Boulder, CO: Westview, 1989).
36. Bahgat Korany, "Restricted Democratization from Above: Egypt," in Bahgat Korany, Rex Brynen, and Paul Noble (eds), *Political Liberalization and Democratization in the Arab World, Vol. 2, Comparative Experiences* (Boulder, CO: Lynne Rienner, 1998).
37. Denis J. Sullivan, *Private Voluntary Organizations in Egypt* (Gainesville, FL: University Press of Florida, 1994), p. xiii.
38. See Bahey el-Din Hassan (ed.), *Challenges Facing the Arab Human Rights Movement* (Cairo: Cairo Institute for Human Rights Studies, 1998); and "Human Rights: Egypt and the Arab World," Special Issue of *Cairo Papers in Social Science*, Vol. 17, No. 3 (Fall 1994), Cairo: American University in Cairo.
39. Keck and Sikkink, *Activists Beyond Borders*, pp. 12–13.
40. Egyptian Organization for Human Rights, "El Kusheh Village," September 28, 1998, Cairo (photocopy).
41. Christina Lamb, "Egyptian Police 'Crucify' and Rape Christians," *Sunday Telegraph*, October 25, 1998.
42. For example, Ibrahim Nafie, "The Same Old Game," *Al-Ahram Weekly*, November 12–18, 1998.
43. Interview by author with Egyptian human rights activist, Cairo, June 17, 2000.
44. The vague charges were dropped after a meeting in March 2000 in Paris between Abu Saeda and one of President Mubarak's top advisors. This was the first meeting between an Egyptian human rights activist and top government leaders. See "Wild Check Chase," *Cairo Times*, March 2000.
45. Interviews by author with officials at Middle East Watch, Washington, DC, February 25, 1999.

46. Nadia Abou El-Magd, "Root Solutions This Time Around?" *Al-Ahram Weekly*, January 20–26, 2000; Amira Elghawaby, "Has the State Failed to Diffuse Sectarian Strife?" *Middle East Times*, January 13–19, 2000.
47. Saad Eddin Ibrahim, "A Reply to My Accusers," *Journal of Democracy*, Vol. 11, No. 4 (2000), pp. 58–63; Mary Anne Weaver, "Egypt on Trial," *New York Times Magazine*, June 17, 2001; Susan Sachs, "Egypt Clears Rights Activist Whose Jailing Drew World Protest," *New York Times*, March 19, 2003; Glenn Frankel, "Egypt Muzzles Calls for Democracy," *Washington Post*, January 6, 2004.

CHAPTER 2

1. For general history of the rise of NGOs, see Akira Iriye, "A Century of NGOs," *Diplomatic History*, Vol. 23, No. 3 (1999), pp. 421–35; and Steve Charnovitz, "Two Centuries of Participation: NGOs and International Governance," *Michigan Journal of International Law*, Vol. 18 (1997), pp. 183–286.
2. For introductions to these issue-areas, see Thomas Risse, Stephen C. Ropp, and Kathryn Sikkink (eds), *The Power of Human Rights: International Norms and Domestic Change* (Cambridge: Cambridge University Press, 1999); Brian H. Smith, *More Than Altruism: The Politics of Private Foreign Aid* (Princeton, NJ: Princeton University Press, 1990); Larry Minear and Thomas G. Weiss, *Mercy under Fire: War and the Global Humanitarian Community* (Boulder, CO: Westview Press, 1995); Thomas Princen and Matthias Finger, *Environmental NGOs in World Politics: Linking the Local and the Global* (New York: Routledge, 1994); Amrita Basu (ed.), *The Challenge of Local Feminisms: Women's Movements in Global Perspective* (Boulder, CO: Westview, 1995); Jason L. Finkle and C. Alison McIntosh (eds), *The New Politics of Population: Conflict and Consensus in Family Planning* (New York: Oxford University Press, 1994); Chester A. Crocker, Fen Osler Hampson, and Pamela Aall (eds), *Managing Global Chaos: Sources of and Responses to International Conflict* (Washington, DC: United States Institute of Peace Press, 1996); and Larry Diamond, *Promoting Democracy in the 1990s: Actors and Instruments, Issues and Imperatives* (New York: Carnegie Commission of New York, 1995).
3. Tadashi Yamamoto (ed.), *Emerging Civil Society in the Asia Pacific Community*, 2nd edn (Seattle, WA: University of Washington Press, 1996); Augustus Richard Norton (ed.), *Civil Society in the Middle East*, Vols 1 and 2 (Leiden: E. J. Brill, 1995, 1996).
4. See Lester M. Salamon, "The Rise of the Nonprofit Sector," *Foreign Affairs*, Vol. 73, No. 4 (1994), pp. 109–22; Ronnie D. Lipschutz, "Reconstructing World Politics: The Emergence of Global Civil Society," *Millennium: Journal of International Studies*, Vol. 21 (1992), pp. 389–420; Laura Macdonald, "Globalising Civil Society: Interpreting International NGOs in Central America," *Millennium: Journal of International Studies*, Vol. 23 (1994), pp. 267–85.
5. Stanley Hoffmann, "An American Social Science: International Relations," *Daedalus*, Vol. 106 (1977), pp. 41–60.

6. Key works of the 1970s transnationalism include Robert O. Keohane and Joseph S. Nye, Jr. (eds), *Transnational Relations and World Politics* (Cambridge, MA: Harvard University Press, 1972); John W. Burton, *World Society* (Cambridge University Press, 1972); Richard W. Mansbach, Yale H. Ferguson, and Donald E. Lampert, *The Web of World Politics: Non-State Actors in the Global System* (Englewood Cliffs, NJ: Prentice Hall, 1976); Harold K. Jacobson, *Networks of Interdependence: International Organizations and the International Political System* (New York: Knopf, 1979); and Peter Willets (ed.), *Pressure Groups in the Global System: The Transnational Relations of Issue-Oriented Non-Governmental Organizations* (London: Pinter, 1982).

7. Two popular surveys of International Relations theory published in the 1980s contain nary a reference to NGOs: James E. Dougherty and Robert L. Pfaltzgraff, Jr., *Contending Theories of International Relations: A Comprehensive Survey*, 2nd edn (New York: Harper & Row, 1981); Paul R. Viotti and Mark V. Kauppi, *International Relations Theory* (New York: Macmillan, 1987). Viotti and Kauppi do acknowledge transnational theory with an excerpt from John W. Burton's *World Society*.

8. Peter Willetts, "Transnational Actors and International Organizations in Global Politics," in John Baylis and Steve Smith (eds), *The Globalization of World Politics*, 2nd edn (Oxford University Press, 2001), p. 382.

9. Robert O. Keohane and Joseph S. Nye, Jr., *Power and Interdependence: World Politics in Transition* (Boston: Little, Brown, 1977).

10. I do not attempt an exhaustive survey of the literature, but cite a few representative examples of research in each school. By associating a particular work with one of the three schools, I am claiming that it takes as its primary point of departure the theoretical orientation of that school, not that its findings or explanations are limited to the assumptions of the school as I define it.

11. Much of the early transnational literature falls somewhere in the pluralist camp, including Burton, *World Society*; Mansbach et al., *The Web of World Politics*; and Willetts, *Pressure Groups in the Global System*. Keohane and Nye in *Transnational Relations and World Politics* evince a pervasive interest in the implications of transnational relations for government policy, and particularly U.S. foreign policy, that renders them somewhat of an anomaly among the pluralists.

12. Key works include Goren Hyden and Michael Bratton (eds), *Governance and Politics in Africa* (Boulder, CO: Lynne Rienner, 1992); Yamamoto (ed.), *Emerging Civil Society in the Asia Pacific Community*; and Norton (ed.), *Civil Society in the Middle East*.

13. For a range of pluralist accounts of NGOs, see Lester M. Salamon and Helmut K. Anheier, *The Emerging Sector: The Nonprofit Sector in Comparative Perspective—An Overview* (Baltimore, MD: Johns Hopkins University Institute for Policy Studies, 1994); Thomas Risse-Kappen (ed.), *Bringing Transnational Relations Back In: Non-State Actors, Domestic Structures and International Institutions* (Cambridge: Cambridge University Press, 1995); Laura MacDonald, *Supporting Civil Society: The Political Role of Non-Governmental Organizations in Central America* (New York: St. Martin's Press, 1995); Seyom Brown, *New Forces, Old Forces, and the Future of*

World Politics, Post-Cold War edn (New York: HarperCollins, 1995); Paul Wapner, *Environmental Activism and World Civic Politics* (Albany, NY: State University of New York Press, 1996); Jackie Smith, Charles Chatfield, and Ron Pagnucco (eds), *Transnational Social Movements and Global Politics: Solidarity Beyond the State* (Syracuse, NY: Syracuse University Press, 1997); Margaret E. Keck and Kathryn Sikkink, *Activists Beyond Borders: Advocacy Networks in International Politics* (Ithaca, NY: Cornell University Press, 1998); Julie Fisher, *Nongovernments: NGOs and the Political Development of the Third World* (West Hartford, CT: Kumarian, 1998); and Ann M. Florini (ed.), *The Third Force: The Rise of Transnational Civil Society* (Washington, DC: Carnegie Endowment for International Peace, 2000).

14. For example, see Robert O'Brien, Anne Marie Goetz, Jan Aart Scholte, and Marc Williams, *Contesting Global Governance: Multilateral Economic Institutions and Global Social Movements* (Cambridge: Cambridge University Press, 2000); Maryann K. Cusimano, *Beyond Sovereignty: Issues for a Global Agenda* (Boston: Bedford and St. Martin's Press, 2000); Gene M. Lyons and Michael Mastanduno (eds), *Beyond Westphalia? State Sovereignty and International Intervention* (Baltimore, MD: Johns Hopkins University Press, 1995).

15. For a sampling of early 1990s debate on the moderate left, see Alan Fowler, "Non-governmental Organizations as Agents of Democratization: An African Perspective," *Journal of International Development*, Vol. 5, No. 3 (1993), pp. 325–39; Paul Ghils, "International Civil Society: International Non-governmental Organizations in the International System," *International Social Science Journal*, Vol. 133 (1992), pp. 417–29; Martin Shaw, "Civil Society and Global Politics: Beyond a Social Movements Approach," *Millennium: Journal of International Studies*, Vol. 23, No. 3 (1994), pp. 647–67; Lipschutz, "Reconstructing World Politics"; and Macdonald, "Globalising Civil Society."

16. See Rajni Kothari, "On the Non-Party Political Process: The NGOs, the State and World Capitalism," *Lokayan Bulletin*, Vol. 4, No. 5 (1986), pp. 6–26, reprinted as Chapter 5 in Rajni Kothari, *State against Democracy: In Search of Humane Governance* (New Delhi: Ajanta, 1989), pp. 72–87; Rajni Kothari, "The Yawning Vacuum: A World without Alternatives," *Alternatives*, Vol. 18 (1993), pp. 119–39; Robert Fatton, Jr., *Predatory Rule: State and Civil Society in Africa* (Boulder, CO: Lynne Rienner, 1992); and James Petras, "NGOs: In Service of Imperialism," *Journal of Contemporary Asia*, Vol. 29, No. 4 (1999), pp. 429–40.

17. For globalist perspectives on NGOs, see Harold K. Jacobson, *Networks of Interdependence: International Organizations and the International Political System* (New York: Knopf, 1979); Peter Willetts (ed.), *"The Conscience of the World": The Influence of Non-governmental Organizations in the U.N. System* (Washington, DC: Brookings, 1996); Larry Minear and Thomas G. Weiss, *Mercy under Fire: War and the Global Humanitarian Community* (Boulder, CO: Westview Press, 1995); Thomas G. Weiss and Leon Gordenker (eds), *NGOs, The UN, and Global Governance* (Boulder, CO: Lynne Rienner, 1996); Thomas G. Weiss (ed.), *Beyond UN Subcontracting: Task-Sharing with Regional Security Arrangements and Service-Providing NGOs* (London: Macmillan, 1998); Michael G. Schechter (ed.), *United Nations-Sponsored*

World Conferences: Focus on Impact and Follow-up (Tokyo and New York: United Nations University Press, 2001); Chadwick F. Alger (ed.), *The Future of the United Nations: Potential for the Twenty-first Century* (Tokyo and New York: United Nations University Press, 1998); Ann Marie Clark, *Diplomacy of Conscience: Amnesty International and Changing Human Rights Norms* (Princeton, NJ: Princeton University Press, 2001).

18. The 1980s literature on "international regimes" was centrally concerned with identifying the causal power of norms created within international organizations, but was resolutely state-centered and very slow to recognize the role of NGOs *vis-à-vis* international norms. NGOs are almost completely ignored in the seminal regime literature. For example, see Stephen D. Krasner (ed.), *International Regimes* (Ithaca, NY: Cornell University Press, 1983); and Jack Donnelly, "International Human Rights: a Regime Analysis," *International Organization*, Vol. 40 (1986), pp. 599–642.

19. Ann Marie Clark, Elisabeth J. Friedman, and Kathryn Hochstetler, "The Sovereign Limits of Global Civil Society: A Comparison of NGO Participation in UN World Conferences on the Environment, Human Rights, and Women," *World Politics*, Vol. 51, No. 1 (1998), pp. 1–35; Kerstin Martens, "NGO Participation at International Conferences: Assessing Theoretical Accounts," *Transnational Associations*, Vol. 3 (2000), pp. 115–26.

20. For a realist case against institutional impact, see John J. Mearsheimer, "The False Promise of International Institutions," *International Security*, Vol. 19, No. 3 (Winter 1994/95), pp. 5–49. For realist views that acknowledge some significance for transnational institutions, see Samuel P. Huntington, "Transnational Organizations in World Politics," *World Politics*, Vol. 25, No. 3 (1973), pp. 333–68; and Stephen D. Krasner, "Power Politics, Institutions, and Transnational Relations," in Risse-Kappen (ed.), *Bringing Transnational Relations Back In*.

21. The inadvertent and tragic consequences of political action are recognized by classic realists. See Reinhold Niebuhr, *The Children of Light and the Children of Darkness* (New York: Scribner, 1945); and Hans J. Morgenthau, *Politics Among Nations*, 2nd edn (New York: Alfred Knopf, 1954).

22. John Boli and George M. Thomas (eds), *Constructing World Culture: International Nongovernmental Organizations Since 1875* (Stanford, CA: Stanford University Press, 1999); George M. Thomas, John W. Meyer, Francisco O. Ramirez, and John Boli, *Institutional Structure: Constituting State, Society, and the Individual* (Beverly Hills, CA: Sage, 1987).

23. For a glimpse of the agent–structure debate in international relations, see Vendulka Kubalkova, Nicholas Onuf, and Paul Kowert (eds), *International Relations in a Constructed World* (Armonk, NY: M. E. Sharpe, 1998); Alexander Wendt, *Social Theory of International Politics* (Cambridge: Cambridge University Press, 1999); and Peter Katzenstein (ed.), *The Culture of National Security* (New York: Columbia University Press, 1996).

24. Clifford Geertz, *The Interpretation of Cultures* (New York: Basic Books, 1973), p. 5.

25. See Janice E. Thomson, "State Sovereignty in International Relations," *International Studies Quarterly*, Vol. 39, No. 2 (1995), pp. 213–33; and Salamon and Anheier, *The Emerging Sector*.

26. Kothari, "On the Non-Party Political Process," p. 22.
27. Jane Fritsch, "Green Cover for Companies," *New York Times*, March 25, 1996; Joyce Nelson, "Great Global Greenwash: Burson-Marsteller, Pax Trilateral, and the Brundtland Gang vs. the Environment," *CovertAction*, No. 44 (Spring 1993), pp. 216–33, 57–8.
28. On the legitimacy problems of authoritarian rule, see Samuel P. Huntington, *The Third Wave: Democratization in the Late Twentieth Century* (Norman, OK: University of Oklahoma Press, 1991), pp. 46–58.
29. Stephen Kinzer, "Istanbul Deters Muslim Quake Help," *International Herald Tribune*, August 28–29, 1999.
30. William DeMars, "Contending Neutralities: Humanitarian Organizations and War in the Horn of Africa," in Smith, Chatfield and Pagnucco (eds), *Transnational Social Movements and Global Politics*.
31. Kenneth E. Boulding, *Three Faces of Power* (Newbury Park, CA: Sage, 1990).
32. See Barbara G. Haskel, "Access to Society: A Neglected Dimension of Power," *International Organization*, Vol. 34, No. 1 (1980), pp. 89–120.
33. Sidney Tarrow, *Power in Movement: Social Movements and Contentious Politics*, 2nd edn (Cambridge: Cambridge University Press, 1998); Smith, Chatfield, and Pagnucco, *Transnational Social Movements and Global Politics*.
34. Stephen N. Ndegwa, *The Two Faces of Civil Society: NGOs and Politics in Africa* (West Hartford, CT: Kumarian Press, 1996).
35. Interviews by the author with NGO staff in Guatemala City, August 1989.
36. Jarat Chopra and Thomas G. Weiss, "Sovereignty is No Longer Sacrosanct: Codifying Humanitarian Intervention," *Ethics & International Affairs*, Vol. 6 (1992), pp. 95–117.
37. For NGOs in warlord conflicts, see Ian Smillie, "NGOs in Complex Emergencies: The Case of Sierra Leone," Working Paper No. 1, CARE Canada, NGOs in Complex Emergencies Project (September 1996); and Hugo Slim, "The Continuing Metamorphosis of the Humanitarian Practitioner: Some New Colours for an Endangered Chameleon," *Disasters*, Vol. 19, No. 2 (1995), pp. 110–26.
38. Interview by author in Cairo, October 1999.
39. I have adapted the concept of NGO latent and salient agendas from the perceptive analysis by Brian H. Smith in *More Than Altruism: The Politics of Private Foreign Aid* (Princeton, NJ: Princeton University Press, 1990).
40. Lowell W. Livezey, *Nongovernmental Organizations and the Ideas of Human Rights*, World Order Studies Program Occasional Paper No. 15 (Princeton University, Center of International Studies, 1988). On the emergence of Islamic NGOs, see Jonathan Benthall, "Financial Worship: The Quranic Injunction to Almsgiving," *Journal of the Royal Anthropological Institute*, Vol. 5, No. 1 (1999), pp. 27–42; and African Rights, *Food and Power in Sudan: A Critique of Humanitarianism* (London: African Rights, 1997), Chapter 9, "The 'Comprehensive Call'."
41. See Smith, *More Than Altruism*, Chapter 4, "European and Canadian Private Foreign Aid Since World War II."

42. The notion that organizations are the "recalcitrant tools" of their creators is from sociologist Philip Selznick, *Leadership in Administration* (New York: Harper & Row, 1957). For the application of organizational theory to international organizations, see Gayl D. Ness and Steven R. Brechin, "Bridging the Gap: International Organizations as Organizations," *International Organization*, Vol. 42, No. 2 (1988), pp. 245–73.

43. The analysis is from Smith, *More Than Altruism*, p. 34. See also Benjamin M. Weissman, *Herbert Hoover and Famine Relief to Soviet Russia: 1921–1923* (Stanford, CA: Hoover Institution Press, 1974).

44. Michael Edwards and David Hulme (eds), *Beyond the Magic Bullet: NGO Performance and Accountability in the Post-Cold War World* (West Hartford, CT: Kumarian, 1996).

45. See John Prendergast, *Frontline Diplomacy: Humanitarian Aid and Conflict in Africa* (Boulder, CO: Lynne Rienner, 1996); and William E. DeMars, "Transnational Non-Governmental Organizations: The Edge of Innocence," in E. Wayne Nafziger and Raimo Väyrynen (eds), *The Prevention of Humanitarian Emergencies* (New York: Palgrave, 2002).

46. Phil Williams, "The Nature of Drug-Trafficking Networks," *Current History* (April 1998), p. 156.

47. David Ronfeldt and Cathryn L. Thorup, *North America in the Era of Citizen Networks: State, Society, and Security* (Santa Monica, CA: RAND, 1995); Phil Williams, "Transnational Criminal Organizations: Strategic Alliances," *The Washington Quarterly*, Vol. 18, No. 1 (1995), pp. 57–72; Walter W. Powell, "Neither Market nor Hierarchy: Network Forms of Organization," *Research in Organizational Behavior*, Vol. 12 (1990), pp. 295–336.

48. Craig N. Murphy, *International Organizations and Industrial Change: Global Governance Since 1850* (Oxford: Oxford University Press, 1994), pp. 214–18; Ondine Barrow and Michael Jennings (eds), *The Charitable Impulse: NGOs and Development in East and North-East Africa* (London: James Currey, 2001).

49. Terje Tvedt, *Angels of Mercy or Development Diplomats? NGOs and Foreign Aid* (Trenton, NJ: Africa World Press, 1998); Ndegwa, *The Two Faces of Civil Society.*

50. Jean-François Bayart, Stephen Ellis, and Béatrice Hibou, *The Criminalization of the State in Africa* (Oxford: James Currey, 1999); William Reno, *Warlord Politics and African States* (Boulder, CO: Lynne Rienner, 1998).

51. Andrea Bartoli, "Mediating Peace in Mozambique: Successful Synergies and the Role of the Community of St. Egidio," and Aldo Ajello, "Mozambique: Implementation of the 1992 Peace Agreement," both in Chester A. Crocker, Fen Osler Hampson, and Pamela Aall (eds), *Herding Cats: Multiparty Mediation in a Complex World* (Washington, DC: United States Institute of Peace Press, 1999).

52. De Waal, *Famine Crimes*; Joanna Macrae and Anthony Zwi (eds), *War and Hunger: Rethinking International Responses to Complex Emergencies* (London: Zed Books, 1994).

53. "Multi-sited ethnography" is used by anthropologists attempting to trace transnational flows of people, money, and symbols. See George E. Marcus, "Ethnography in/of the World System: The Emergence of

Multi-Sited Ethnography," *Annual Review of Anthropology*, Vol. 24 (1995), pp. 95–117.

54. J. D. Armstrong, "The International Committee of the Red Cross and Political Prisoners," *International Organization*, Vol. 39, No. 4 (1985), pp. 616–42.

55. Alex de Waal and Rakiya Omaar, "Can Military Intervention be 'Humanitarian'?" *Middle East Report*, Vol. 187/188 (1994), p. 7.

56. Andrew S. Natisos, *The Great North Korean Famine: Famine, Politics, and Foreign Policy* (Washington, DC: United States Institute of Peace Press, 2001).

57. William DeMars, "Waiting for Early Warning: Humanitarian Action After the Cold War," *Journal of Refugee Studies*, Vol. 8, No. 4 (1995), pp. 390–410.

58. Scott Anderson, *The Man Who Tried to Save the World: The Dangerous Life and Mysterious Disappearance of Fred Cuny* (New York: Doubleday, 1999).

59. Janie Leatherman, William DeMars, Patrick Gaffney, and Raimo Väyrynen, *Breaking Cycles of Violence: Conflict Prevention in Intrastate Crises* (West Hartford, CT: Kumarian, 1999); Prendergast, *Frontline Diplomacy*; Crocker, Hampson, and Aall (eds), *Managing Global Chaos*; International Crisis Group, <www.crisisweb.org>.

60. William E. DeMars, "Hazardous Partnership: NGOs and United States Intelligence in Small Wars," *International Journal of Intelligence and CounterIntelligence*, Vol. 14, No. 2 (2001), pp. 193–222.

61. On political learning, see Peter M. Haas and Ernst B. Haas, "Learning to Learn: Improving International Governance," *Global Governance*, Vol. 1 (1995), pp. 255–85; and Judith Goldstein and Robert E. Keohane (eds), *Ideas and Foreign Policy: Beliefs, Institutions, and Political Change* (Ithaca, NY: Cornell University Press, 1993).

62. Robert W. Cox, "Gramsci, Hegemony, and International Relations: An Essay in Method," *Millennium: Journal of International Studies*, Vol. 12, No. 2 (1983), pp. 162–75; reprinted in Robert W. Cox and Timothy J. Sinclair, *Approaches to World Order* (Cambridge: Cambridge University Press, 1996), quotation from p. 139.

63. Katzenstein (ed.), *The Culture of National Security*.

64. Iain Guest, *Behind the Disappearances: Argentina's Dirty War Against Human Rights and the United Nations* (Philadelphia, PA: University of Pennsylvania Press, 1990); Lawrence Weschler, *A Miracle, a Universe: Settling Accounts with Torturers* (New York: Pantheon, 1990).

65. Arie M. Kacowitz, "Latin America as an International Society," *International Politics*, Vol. 37 (June 2000), pp. 143–62.

66. Kathryn Sikkink, "The Emergence, Evolution, and Effectiveness of the Latin American Human Rights Network," in Elizabeth Jelin and Eric Hershberg (eds), *Constructing Democracy: Human Rights, Citizenship, and Society in Latin America* (Boulder, CO: Westview, 1996); Liam Mahoney and Luis Enrique Eguren, *Unarmed Bodyguards: Case Studies in Protective International Accompaniment* (West Hartford, CT: Kumarian, 1997).

67. Mehran Kamrava and Frank O. Mora, "Civil Society and Democratisation in Comparative Perspective: Latin America and the Middle East," *Third*

World Quarterly, Vol. 19, No. 5 (1998), pp. 893–916; Larry Diamond, *Promoting Democracy in the 1990s: Actors and Instruments, Issues and Imperatives*, A Report to the Carnegie Commission on Preventing Deadly Conflict (New York: Carnegie Commission of New York, 1995).

68. Guy Nicholas, "Victime ou Martyr," *Cultures et Conflits* 11 (Automne 1993); Amir Pasic and Thomas G. Weiss, "Humanitarian Recognition in the Former Yugoslavia: The Limits of Non-State Politics," *Security Studies*, Vol. 7, No. 1 (1997), pp. 194–228.

69. William DeMars, "War and Mercy in Africa," *World Policy Journal*, Vol. 17, No. 2 (Summer 2000), pp. 1–10.

70. Gabriel Almond, "Review Article: The International–National Connection," *British Journal of Political Science*, Vol. 19 (1989), pp. 237–59; Peter Gourevitch, "The Second Image Reversed: The International Sources of Domestic Politics," *International Organization*, Vol. 32, No. 4 (1978), pp. 881–912.

71. Stephen D. Krasner, "Sovereignty: an Institutional Perspective," in James A. Caporaso (ed.), *The Elusive State: International and Comparative Perspectives* (Newbury Park, CA: Sage, 1989).

CHAPTER 3

1. Stephen Toulmin, historian and philosopher of science, questions this received view and offers a modified explanation for the rise of modernity in *Cosmopolis: The Hidden Agenda of Modernity* (New York: Free Press, 1990).

2. Paul Ghils, "International Civil Society: International Non-governmental Organizations in the International System," *International Social Science Journal*, Vol. 44, No. 133 (1992), p. 428. On this point Ghils cites Bernard Badie, *Les Deux Etats: Pouvoir et Société en Occident et en Terre d'Islam* (Paris: Fayard, 1986).

3. Ghils, "International Civil Society," p. 428.

4. Margaret E. Keck and Kathryn Sikkink, *Activists Beyond Borders: Advocacy Networks in International Politics* (Ithaca, NY: Cornell University Press, 1998), Chapter 2, "Historical Precursors to Modern Transnational Advocacy Networks."

5. Robert William Fogel, *The Fourth Great Awakening and the Future of Egalitarianism* (Chicago, IL: University of Chicago Press, 2000), p. 11.

6. Ethan A. Nadelman, "Global Prohibition Regimes: The Evolution of Norms in International Society," *International Organization*, Vol. 44, No. 4 (1990), p. 497.

7. David Brion Davis, *Slavery and Human Progress* (Oxford University Press, 1984), p. 143.

8. For the emerging literature on the role of ideas in international relations, see Judith Goldstein and Robert O. Keohane (eds), *Ideas and Foreign Policy: Beliefs, Institutions, and Political Change* (Ithaca, NY: Cornell University Press, 1993); Peter J. Katzenstein (ed.), *The Culture of National Security: Norms and Identity in World Politics* (New York: Columbia University Press, 1996); and Daniel Philpott, *Revolutions in Sovereignty: How Ideas Shaped*

Modern International Relations (Princeton, NJ: Princeton University Press, 2001).

9. Thomas L. Haskell, "Capitalism and the Origins of the Humanitarian Sensibility, Part 1," *American Historical Review*, Vol. 90, No. 2 (1985), pp. 339–61; and "Capitalism and the Origins of the Humanitarian Sensibility, Part 2," *American Historical Review*, Vol. 90, No. 3 (1985), pp. 547–66.

10. Davis, *Slavery and Human Progress*, p. 132.

11. Ibid., p. 135.

12. Ibid., p. 143.

13. David Butler, *Methodists and Papists: John Wesley and the Catholic Church in the Eighteenth Century* (London: Darton, Longman and Todd, 1995).

14. Quoted in Warren Thomas Smith, *John Wesley and Slavery* (Nashville, TN: Abingdon Press, 1986), p. 90.

15. Davis, *Slavery and Human Progress*, p. 140.

16. Ibid., p. 148, citing M. H. Abrams, *Natural Supernaturalism: Tradition and Revolution in Romantic Literature* (New York: Norton, 1971), pp. 356–72.

17. Davis, *Slavery and Human Progress*, p. 148.

18. Suzanne Miers and Richard Roberts (eds), *The End of Slavery in Africa* (Madison, WI: University of Wisconsin Press, 1988).

19. Tim Jeal, *Livingstone* (New York: G. P. Putnam's Sons, 1973).

20. Much of this section relies on the gripping and exhaustively researched book by Adam Hochschild, *King Leopold's Ghost* (New York: Houghton Mifflin, 1998).

21. Ibid., p. 45.

22. Ibid., p. 46.

23. Quoted in ibid., *King Leopold's Ghost*, p. 72.

24. In ibid., Chapter 5, "From Florida to Berlin."

25. Ibid., Chapter 15, "A Reckoning."

26. Ibid., p. 211.

27. Ibid., pp. 174, 239, 251.

28. Ibid., pp. 275–83; David Northrup, "The Ending of Slavery in the Eastern Belgian Congo," in Miers and Roberts (eds), *The End of Slavery in Africa*.

29. Deborah Barrett, "Reproducing Persons as a Global Concern: The Making of an Institution" (PhD Dissertation, Stanford University, 1995); Deborah Barrett and David John Frank, "Population Control for National Development: From World Discourse to National Policies," in John Boli and George M. Thomas (eds), *Constructing World Culture: International Nongovernmental Organizations since 1875* (Stanford, CA: Stanford University Press, 1999); Deborah Barrett and Amy Ong Tsui, "Policy as Symbolic Statement: International Response to National Population Policies," *Social Forces*, Vol. 78, No. 1 (1999), pp. 213–33.

30. Barrett and Frank, "Population Control for National Development," p. 198.

31. Ibid., p. 210.

32. Barrett, "Reproducing Persons as a Global Concern."

33. Daniel J. Kevles, *In the Name of Eugenics: Genetics and the Uses of Human Heredity* (New York: Alfred A. Knopf, 1985), p. 63.

34. Barrett and Frank, "Population Control for National Development," p. 218.

35. Akira Iriye, "A Century of NGOs," *Diplomatic History*, Vol. 23, No. 3 (1999), p. 424.
36. Stephen D. Krasner, "Power Politics, Institutions, and Transnational Relations," in Thomas Risse-Kappen (ed.), *Bringing Transnational Relations Back In: Non-State Actors, Domestic Structures and International Institutions* (Cambridge: Cambridge University Press, 1995), p. 266.
37. Alexis de Tocqueville, edited by J. P. Mayer, translated by George Lawrence, *Democracy in America* (Garden City, NY: Doubleday, 1969), p. 513.
38. Walt Whitman, "Democratic Vistas," in Walt Whitman, edited by Floyd Stoval, *Prose Works 1892*, Volume II (New York: New York University Press, 1964), pp. 379–80.
39. Samuel P. Huntington, "Transnational Organizations in World Politics," *World Politics*, Vol. 25, No. 3 (1973), pp. 333–68.
40. Ibid., p. 335.
41. Ibid., p. 342.
42. See Sidney Tarrow, *Power in Movement: Social Movements and Contentious Politics*, 2nd edn (Cambridge University Press, 1998), pp. 43–53, 179–83.
43. Huntington, "Transnational Organizations in World Politics," p. 343, emphasis added.
44. Ibid., pp. 355–6.
45. For the political dynamics of Third World governments financing themselves through international partners, see Christopher Clapham, *Africa in the International System: The Politics of Survival* (Cambridge: Cambridge University Press, 1996); Mark Duffield, *Global Governance and the New Wars: The Merging of Development and Security* (London: Zed Books, 2001).
46. Huntington, "Transnational Organizations in World Politics," pp. 345–6.
47. Ibid., p. 358.
48. Joseph S. Nye, "The Changing Nature of World Power," *Political Science Quarterly*, Vol. 105, No. 2 (1990), pp. 177–92.

CHAPTER 4

1. The Argentina network of the late 1970s is the paradigm case for the "boomerang pattern" by which "transnational advocacy networks" bring pressure on target governments through international allies. See Margaret E. Keck and Kathryn Sikkink, *Activists Beyond Borders: Advocacy Networks in International Politics* (Ithaca, NY: Cornell University Press, 1998), pp. vii–viii, 92–4, and 103–110. See also Ann Marie Clark, *Diplomacy of Conscience: Amnesty International and Changing Human Rights Norms* (Princeton, NJ: Princeton University Press, 2001), Chapter 4, "Disappearances"; and Jack Donnelly, *International Human Rights* (Boulder, CO: Westview, 1993), Chapter 3, "The Domestic Politics of Human Rights: The Case of the Southern Cone."
2. Frederick C. Turner and José Enrique Miguens (eds), *Juan Perón and the Reshaping of Argentina* (Pittsburgh, PA: University of Pittsburgh Press, 1983).

3. See Alison Brysk, "The Politics of Measurement: The Contested Count of the Disappeared in Argentina," *Human Rights Quarterly*, Vol. 16, No. 4 (1994), pp. 676–92; and new data from Argentine Intelligence Battalion 601 suggesting that disappearances numbered at least 22,000, in John Dinges, *The Condor Years: How Pinochet and His Allies Brought Terrorism to Three Continents* (New York: The New Press, 2004), pp. 139–40.

4. Iain Guest, *Behind the Disappearances: Argentina's Dirty War Against Human Rights and the United Nations* (Philadelphia, PA: University of Pennsylvania Press, 1990), p. 52.

5. Ibid., pp. 68–9.

6. Ron Pagnucco, "The Transnational Strategies of the Service for Peace and Justice in Latin America," in Jackie Smith, Charles Chatfield, and Ron Pagnucco (eds), *Transnational Social Movements and Global Politics: Solidarity Beyond the State* (Syracuse, NY: Syracuse University Press, 1997).

7. For a sampling of the extensive literature on Las Madres, see Marguerite Guzman Bouvard, *Revolutionizing Motherhood: The Mothers of the Plaza De Mayo* (Wilmington, DE: Scholarly Resources, 2002); Matilde Mellibovsky, translated by Maria and Matthew Proser, *Circle of Love over Death: Testimonies of the Mothers of the Plaza de Mayo* (Willimantic, CT: Curbstone Press, 1997); Alison Brysk, *The Politics of Human Rights in Argentina: Protest, Change, and Democratization* (Stanford, CA: University of California Press, 1994); Jean Bethke Elshtain, "The Mothers of the Disappeared," in Donna Bassin, Margaret Honey, and Marlyle Mohrer Kaplan (eds), *Representations of Motherhood* (New Haven, CT: Yale University Press, 1994); and Andrea Malin, "Mothers Who Won't Disappear," *Human Rights Quarterly*, Vol. 15 (1994), pp. 187–213.

8. Alison Brysk, "From Above and Below: Social Movements, the International System, and Human Rights in Argentina," *Comparative Political Studies*, Vol. 26, No. 3 (1993), pp. 264–5.

9. David P. Forsythe, *Human Rights and World Politics* (Lincoln, NE: University of Nebraska Press, 1983), p. 141.

10. Pagnucco, "The Transnational Strategies of the Service for Peace and Justice in Latin America," p. 130.

11. Clark, *Diplomacy of Conscience*, p. 76.

12. Guest, *Behind the Disappearances*, pp. 76–86.

13. Ibid., pp. 151–63.

14. Roberta Cohen, "Human Rights Decision-Making in the Executive Branch: Some Proposals for a Coordinated Strategy," in Donald P. Kommers and Gilburt D. Loescher (eds), *Human Rights and American Foreign Policy* (Notre Dame, IN: University of Notre Dame Press, 1979), p. 224.

15. William Korey, *NGOs and the Universal Declaration of Human Rights* (New York: St. Martin's Press, 1998), pp. 188–9; Guest, *Behind the Disappearances*, pp. 173–243.

16. Reported in Keck and Sikkink, *Activists Beyond Borders*, p. 108.

17. Thomas C. Wright, *Latin America and the Cuban Revolution* (New York: Praeger, 1991); Timothy P. Wickham-Crowley, "A Qualitative Comparative Approach to Latin American Revolutions," *International Journal of Comparative Sociology*, Vol. 32, Nos. 1–2 (1991), pp. 82–109; Raj

Desai and Harry Eckstein, "Insurgency: The Transformation of Peasant Rebellion," *World Politics*, Vol. 42 (1990), pp. 441–66.

18. Jorge G. Castañeda, *Utopia Unarmed: The Latin American Left After the Cold War* (New York: Alfred A. Knopf, 1993), p. 16.

19. Timothy P. Wickham-Crowley, "Winners, Losers, and Also-Rans: Toward a Comparative Sociology of Latin American Guerrilla Movements," in Susan Eckstein (ed.), *Power and Popular Protest* (Berkeley, CA: University of California Press, 1989), p. 138.

20. Castañeda, *Utopia Unarmed*, pp. 68–74.

21. María José Moyano, *Argentina's Lost Patrol: Armed Struggle, 1969–1979* (New Haven, CT: Yale University Press, 1995), p. 104.

22. Ibid., pp. 90 and 93.

23. Ibid., p. 64.

24. Ibid., pp. 96–8.

25. Ibid., p. 108.

26. Kathryn Sikkink, "The Emergence, Evolution, and Effectiveness of the Latin American Human Rights Network," in Elizabeth Jelin and Eric Hershberg (eds), *Constructing Democracy: Human Rights, Citizenship, and Society in Latin America* (Boulder, CO: Westview Press, 1996), p. 63.

27. Paul Heath Hoeffel and Peter Kornbluh, "The War at Home: Chile's Legacy in the United States," *NACLA Report on the Americas*, Vol. 17 (September–October, 1983), pp. 27–39.

28. David P. Forsythe, "The United Nations and Human Rights, 1945–1985," *Political Science Quarterly*, Vol. 100, No. 1 (1985), pp. 249–69.

29. Hoeffel and Kornbluh, "The War At Home," p. 31.

30. Virginia Bouvier, "The Washington Office on Latin America: Charting a New Path in U.S.–Latin American Relations," in Robert S. Pelton (ed.), *From Power to Communion: Toward a New Way of Being Church Based on the Latin American Experience* (South Bend, IN: University of Notre Dame Press, 1994).

31. Korey, *NGOs and the Universal Declaration*, p. 186, based on William Korey's 1996 interview with Joseph Eldridge.

32. Gil Loescher, *Beyond Charity: International Cooperation and the Global Refugee Crisis* (Oxford University Press, 1993), pp. 84–6.

33. Guest, *Behind the Disappearances*, p. 69.

34. Lawrence Weschler, *A Miracle, A Universe: Settling Accounts with Torturers* (New York: Pantheon, 1990); Brian H. Smith, *The Church and Politics in Chile* (Princeton, NJ: Princeton University Press, 1982).

35. Guest, *Behind the Disappearances*, pp. 59, 238–40.

36. Brysk, *The Politics of Human Rights in Argentina*, p. 48.

37. Elshtain, "The Mothers of the Disappeared."

38. Ariel C. Armony, *Argentina, the United States, and the Anti-Communist Crusade* (Athens, OH: Ohio University Press, 1997), p. 165; and Margaret E. Crahan, "Religion, Revolution, and Counterrevolution: The Role of the Religious Right in Central America," in Douglas A. Chalmers, Maria do Carmo Campello de Souza, and Atilio A. Boron (eds), *The Right and Democracy in Latin America* (New York: Praeger, 1992).

39. Human Rights Watch, which today is the second NGO to conduct continuous monitoring of human rights abuses in all countries,

was founded piecemeal beginning with Helsinki Watch in 1979 and culminating with Middle East Watch in 1989.

40. From *First Annual Report, 1961–62* (London: Amnesty International, 1962), quoted in Korey, *NGOs and the Universal Declaration*, p. 162. See also Edy Kaufman, "Prisoners of Conscience: The Shaping of a New Human Rights Concept," *Human Rights Quarterly*, Vol. 13 (1991), pp. 339–67; and Clark, *Diplomacy of Conscience*.

41. Indeed, the experience and historical memory of the Argentina network has shaped human rights scholarship to the degree that the dominant theoretical approaches of pluralism and globalism both reinforce inattention to political and military conflict in the contexts of advocacy campaigns (see chapter 2).

42. See Keck and Sikkink, *Activists Beyond Borders*, fn. 72, p. 104; and Carlos H. Acuña and Catalina Smulovitz, "Adjusting the Armed Forces to Democracy: Successes, Failures, and Ambiguities in the Southern Cone," in Elizabeth Jelin and Eric Hershberg (eds), *Constructing Democracy: Human Rights, Citizenship, and Society in Latin America* (Boulder, CO: Westview Press, 1996), p. 15.

43. This observation originates in my conversation with a leader of Amnesty International USA at its annual general meeting held in Minneapolis in June 1977.

44. On the tactic of disappearances in Guatemala, used earlier and on a larger scale than in Argentina, see Lisa L. Martin and Kathryn Sikkink, "U.S. Policy and Human Rights in Argentina and Guatemala, 1973–80," in Peter B. Evans, Harold K. Jacobson, and Robert D. Putnam (eds), *Double-Edged Diplomacy: International Bargaining and Domestic Politics* (Berkeley, CA: University of California Press, 1993).

45. On the expansion of human rights NGOs in the U.S. during the 1970s, see Kenneth Cmiel, "The Emergence of Human Rights Politics in the United States," *The Journal of American History*, Vol. 86, No. 3 (1999), pp. 1231–50.

46. Emilio Mignone, *Derechos Humanos y Sociedad: El Caso Argentino* (Buenos Aires: Ediciones del Pensamiento Nacional and Centro de Estudios Legales y Sociales, 1991), p. 66, quoted in Kathryn Sikkink, "Human Rights, Principled Issue-Networks, and Sovereignty in Latin America," *International Organization*, Vol. 47, No. 3 (1993), fn. 37, p. 423.

47. Armony, *Argentina, the United States, and the Anti-Communist Crusade in Central America, 1977–1984*, pp. 4–14.

48. Moyano, *Argentina's Lost Patrol*, pp. 1–3.

49. Ibid., p. 157.

50. Ibid., p. 93.

51. Ibid., p. 102.

52. Ibid., p. 105.

53. Ibid., p. 108.

54. Keck and Sikkink, *Activists Beyond Borders*, p. 109, using data from the 1984 Argentine National Commission on the Disappeared (CONADEP).

55. See ibid., Figure 3, "Disappearances in Argentina, 1971–1983," p. 108 (using data from the report of CONADEP, the Argentine National Commission on the Disappeared); and Moyano, *Argentina's Lost*

Patrol, Figure 6.2, "Incidents of Agitational and Enforcement Violence, 1969–79," p. 94 (using data compiled by Moyano from contemporary press reports).

56. Moyano, *Argentina's Lost Patrol*, p. 155.
57. Ibid., p. 93.
58. Ibid., p. 96. Also see Ariel C. Armony, *The Dubious Link: Civic Engagement and Democratization* (Palo Alto, CA: Stanford University Press, 2004).
59. Armony, *Argentina, the United States, and the Anti-Communist Crusade*, pp. 28–9.
60. Ibid., p. 152.
61. Dinges, *The Condor Years*.
62. Armony, *Argentina, the United States, and the Anti-Communist Crusade*, Chapter 4, "Argentina and the Nicaraguan Contras."
63. Cohen, "Human Rights Decision-Making," p. 222.
64. Armony, *Argentina, the United States, and the Anti-Communist Crusade*, pp. 46–7 and 145–52.
65. Ibid., p. 45.
66. Ibid., p. 64.
67. Brysk, *The Politics of Human Rights in Argentina*, p. 6.
68. Samuel P. Huntington, *The Third Wave: Democratization in the Late Twentieth Century* (Norman, OK: University of Oklahoma Press, 1991).
69. Arie M. Kacowicz, "Latin America as an International Society," *International Politics*, Vol. 37 (2000), pp. 143–62.
70. See Tamar Jacoby, "The Reagan Turnaround on Human Rights," *Foreign Affairs*, Vol. 64 (Summer, 1986), pp. 1066–86; and Aryeh Neier, "Human Rights in the Reagan Era: Acceptance in Principle," *The Annals of the American Academy of Political and Social Science*, Vol. 506 (November 1989), pp. 30–41.
71. Korey, *NGOs and the Universal Declaration*, p. 111. See also Daniel C. Thomas, *The Helsinki Effect: International Norms, Human Rights, and the Demise of Communism* (Princeton, NJ: Princeton University Press, 2001).
72. Jeane Kirkpatrick, "Dictatorships and Double Standards," *Commentary* (November 1979), pp. 34–45.
73. Ronald Reagan, "Promoting Democracy and Peace," United States Department of State Bureau of Public Affairs, Washington, DC, Speech delivered before the British Parliament, London, June 8, 1982, <www.ned.org/about/reagan-060882.html>.
74. David Lowe, "Idea to Reality: A Brief History of the National Endowment for Democracy" (Washington, DC: The National Endowment for Democracy, 2001), <www.ned.org/about/nedhistory.html>.
75. See Roland Rich, "Bringing Democracy into International Law," *Journal of Democracy*, Vol. 12, No. 3 (July 2001), pp. 20–34.
76. See Jacoby, "The Reagan Turnaround on Human Rights."
77. Juan Linz and Alfred Stepan, "Political Crafting of Democratic Consolidation or Destruction: European and South American Comparisons," in Robert A. Pastor (ed.), *Democracy in the Americas: Stopping the Pendulum* (New York: Holmes and Meier, 1989), p. 47. For a recent expression of this

idea, see Fernando Henrique Cardoso, "Democracy as a Starting Point," *Journal of Democracy*, Vol. 12, No. 1 (2001), pp. 5–14.
78. Mehran Kamrava and Frank O. Mora, "Civil Society and Democratization in Comparative Perspective: Latin America and the Middle East," *Third World Quarterly*, Vol. 19, No. 5 (1998), p. 902, quoting Francisco Weffort, *Qual Democracia?* (São Paulo: Companhia Das Letras, 1992), pp. 42–69.
79. Castañeda, *Utopia Unarmed*, p. 308.
80. Ibid., p. 235.

CHAPTER 5

1. Daniel C. Thomas, *The Helsinki Effect: International Norms, Human Rights, and the Demise of Communism* (Princeton, NJ: Princeton University Press, 2001); Peter Ackerman and Jack Duvall, *A Force More Powerful: A Century of Nonviolent Conflict* (New York: Palgrave, 2000); Guillermo O'Donnell and Philippe C. Schmitter, *Transitions from Authoritarian Rule: Tentative Conclusions about Uncertain Democracies* (Baltimore, MD: Johns Hopkins University Press, 1986).
2. Rewards For Justice, Diplomatic Security Service, U.S. Department of State, <www.dssrewards.net>.
3. Gil Loescher, *Beyond Charity: International Cooperation and the Global Refugee Crisis* (Oxford: Oxford University Press, 1993); Roberta Cohen and Francis Deng, *Masses in Flight: The Global Crisis of Internal Displacement* (Washington, DC: Brookings, 1998); David P. Forsythe, *Human Rights in International Relations* (Cambridge: Cambridge University Press, 2000); Samantha Power, *"A Problem From Hell": America and the Age of Genocide* (New York: Basic Books, 2002); Brian H. Smith, *More than Altruism: The Politics of Private Foreign Aid* (Princeton, NJ: Princeton University Press, 1990); John F. Hutchinson, *Champions of Charity: War and the Rise of the Red Cross* (Boulder, CO: Westview, 1996); John Paul Lederach, *Building Peace: Sustainable Reconciliation in Divided Societies* (Washington, DC: United States Institute of Peace Press, 1998)
4. Mark R. Duffield, *Global Governance and the New Wars: The Merging of Development and Security* (London: Zed Books, 2001); William DeMars, "War and Mercy in Africa," *World Policy Journal*, Vol. 17, No. 2 (Summer 2000), pp. 1–10; Alex de Waal, *Famine Crimes: Politics and the Disaster Relief Industry in Africa* (Oxford: James Currey, 1997).
5. William E. DeMars, "Hazardous Partnership: NGOs and United States Intelligence in Small Wars," *International Journal of Intelligence and CounterIntelligence*, Vol. 14, No. 2 (2001), pp. 193–222.
6. For the distinction between the view of Balkan wars as the upwelling of "primordial nationalism," and the alternate "instrumentalist conception of nationalism" followed here, see Mary Kaldor, *New and Old Wars: Organized Violence in a Global Era* (Stanford, CA: Stanford University Press, 1999), pp. 32–44.
7. Susan Woodward, *Balkan Tragedy: Chaos and Dissolution after the Cold War* (Washington, DC: Brookings, 1995).
8. Kaldor, *New and Old Wars*.

9. Norman Cigar, *Genocide in Bosnia: The Policy of "Ethnic Cleansing"* (College Station, TX: Texas A&M University Press, 1995).

10. David Keen and John Ryle, "Editorial: The Fate of Information in the Disaster Zone," *Disasters*, Vol. 20, No. 3 (1996), pp. 169–72; Mark Duffield, "The Symphony of the Damned: Racial Discourse, Complex Political Emergencies and Humanitarian Aid," *Disasters*, Vol. 20, No. 3 (1996), pp. 173–93.

11. De Waal, *Famine Crimes*, p. 83.

12. See Roy Gutman, *A Witness to Genocide* (New York: Macmillan, 1993); Ed Villiamy, *Seasons in Hell: Understanding Bosnia's War* (London: Simon & Schuster, 1994).

13. Quoted in Power, *"A Problem From Hell,"* p. 279.

14. Ibid., pp. 265–81.

15. Charles Lane and Thom Shanker, "Bosnia: What the CIA Didn't Tell Us," *The New York Review of Books*, May 9, 1996, p. 10.

16. Power, *"A Problem From Hell,"* p. 556, fn. 62.

17. Roger Cohen, "C.I.A. Report Finds Serbs Guilty of Majority of Bosnia War Crimes," *New York Times*, March 9, 1995. See also Lane and Shanker, "Bosnia: What the CIA Didn't Tell Us," p. 12.

18. Power, *"A Problem From Hell,"* p. 264.

19. Larry Minear, Jeffrey Clark, Roberta Cohen, Dennis Gallagher, Iain Guest, and Thomas G. Weiss, *Humanitarian Action in the Former Yugoslavia: The U.N.'s Role 1991–1993* (Occasional Paper #18, Thomas J. Watson Jr. Institute for International Studies, Brown University, 1994), pp. 40–3.

20. Interview by author with Nancy Bearg Dyke, 1989–93 Director of International Programs and Public Diplomacy for the National Security Council, September 28, 1995, Washington, DC.

21. Scott Anderson, *The Man Who Tried to Save the World* (New York: Doubleday, 1999), p. 130; Richard Holbrooke, *To End a War* (New York: Random House, 1998), p. 340.

22. Anderson, *The Man Who Tried to Save the World*, pp. 132–52.

23. William Korey, *NGOs and the Universal Declaration of Human Rights* (New York: St. Martin's Press, 1998), p. 320.

24. Helsinki Watch, *War Crimes in Bosnia-Hercegovina* (New York: Human Rights Watch, August 1992), pp. vii, 1, and 6.

25. Roy Gutman, "Prisoners of Serbia's War," *Newsday*, July 19, 1992.

26. Helsinki Watch, *War Crimes in Bosnia-Hercegovina*, pp. 66–7.

27. Power, *"A Problem From Hell,"* pp. 264–5.

28. Lane and Shanker, "Bosnia: What the CIA Didn't Tell Us," pp. 10 and 12.

29. The phrase is from Kaldor, *New and Old Wars*, p. 4.

30. For an account based heavily on reports of local journalists, see Cigar, *Genocide in Bosnia*.

31. Gary Jonathan Bass, *Stay the Hand of Vengeance: The Politics of War Crimes Tribunals* (Princeton, NJ: Princeton University Press, 2000), p. 33.

32. On his purposeful inattention to nonstate actors, see ibid., p. 280.

33. Aryeh Neier, *War Crimes: Brutality, Genocide, Terror, and the Struggle for Justice* (New York: Times Books, 1998), p. 120.

34. Neier, *War Crimes*, pp. 120–33; Bass, *Stay the Hand of Vengeance*, p. 210; Power, *"A Problem From Hell,"* pp. 288–92.
35. Neier, *War Crimes*, p. 135.
36. Minear et al., *Humanitarian Action in the Former Yugoslavia*, pp. 42, 69.
37. Michael Ignatieff, *The Warrior's Honor: Ethnic War and the Modern Conscience* (New York: Henry Holt, 1997), p. 136.
38. Nicholas O. Berry, *War and the Red Cross: The Unspoken Mission* (New York: St. Martin's Press, 1997), p. 73.
39. For the charge and a reproduction of the UN memo, see Helsinki Watch, *War Crimes in Bosnia-Hercegovina*, pp. 15, 228–9.
40. Bass, *Stay the Hand of Vengeance*, p. 207 (emphasis in original).
41. Ibid., p. 211.
42. M. Cherif Bassiouni, "Opening Remarks," Conference sponsored by the Center for Civil and Human Rights at Notre Dame Law School, "From Ad Hoc Tribunals for the former Yugoslavia and Rwanda to a Permanent International Criminal Court: Reflections and Recommendations," University of Notre Dame, Indiana, March 23, 1996. Also see M. Cherif Bassiouni, "Former Yugoslavia: Investigating Violations of International Law and Establishing an International Criminal Tribunal," *Fordham International Law Journal*, Vol. 18, No. 4 (1995), pp. 1191–1211.
43. Lane and Shanker, "Bosnia: What the CIA Didn't Tell Us," pp. 10, 12.
44. International Human Rights Law Institute, DePaul University College of Law, <www.depaul.edu/opportunities/institutes_centers/ihrli/default.asp>.
45. "WCL Inaugurates War Crimes Tribunal Research Office," *The Human Rights Brief*, Vol. 3, No. 1 (Fall 1995), Center for Human Rights and Humanitarian Law, Washington College of Law at American University, p. 20.
46. Scott Johnson, "Next Big Trial Will Expose Bosnian Horror," *Buffalo News*, November 10, 1995.
47. Korey, *NGOs and the Universal Declaration*, p. 322.
48. Neier, *War Crimes*, pp. 9–11.
49. Christopher Joyce and Eric Stover, *Witnesses from the Grave: The Stories Bones Tell* (Boston: Little, Brown, 1991); Margaret E. Keck and Kathryn Sikkink, *Activists Beyond Borders* (Ithaca, NY: Cornell University Press, 1998), pp. 94, 109–10.
50. William D. Haglund, Melissa Connor, and Douglas D. Scott, "The Archeology of Mass Graves," *Historical Archeology*, Vol. 35, No. 1 (2000), pp. 57–69; Eric Stover and Gilles Peress, *The Graves: Srebrenica and Vukovar* (Berlin: Scalo, 1998); Elizabeth Neuffer, *The Key to My Neighbor's House: Seeking Justice in Bosnia and Rwanda* (New York: Picador, 2001), pp. 221–47; Korey, *NGOs and the Universal Declaration*, Chapter 17, "The 'Unexplored Continent' of Physicians Involvement in Human Rights"; Bass, *Stay the Hand of Vengeance*, pp. 224–5.
51. *Non-Governmental Organizations and the Tribunals: A New Partnership* (Oslo: The Royal Norwegian Ministry of Foreign Affairs, 1996), p. 108, quoted in Korey, *NGOs and the Universal Declaration*, p. 337.
52. Korey, *NGOs and the Universal Declaration*, p. 331.
53. Holbrooke, *To End a War*, pp. 35, 46.

54. See Korey, *NGOs and the Universal Declaration*, pp. 334–6; and the website of the Coalition for International Justice, <www.cij.org>.

55. For example, see Anthony Lloyd, "Srebrenica's Exiles Tell Grimly Familiar Stories of Murder," *The Times* (London), July 15, 1995. In another NGO connection, Richard Holbrooke's son Stanley worked for Refugees International, and went to Tuzla with Lionel Rosenblatt to interview refugees from Srebrenica: see Holbrooke, *To End a War*, p. 69.

56. Korey, *NGOs and the Universal Declaration*, pp. 327–8.

57. Stephen Engelberg and Tim Weiner, "Srebrenica: The Days of Slaughter," *New York Times*, October 29, 1995.

58. Eric Schmitt, "Spy Photos Indicate Mass Grave at Serb-Held Town, U.S. Says," *New York Times*, August 10, 1995; Barbara Crossette, "U.S. Seeks to Prove Mass Killings," *New York Times*, August 11, 1995.

59. The Hague Tribunal issued indictments of two Croatian generals in 2001 for their role in Operation Storm. See Carlotta Gall and Marlise Simons, "Croatia in Turmoil after Agreeing to Send 2 to Tribunal," *New York Times*, July 9, 2001.

60. Holbrooke, *To End a War*, pp. 72–3.

61. The accusation first emerged in Yves Goulet, "Washington's Freelance Advisors," *Jane's Intelligence Review*, Vol. 10, No. 7 (1998), pp. 38–41. See also, Leslie Wayne, "America's For-Profit Secret Army," *New York Times*, October 13, 2002; and Raymond Bonner, "War Crimes Panel Finds Croat Troops 'Cleansed' the Serbs," *New York Times*, March 21, 1999.

62. Holbrooke, *To End a War*, p. 98.

63. Quoted in Bass, *Stay the Hand of Vengeance*, p. 239.

64. Ibid., pp. 244–5.

65. Ibid., p. 236.

66. Ibid., p. 245.

67. Michael Ignatieff, *Virtual War: Kosovo and Beyond* (New York: Henry Holt: 2000).

68. Hugh Griffiths, "Evidence Gathering: The Role of NGOs," *The Tribunals*, Magazine of the Crimes of War Project, May 2001, <www.crimesofwar. org/tribun-mag/relate_ngo_print.html>. For the 290 page public report of the mission, see International Crisis Group, *Reality Demands: Documenting Violations of International Humanitarian Law in Kosovo 1999*, June 27, 2000, <www.crisisweb.org/projects/balkans/kosovo/reports/A400057_ 27062000.pdf>.

69. On the intelligence sought by the Tribunal, and provided by the U.S., see Marlise Simons, "War Crimes Panel Seeks NATO Aid on Milosevic," *International Herald Tribune*, April 15, 1999; and William Branigan, "The Shadow of Intelligence: U.S. Gave Tribunal Classified Data," *International Herald Tribune*, May 29–30, 1999. On Louise Arbour's denial that U.S. intelligence determined the timing of the indictment, see Ignatieff, *Virtual War*, pp. 118–25.

70. On the indictments and trial of Milosevic, see websites for the International Criminal Tribunal for the Former Yugoslavia, <www.un.org/icty>; and the Coalition for International Justice, <www.cij.org>.

71. Peter Ackerman and Jack Duvall, *A Force More Powerful: A Century of Nonviolent Conflict* (New York: Palgrave, 2000), pp. 478–89; "Strategic

Nonviolent Action Key to Serbia's Revolution," *PeaceWatch*, Journal of the United States Institute of Peace, Vol. 7, No. 1 (December 2000); "Bringing Down a Dictator: In His Own Words—Col. Robert Helvey," Excerpt from interview with Steve York, Belgrade, January 29, 2002, on website for PBS documentary, *Bringing Down a Dictator*, <www.pbs.org/weta/dictator/otpor/ownwords/helvey.html>.

72. Bass, *Stay the Hand of Vengeance*, pp. 311–24.

73. The term "NGO-ization" was coined by Paul Gifford in reference to the reliance of African churches on international NGOs. See Paul Gifford, "Some Recent Developments in African Christianity," *African Affairs*, Vol. 93 (1994), p. 521.

74. James R. Steinberg, "International Involvement in the Yugoslav Conflict," in Lori Fisler Damrosch (ed.), *Enforcing Restraint: Collective Intervention in Internal Conflicts* (New York: Council on Foreign Relations Press, 1993); Susan Woodward, "International Aspects of the Wars in Former Yugoslavia," in Jasminka Udovicki and James Ridgeway (eds), *Burn This House: The Making and Unmaking of Yugoslavia* (Durham, NC: Duke University Press, 1997).

75. On UN human rights investigations and reports, see Minear et al., *Humanitarian Action in the Former Yugoslavia*, pp. 31–4. On charges that UN civilian or military personnel withheld information on atrocities in Bosnia, see Helsinki Watch, *War Crimes in Bosnia-Hercegovina*, p. 15; and Neuffer, *The Key to My Neighbor's House*, pp. 325–6. On the general fecklessness of UNPROFOR in Bosnia, see Roger Cohen, *Hearts Grown Brutal: Sagas of Sarajevo* (New York: Random House, 1998), Chapter 18, "A Death Observed."

76. Thomas G. Weiss and Amir Pasic, "Reinventing UNHCR: Enterprising Humanitarians in the Former Yugoslavia, 1991–1995," *Global Governance*, Vol. 3 (1997), pp. 41–57; Amir Pasic and Thomas Weiss, "The Politics of Rescue: Yugoslavia's Wars and the Humanitarian Impulse," *Ethics and International Affairs*, Vol. 11 (1997), pp. 105–31.

77. See Woodward, "International Aspects of the Wars in Former Yugoslavia," pp. 235–6.

78. Ignatieff, *The Warrior's Honor*, pp. 136–7.

79. Alan J. Kuperman, "Transnational Causes of Genocide: How the West Inadvertently Exacerbates Ethnic Conflict," in Raju G. C. Thomas (ed.), *Yugoslavia Unraveled: Sovereignty, Self-Determination, Intervention* (Lanham, MD: Lexington Books, 2003).

80. On journalists and the Bosnian strategy, see Nik Gowing, "Real-Time Television Coverage of Armed Conflicts and Diplomatic Crises: Does it Pressure or Distort Foreign Policy Decisions?" The Joan Shorenstein Barone Center on the Press, Politics and Public Policy, Harvard University, Working Paper 94–1 (June 1994), pp. 59–66.

81. Steven Erlanger, "Tribunal Plays Down Kosovo Study," *International Herald Tribune*, December 30, 1999; Barbara Crossette, "Helms Blasts UN, and UN Fires Back," *International Herald Tribune*, January 21, 2000.

82. Fanny Benedetti and John L. Washburn, "Drafting the International Criminal Court Treaty: Two Years to Rome and an Afterword on the Rome Diplomatic Conference," *Global Governance*, Vol. 5, No. 1 (1999),

pp. 1–37; and Korey, *NGOs and the International Declaration*, pp. 524–33.

83. See Coalition for an International Criminal Court, website at <www. iccnow.org>.

84. Peter Slevin, "U.S. Presses Allies on War Crimes Court," *Washington Post*, August 27, 2002.

85. David Rieff, "A New Age of Liberal Imperialism?" *World Policy Journal*, Vol. 16, No. 2 (1999), pp. 1–10.

86. See Marc Weller, "Undoing the Global Constitution: UN Security Council Action on the International Criminal Court," *International Affairs*, Vol. 78, No. 4 (2002), pp. 693–712; and David B. Rivkin, Jr., Lee A. Casey and Darin R. Bartram, "When Justice for All isn't Fair," *Washington Post*, April 7, 2002.

CHAPTER 6

1. Stanley Johnson, *Politics of Population: The International Conference on Population and Development, Cairo 1994* (London: Earthscan, 1995).

2. For United Nations documents concerning the Cairo conference, see United Nations Population Information Network, International Conference on Population and Development, <www.un.org/popin/icpd2. htm>.

3. Margaret E. Keck and Kathryn Sikkink, *Activists Beyond Borders: Advocacy Networks in International Politics* (Ithaca, NY: Cornell University Press, 1998), pp. 189–90.

4. Betsy Hartmann, *Reproductive Rights and Wrongs: The Global Politics of Population Control* (Boston: South End Press, 1995), p. xviii.

5. Ibid., p. 137.

6. Ibid., p. 134.

7. Ibid., p. 140.

8. Ibid., p. 138.

9. Ann Marie Clark, Elisabeth J. Friedman, and Kathryn Hochstetler, "The Sovereign Limits of Global Civil Society: A Comparison of NGO Participation in UN World Conferences on the Environment, Human Rights, and Women," *World Politics*, Vol. 51, No. 1 (1998), p. 23. See also Kerstin Martens, "NGO Participation at International Conferences: Assessing Theoretical Accounts," *Transnational Associations*, Vol. 3 (2000), p. 119.

10. Tanya Melich, *The Republican War Against Women: An Insider's Report from Behind the Lines* (New York: Bantam, 1996).

11. Alejandro Bermudez, "Why Latin American Countries Aren't Pro-Life at the U.N.," *National Catholic Register*, Vol. 78, No. 28 (July 14–20, 2002), p. 1.

12. Deborah Barrett, "Reproducing Persons as a Global Concern: The Making of an Institution" (PhD Dissertation, Stanford University, 1995); Deborah Barrett and David John Frank, "Population Control for National Development: From World Discourse to National Policies," in John Boli and George M. Thomas (eds), *Constructing World Culture:*

International Nongovernmental Organizations since 1875 (Stanford, CA: Stanford University Press, 1999).

13. Linda Gordon, *Woman's Body, Woman's Right: A Social History of Birth Control in America* (New York: Grossman, 1976), p. 394.
14. Donald T. Critchlow, *Intended Consequences: Birth Control, Abortion, and the Federal Government in Modern America* (Oxford: Oxford University Press, 1999), p. 20.
15. Gordon, *Woman's Body, Woman's Right*, p. 396.
16. Barrett and Frank, "Population Control for National Development," p. 214.
17. Ibid., pp. 218–19.
18. David John Frank, Ann Hironka, John M. Meyer, Evan Shofer, and Nancy Brandon Tuma, "The Rationalization and Organization of Nature in World Culture," in Boli and Thomas (eds), *Constructing World Culture*, p. 85.
19. Barrett, "Reproducing Persons as a Global Concern," p. 214.
20. Nitza Berkovitch, "The Emergence and Transformation of the International Women's Movement," in Boli and Thomas (eds), *Constructing World Culture*, p. 122.
21. Hartmann, *Reproductive Rights and Wrongs*, pp. 141–2.
22. See Brad Erickson, *Call to Action: Handbook for Ecology, Peace and Justice* (San Francisco: Sierra Club Books, 1990), cited in Hartmann, *Reproductive Rights and Wrongs*, p. 335.
23. Hartmann, *Reproductive Rights and Wrongs*, pp. 143–4.
24. Berkovitch, "The Emergence and Transformation of the International Women's Movement," p. 122.
25. Keck and Sikkink, *Activists Beyond Borders*, pp. 171–81.
26. Ibid., p. 182.
27. Ibid., p. 187.
28. Hartmann, *Reproductive Rights and Wrongs*, p. 120.
29. Currently, the Ford Foundation maintains regional offices in Mexico City, Rio de Janeiro, Santiago, Cairo, Lagos, Nairobi, Johannesburg, Moscow, New Delhi, Hanoi, Jakarta, Manila, and Beijing, <www.fordfound.org>. I administered three small Ford Foundation grants in Cairo, Egypt during 1996.
30. Population Council, *Annual Report 2002* (New York, 2003), and interviews by author at Population Council office in Nairobi, Kenya, in September 1999.
31. Rajni Kothari, "The Yawning Vacuum: A World without Alternatives," *Alternatives*, Vol. 18, No. 2 (1993), pp. 133–4.
32. Hartmann, *Reproductive Rights and Wrongs*, pp. 123–4.
33. Ibid., pp. 146–7.
34. Ibid., pp. 148–9.
35. Archbishop Jean-Louis Tauran, "The Presence of the Holy See in the International Organizations," Lecture at the Catholic University of the Sacred Heart, Milan, Italy (April 22, 2002), emphasis in original, <www.vatican.va/roman_curia/secretariat_state/documents/rc_seg-st_doc_20020422_tauran_en.html>.

36. For more NGO wars over family politics, see Doris Buss and Didi Herman, *Globalizing Family Values: The Christian Right in Global Politics* (Minneapolis, MN: University of Minnesota Press, 2003).
37. Malcolm Gladwell, "John Rock's Error," *The New Yorker* (March 10, 2000), <www.gladwell.com/2000/2000_03_10_a_rock.htm>.
38. Charles B. Keely, "Limits to Papal Power: Vatican Inaction after *Humanae Vitae*," and Barbara B. Crane, "The Transnational Politics of Abortion," both in Jason L. Finkle and C. Alison McIntosh (eds), *The New Politics of Population: Conflict and Consensus in Family Planning* (New York: The Population Council, 1994).
39. "A Mouse That Roars Turns 25: An Interview with CFFC President Frances Kissling" (May 1998), Catholics For a Free Choice, <www.cath4choice.org/aboutus2.htm>.
40. "CFFC See Change Campaign," Catholics For a Free Choice, <www.seechange.org/bluebottom5c.htm>.
41. "Holy See Campaign," Catholic Family and Human Rights Institute, <www.c-fam.org/HolySee/index.html>.
42. As of April 2003, Catholics For a Free Choice had garnered more than 700 NGO endorsers for the See Change campaign, and the Catholic Family and Human Rights Institutes had assembled more than 4,000 for its Holy See counter-campaign.
43. Hartmann, *Reproductive Rights and Wrongs*, p. 22, citing Paul R. Ehrlich and Anne H. Ehrlich, *The Population Explosion* (New York: Simon and Schuster, 1990), p. 58.
44. Barrett and Frank, "Population Control for National Development," pp. 209–10.

CHAPTER 7

1. INFACT, "Challenging Corporate Abuse, Building Grassroots Power Since 1977," <www.infact.org/aboutinf.html>.
2. INFACT Canada, <www.infactcanada.ca/InfactHomePage.htm>.
3. Carlos Osorio (ed.), "State Department Opens Files on Argentina's Dirty War," National Security Archive Briefing Book No. 73 (August 21, 2002), <www.gwu.edu/~nsarchiv/NSAEBB/NSAEBB73/>; Centro de Estudios Legales y Sociales, "El Estado Terrorista Desenmascarado," Selección de documentos realizada por The National Security Archive y el Centro de Estudios Legales y Sociales (October 2001), <www.cels.org.ar/Site_cels/ejes/a_justicia/justicia_archivos/estado_terr.html>.
4. Kevin Gray, "Argentina 'Dirty War' Moms Claim Victory," *Washington Post*, August 21, 2003; Abuelas de Plaza de Mayo, <www.abuelas.org.ar>.
5. "FACTBOX-NGOs Responding to Iran Earthquake," Reuters AlertNet, December 29, 2003.
6. Andrew S. Natsios, *The Great North Korean Famine* (Washington, DC: U.S. Institute of Peace Press, 2001).
7. Interviews by author in Nairobi, during September 1999.
8. International Rescue Committee, "Mortality in the Democratic Republic of Congo: Results from a Nationwide Survey," International Rescue

Committee (April 2003), <intranet.theirc.org/docs/drc_mortality_iii_full. pdf>, p. i.

9. International Rescue Committee, "The IRC in the Democratic Republic of Congo," <www.theirc.org/DRCongo/index.cfm>; International Rescue Committee, "Mortality in the Democratic Republic of Congo," pp. 4 and 7.

10. Tom Clynes, "Militia OK'd to Shoot Poachers in Africa," *National Geographic News*, September 24, 2002, <news.nationalgeographic.com/ news/2002/09/0924_020924_poaching.html>. Also see "Q&A: Africa's Deadliest Conservationist," *National Geographic Adventure* (January/ February 2002), <www.nationalgeographic.com/adventure/0201/q_n_ a.html>.

11. "Chinko River," Africa Rainforest and River Conservation, Inc., <www. Africa-rainforest.org/expeditions.html>.

12. Jarol B. Manheim, *The Death of a Thousand Cuts: Corporate Campaigns and the Attack on the Corporation* (Mahwah, NJ: Lawrence Erlbaum Associates, 2001).

13. Manheim, *The Death of a Thousand Cuts*, Appendix B, "Anticorporate Campaigns Launched by Nonlabor Entities, 1989–1999," pp. 341–6.

14. Joyce Nelson, "Great Global Greenwash: Burson-Marstellar, Pax Trilateral, and the Brundtland Gang vs. the Environment," *Covert Action Quarterly*, No. 44 (Spring 1993), pp. 26–33, 57–8.

15. John Gerard Ruggie, "global_governance.net: The Global Compact as Learning Network," *Global Governance*, Vol. 7, No. 4 (2001), pp. 371–8.

16. Kenny Bruno and Joshua Karliner, "Tangled up in Blue: Corporate Partnerships at the United Nations," TRAC—Transnational Resource and Action Center (September 2000), <www.corpwatch.org/upload/ document/tangled.pdf>.

17. "Who we are," SustainAbility, <www.sustainability.com/philosophy/who-we-are/default.asp>, September 2003.

18. See SustainAbility, *The 21st Century NGO: In the Market for Change* (Brooklyn, NY: SustainAbility, 2003); and the companion report, "The 21st Century NGO—White Paper" (2003), SustainAbility, <www.sustainability. com/programs/pressure-front/21-NGO-white-paper.pdf>.

19. "Chad Pipeline Plays a Role in Development," *Wall Street Journal*, June 25, 2003.

20. Marina Ottaway, "Corporatism Goes Global: International Organizations, Nongovernmental Organization Networks, and Transnational Business," *Global Governance*, Vol. 7, No. 3 (2001), p. 287.

21. Karl Taro Greenfeld, "The New Philanthropy," *Time Magazine*, July 24, 2000.

22. Ron Kampeas, "New Philanthropy: Billionaires Decide Exactly Where Dollars Go," Associated Press, February 6, 2001.

23. The Turner Foundation, <www.turnerfoundation.org>; The United Nations Foundation, <www.unfoundation.org>.

24. The Bill and Melinda Gates Foundation, "Grant Highlights," June 2003, <www.gatesfoundation.org/Grants>; Bill and Melinda Gates Foundation, *2002 Annual Report* (Seattle, WA: Bill and Melinda Gates Foundation,

2002); and *2001 Annual Report* (Seattle, WA: Bill and Melinda Gates Foundation, 2001).

25. Judith Miller, "A Giver's Agenda," *New York Times*, December 17, 1996.
26. Open Society Institute, *Building Open Societies: Soros Foundations Network 2002 Report* (New York: Open Society Institute, 2003).
27. Repromed International, <www.repromedinternational.com>.
28. Reproductive Cloning Network, <www.reproductivecloning.net>; and Human Cloning Foundation, <www.humancloning.org>.
29. Clonaid, <www.clonaid.com/index.html>, emphasis added.
30. Clonaid, <www.clonaid.com/index.html>.
31. BBC News, "On 23 November 2003, Sir David Frost interviewed Dr Brigitte Boisselier and Nigel Cameron," BBC Breakfast with Frost, November 23, 2003, <news.bbc.co.uk/1/programmes/breakfast_with_frost/3231072.stm>.
32. World Transhumanist Association, "Meet the WTA Board of Directors," <www.transhumanism.org/board.htm>.
33. World Transhumanist Association, "The Transhumanist Declaration," <www.transhumanism.org/declaration.htm>.
34. Immortality Institute, <www.imminst.org>.
35. BLTC Research, "Mission Statement," <www.bltc.com>.
36. Richard Cohen, "Unsettling, Maybe, But Not Unethical," *Washington Post*, January 2, 2003.
37. Christopher Manes, *Green Rage: Radical Environmentalism and the Unmaking of Civilization* (Boston, MA: Little, Brown and Co., 1990), pp. 69–70. See also Dave Foreman, *Confessions of an Eco-Warrior* (New York: Harmony Books, 1991); and Edward Abbey, *The Monkey Wrench Gang* (Philadelphia, PA: Lippincott, 1975).
38. Dave Foreman (ed.), *Ecodefense: A Field Guide to Monkeywrenching* (Tucson, AZ: Ned Ludd Books, 1985); Bill Devall and George Sessions, *Deep Ecology* (Salt Lake City, UT: Gibbs Smith, 1985); Arne Naess, "The Shallow and the Deep, Long Range Ecology Movements: A Summary," *Inquiry* 16 (Oslo, 1973), pp. 95–100.
39. Devall and Sessions, *Deep Ecology*, p. 67.
40. Foreman, *Confessions of an Eco-Warrior*, pp. 25–7.
41. Manes, *Green Rage*, p. 25.
42. Quoted in Rik Scarce, *Eco-Warriors: Understanding the Radical Environmental Movement* (Chicago: Noble Press, 1990), p. 92.
43. Miss Ann Thropy, "Population and AIDS," *EarthFirst! Journal*, Vol. 8, No. 2 (December 22, 1987), quoted in Scarce, *Eco-Warriors*, p. 92.
44. Robin Webb (ALF Press Officer), "Animal Liberation—By 'Whatever Means Necessary'," Animal Liberation Front, <www.animalliberationfront.com/ALFront/alf_summary.htm>.
45. Monte Morin and Julie Tamaki, "Secret Group Offers Web Terrorism Guide," *Los Angeles Times*, August 23, 2003; Rodney Coronado, "San Diego Fire," *EarthFirst! Journal*, September 2003, <earthliberationfront.com/news/2003/090203a.shmtl>.
46. Earth Liberation Front, <www.earthliberationfront.com>; Animal Liberation Front, <www.animalliberationfront.com>.

47. See contact pages of the ELF and ALF websites, <earthliberationfront. com/media/>, <www.earthliberationfront.com/feedback.shtml>, and <animalliberationfront.com/feedback.htm>.

48. Webb, "Animal Liberation."

49. "Meet the E.L.F.," <www.earthliberationfront.com/about/>, and "What is the ALF?" <www.animalliberationfront.com/ALFront/WhatisALF. htm>.

50. Julie Tamaki, Jia-Rui Chong and Mitchell Landsberg, "Radicals Target SUVs in Series of Southland Attacks," *Los Angeles Times*, August 23, 2003.

51. Quoted in Audrey Hudson, "ELF Admits to Arson at Forest Service Lab," *Washington Times*, September 10, 2002.

52. People for the Ethical Treatment of Animals, <www.peta.org>.

53. "Frequently Asked Questions," PETA, <www.peta.org/fp/gaq.html>.

54. Southern Poverty Law Center, "From Push to Shove," *Intelligence Report*, Issue 107 (Fall 2002), <www.splcenter.org/intelligenceproject/ip-4w3. html>.

55. See, for example, Michael Pollan, "An Animal's Place," *New York Times Magazine*, November 10, 2002.

56. Martin Luther King, Jr., "Letter From Birmingham Jail," in Martin Luther King, Jr., *Why We Can't Wait* (New York: Harper & Row, 1964), p. 85.

57. Jeremy Bentham, *Introduction to the Principles of Morals and Legislation*, Chapter 17; quoted in Peter Singer, *Animal Liberation* (New York: New York Review, 1975), p. 8.

58. Peter Berger (ed.), *The Desecularization of the World: Resurgent Religion and World Politics* (Grand Rapids, WI: Wm. B. Eerdmans, 1999); David Westerlund (ed.), *Questioning the Secular State: The Worldwide Resurgence of Religion in Politics* (London: I. B. Tauris, 1996); Mark Juergensmeyer, *Terror in the Mind of God: The Global Rise of Religious Violence* (Berkeley, CA: University of California, 2000); Scott M. Thomas, "Taking Religious and Cultural Pluralism Seriously: The Global Resurgence of Religion and the Transformation of International Society," *Millennium: Journal of International Studies*, Vol. 29, No. 3 (2000), pp. 815–41.

59. Francis Fukuyama, *The End of History and the Last Man* (New York: Free Press, 1992).

60. Brian W. Smith, *More Than Altruism: The Politics of Private Foreign Aid* (Princeton, NJ: Princeton University Press, 1990).

61. Susanne Hoeber Rudolph, "Introduction: Religions, States, and Transnational Civil Society," in Susanne Hoeber Rudolph and James Piscatori (eds), *Transnational Religion and Failing States* (Boulder, CO: Westview Press, 1997), p. 1.

62. These variations are illustrated by the contributors to Rudolph and Piscatori (eds), *Transnational Religion and Failing States*.

63. Paul Gifford, "Some Recent Developments in African Christianity," *African Affairs*, Vol. 93 (1994), p. 521.

64. Jillian Schwedler (ed.), *Toward Civil Society in the Middle East? A Primer* (Boulder, CO: Lynne Rienner, 1995).

65. "Puebla Institute," Profile by GroupWatch (Albuquerque, NM: Interhemispheric Resource Center, April 1989), <www.namebase.org/ gw/puebla.txt>.

66. William Korey, *NGOs and the Universal Declaration of Human Rights* (New York: St. Martin's Press, 1998), Chapter 18, "Freedom House's Changing Priorities"; Paul Blustein, "Crusader for a Religious Right: Michael Horowitz Hopes to Stop Persecution of Christians," *Washington Post*, September 30, 1997.
67. Korey, *NGOs and the Universal Declaration*, pp. 462–7.
68. United States Commission on International Religious Freedom, <www.uscirf.org>; and Office of International Religious Freedom, U.S. Department of State, <www.state.gov/g/drl/irf/>.
69. Nat Hentoff, "Genocide: Sudan Found Guilty!," *Village Voice*, November 1, 2002; Mike Allen and Paul Blustein, "Unlikely Allies Influenced Bush to Shift Course on AIDS Relief," *Washington Post*, January 30, 2003; Elisabeth Bumiller, "Evangelicals Sway White House on Human Rights Issues Abroad," *New York Times*, October 26, 2003; Holly Burkhalter, "The Politics of AIDS: Engaging Conservative Activists," *Foreign Affairs*, Vol. 83, No. 1 (January/February 2004), pp. 8–14.
70. Doris Buss and Didi Herman, *Globalizing Family Values: The Christian Right in International Politics* (Minneapolis, MN: University of Minnesota Press, 2003).
71. For ongoing coverage and serious analysis, see the Global Civil Society yearbook series, including Marlies Glasius, Mary Kaldor, and Helmut Anheier (eds), *Global Civil Society 2002* (Oxford University Press, 2003); and Mary Kaldor, Helmut Anheier, and Marlies Glasius (eds), *Global Civil Society 2003* (Oxford: Oxford University Press, 2004).
72. Jack Holland, *The American Connection: U.S. Guns, Money, and Influence in Northern Ireland* (Lanham, MD: Roberts Rinehart, 1999), Chapter 2, "NORAID and the Northern Crisis."
73. Rohan Gunaratna, *Inside Al Qaeda: Global Network of Terror* (New York: Columbia University Press, 2002).
74. Ahmed Rashid, *Taliban: Militant Islam, Oil and Fundamentalism in Central Asia* (New Haven, CT: Yale University Press, 2001), pp. 128–31; Simon Henderson (Saudi Strategies, London), "Institutionalized Islam: Saudi Arabia's Islamic Policies and the Threat They Pose," Testimony before the Senate Judiciary Committee, Subcommittee on Terrorism, United States Senate, 10 September 2003.
75. See Marlies Glasius and Mary Kaldor, "The State of Global Civil Society: Before and After September 11," in Glasius, Kaldor, and Anheier (eds), *Global Civil Society 2002*, p. 23; and Jessica Stern, "The Protean Enemy," *Foreign Affairs*, Vol. 82, No. 4 (July/August 2003), p. 33.
76. Francisco Rey Marcos, "Viewpoint: When the Red Cross is the Target," Reuters AlertNet, November 18, 2003; Mike Patterson, "Aid Workers Increasingly Bear Brunt of Attacks in Iraq, Afghanistan," ReliefWeb, from Agence France-Presse, August 21, 2003; Daniel Serwer and Ylber Bajraktari, "Building Civil Society: An Overlooked Aspect of Iraq's Reconstruction?" *USIP Newsbyte*, United States Institute of Peace, July 31, 2003; Research Triangle Institute, "RTI International Granted USAID Contract for Post-War Local Governance Support in Iraq," RTI International, <www.rti.org>.

77. Human Rights Watch, "On the Precipice: Insecurity in Northern Afghanistan," Human Rights Watch Briefing Paper (June 2002).
78. Coalition for International Justice, <www.cij.org>.
79. For board members of the Coalition for International Justice, see <www.cij.org/index.cfm?fuseaction=staff>; for board members of Freedom House, see <www.freedomhouse.org/aboutfh/bod.htm>.
80. The Balkan Action Committee is disbanded, but a critical description can be found in "Balkan Action Committee," *Disinfopedia: The Encyclopedia of Propaganda* (A Project of PRWatch.org, Center for Media and Democracy, Madison, WI), <www.disinfopedia.org/wiki.phtml?title=Balkan_Action_Committee>.
81. "Committee for the Liberation of Iraq," *Disinfopedia: The Encyclopedia of Propaganda* (A Project of PRWatch.org, Center for Media and Democracy, Madison, WI), <www.disinfopedia.org/wiki.phtml?title= Committee_for_the_Liberation_of_Iraq>.
82. "James Woolsey is New Chairman of Freedom House," *Freedom House Monitor*, Vol. 20, No. 1 (Winter/Spring 2003), p. 1.
83. Sebatian Rotella, "Bin Laden is Named in 9/11 Indictment," *Los Angeles Times*, September 18, 2003.
84. Natalie Pompilio, "American Bounty on Saddam," *Hamilton Spectator*, July 4, 2003.
85. "Belgium Court Throws out Bush War Crimes Case," Reuters, September 24, 2003.
86. Michael Wines, "Conflict in Oslo over a Pointed Peace Prize," *New York Times*, October 14, 2002.
87. Paresa Hafezi, "Iranian Nobel Winner Demands Release of Dissidents," Reuters, October 15, 2003.
88. Irwin Abrams, *The Nobel Peace Prize and the Laureates: An Illustrated Biographical History, 1901–2001* (Canton, MA: Science History Publications, 2001).
89. Seyyed Hossein Nasr, *Traditional Islam in the Modern World* (London: Kegan Paul International, 1987).
90. Abdullahi An-Na"im, *Toward an Islamic Reformation* (Syracuse, NY: Syracuse University Press, 1990); Abdulaziz Sachedina, *The Islamic Roots of Democratic Pluralism* (Oxford: Oxford University Press, 2001).
91. Karim Douglas Crow, "Islam, Peace and Nonviolence: A Select Bibliography," Nonviolence International (September 1998), <www.members.tripod.com/nviusa/islam.htm>. See also Glenn D. Paige, Chaiwat Satha-Anand, and Sarah Gilliatt (eds), *Islam and Nonviolence* (Honolulu: Matsunaga Institute for Peace, University of Hawaii, 1993).
92. Muslims Against Terrorism, <www.matusa.org> until August 2003, thereafter Muslim Voices for Peace, <www.mvp-us.org/index.php>.
93. Kenneth Roth, "The Law of War in the War on Terror: Washington's Abuse of 'Enemy Combatants'," *Foreign Affairs*, Vol. 83, No. 1 (January/February 2004), pp. 2–7; Susan Sachs, "Prosecution of Hussein: Decade's Digging is Already Done," *New York Times*, December 17, 2003. For archives of major human rights reports on Iraq see Amnesty International, <web.amnesty.org/library/eng-irq/reports>, and Human Rights Watch, <hrw.org/doc/

?t=mideast&c=iraq>. Also see Indict, a group dedicated to "Bringing Iraqi war criminals to justice," at <www.indict.org.uk/index.php>.

94. See Iraq Occupation Watch, <occupationwatch.org>; and Iraq Revenue Watch, <www.iraqrevenuewatch.org>. The Center for Public Integrity has criticized the finances of the Iraq and Afghanistan occupations in its report, "Winning Contractors: U.S. Contractors Reap the Windfalls of Post-war Reconstruction," Center for Public Integrity, October 30, 2003, <www.publicintegrity.org>.

95. "Millions March Worldwide to Denounce Bush's War Plans," Independent Media Center, February 15, 2003, <www.indymedia.org/en/2003/02/107355.shtml>; Graham Caswell, "The Rise of Open Source, Network-Based Movements," Indymedia Ireland, February 19, 2003, <www.indymedia.ie/newswire.php?id=29627>.

96. Stop the War Coalition, <www.stopwar.org.uk>.

97. Stop the War Coalition, <www.stopwar.org.uk/about.asp>.

Selected Bibliography

Abbey, Edward, *The Monkey Wrench Gang* (Philadelphia, PA: Lippincott, 1975).

Abrams, Irwin, *The Nobel Peace Prize and the Laureates: An Illustrated Biographical History, 1901–2001* (Canton, MA: Science History Publications, 2001).

Ackerman, Peter and Jack Duvall, *A Force More Powerful: A Century of Nonviolent Conflict* (New York: Palgrave, 2000).

Acuña, Carlos H. and Catalina Smulovitz, "Adjusting the Armed Forces to Democracy: Successes, Failures, and Ambiguities in the Southern Cone," in Elizabeth Jelin and Eric Hershberg (eds), *Constructing Democracy: Human Rights, Citizenship, and Society in Latin America* (Boulder, CO: Westview Press, 1996).

African Rights, "The 'Comprehensive Call'," Chapter 9 in *Food and Power in Sudan: A Critique of Humanitarianism* (London: African Rights, 1997).

Ajello, Aldo, "Mozambique: Implementation of the 1992 Peace Agreement," in Chester A. Crocker, Fen Osler Hampson, and Pamela Aall (eds), *Herding Cats: Multiparty Mediation in a Complex World* (Washington, DC: United States Institute of Peace Press, 1999).

Alger, Chadwick F. (ed.), *The Future of the United Nations: Potential for the Twenty-first Century* (Tokyo and New York: United Nations University Press, 1998).

Almond, Gabriel, "Review Article: The International–National Connection," *British Journal of Political Science*, Vol. 19, No. 2 (1989), pp. 237–59.

An-Naim, Abdullahi, *Toward an Islamic Reformation* (Syracuse, NY: Syracuse University Press, 1990).

Anderson, Scott. *The Man Who Tried to Save the World* (New York: Doubleday, 1999).

Armony, Ariel C., *Argentina, the United States, and the Anti-Communist Crusade in Central America, 1977–1984* (Athens, OH: Ohio University Press, 1997).

Armony, Ariel C., *The Dubious Link: Civic Engagement and Democratization* (Palo Alto, CA: Stanford University Press, 2004).

Armstrong, J. D., "The International Committee of the Red Cross and Political Prisoners," *International Organization*, Vol. 39, No. 4 (1985), pp. 616–42.

Badie, Bernard, *Les Deux Etats: Pouvoir et Société en Occident et en Terre d'Islam* (Paris: Fayard, 1986).

Barrett, Deborah, "Reproducing Persons as a Global Concern: The Making of an Institution" (PhD Dissertation, Stanford University, 1995).

Barrett, Deborah and David John Frank, "Population Control for National Development: From World Discourse to National Policies," in John Boli and George M. Thomas (eds), *Constructing World Culture: International Nongovernmental Organizations since 1875* (Stanford, CA: Stanford University Press, 1999).

Barrett, Deborah and Amy Ong Tsui, "Policy as Symbolic Statement: International Response to National Population Policies," *Social Forces*, Vol. 78, No. 1 (1999), pp. 213–33.

Barrow, Ondine and Michael Jennings (eds), *The Charitable Impulse: NGOs and Development in East and North-East Africa* (London: James Currey, 2001).

Bartoli, Andrea, "Mediating Peace in Mozambique: Successful Synergies and the Role of the Community of St. Egidio," in Chester A. Crocker, Fen Osler Hampson, and Pamela Aall (eds), *Herding Cats: Multiparty Mediation in a Complex World* (Washington, DC: United States Institute of Peace Press, 1999).

Bass, Gary Jonathan, *Stay the Hand of Vengeance: The Politics of War Crimes Tribunals* (Princeton, NJ: Princeton University Press, 2000).

Bassiouni, M. Cherif, "Former Yugoslavia: Investigating Violations of International Law and Establishing an International Criminal Tribunal," *Fordham International Law Journal*, Vol. 18, No. 4 (April 1995), pp. 1191–1211.

Basu, Amrita (ed.), *The Challenge of Local Feminisms: Women's Movements in Global Perspective* (Boulder, CO: Westview, 1995).

Bayart, Jean-François, Stephen Ellis, and Béatrice Hibou, *The Criminalization of the State in Africa* (Oxford: James Currey, 1999).

Benedetti, Fanny and John L. Washburn, "Drafting the International Criminal Court Treaty: Two Years to Rome and an Afterword on the Rome Diplomatic Conference," *Global Governance*, Vol. 5, No. 1 (1999), pp. 1–37.

Benthall, Jonathan, "Financial Worship: The Quranic Injunction to Almsgiving," *Journal of the Royal Anthropological Institute*, Vol. 5, No. 1 (1999), pp. 27–42.

Berger, Peter (ed.), *The Desecularization of the World: Resurgent Religion and World Politics* (Grand Rapids, WI: Wm. B. Eerdmans, 1999).

Berkovitch, Nitza, "The Emergence and Transformation of the International Women's Movement," in John Boli and George M. Thomas (eds), *Constructing World Culture: International Nongovernmental Organizations since 1875* (Stanford, CA: Stanford University Press, 1999).

Berry, Nicholas O., *War and the Red Cross: The Unspoken Mission* (New York: St. Martin's Press, 1997).

Boli, John and George M. Thomas (eds), *Constructing World Culture: International Nongovernmental Organizations since 1875* (Stanford, CA: Stanford University Press, 1999).

Boulding, Kenneth E., *Three Faces of Power* (Newbury Park, CA: Sage, 1990).

Boutros-Ghali, Boutros, Foreword to Thomas G. Weiss and Leon Gordenker (eds), *NGOs, the United Nations, and Global Governance* (Boulder, CO: Lynne Rienner, 1996).

Bouvier, Virginia, "The Washington Office on Latin America: Charting a New Path in U.S.–Latin American Relations," in Robert S. Pelton (ed.), *From Power to Communion: Toward a New Way of Being Church Based on the Latin American Experience* (South Bend, IN: University of Notre Dame Press, 1994).

Bratton, Michael (ed.), *Governance and Politics in Africa* (Boulder, CO: Lynne Rienner, 1992).

Brown, Seyom, *New Forces, Old Forces, and the Future of World Politics*, Post-Cold War edn (New York: HarperCollins, 1995).

Bruno, Kenny and Joshua Karliner, "Tangled up in Blue: Corporate Partnerships at the United Nations," TRAC—Transnational Resource and Action Center (September 2000), <www.corpwatch.org/upload/document/tangled.pdf>.

Brysk, Alison, "From Above and Below: Social Movements, the International System, and Human Rights in Argentina," *Comparative Political Studies*, Vol. 26, No. 3 (1993), pp. 259–85.

Brysk, Alison, *The Politics of Human Rights in Argentina: Protest, Change, and Democratization* (Stanford, CA: University of California Press, 1994).

Brysk, Alison, "The Politics of Measurement: The Contested Count of the Disappeared in Argentina," *Human Rights Quarterly*, Vol. 16, No. 4 (1994), pp. 676–92.

Burkhalter, Holly, "The Politics of AIDS: Engaging Conservative Activists," *Foreign Affairs*, Vol. 83, No. 1 (January/February 2004), pp. 8–14.

Burton, John W., *World Society* (Cambridge: Cambridge University Press, 1972).

Buss, Doris, and Didi Herman, *Globalizing Family Values: The Christian Right in Global Politics* (Minneapolis, MN: University of Minnesota Press, 2003).

Butler, David, *Methodists and Papists: John Wesley and the Catholic Church in the Eighteenth Century* (London: Darton, Longman and Todd, 1995).

Cardoso, Fernando Henrique, "Democracy as a Starting Point," *Journal of Democracy*, Vol. 12, No. 1 (2001), pp. 5–14.

Castañeda, Jorge G., *Utopia Unarmed: The Latin American Left After the Cold War* (New York: Alfred A. Knopf, 1993).

Center for Public Integrity, "Winning Contractors: U.S. Contractors Reap the Windfalls of Post-war Reconstruction," Center for Public Integrity, October 30, 2003, <www.publicintegrity.org>.

Charnovitz, Steve, "Two Centuries of Participation: NGOs and International Governance," *Michigan Journal of International Law*, Vol. 18 (1997), pp. 183–286.

Chopra, Jarat and Thomas G. Weiss, "Sovereignty is No Longer Sacrosanct: Codifying Humanitarian Intervention," *Ethics and International Affairs*, Vol. 6 (1992), pp. 95–117.

Cigar, Norman, *Genocide in Bosnia: The Policy of "Ethnic Cleansing"* (College Station, TX: Texas A&M University Press, 1995).

Clapham, Christopher, *Africa in the International System: The Politics of Survival* (Cambridge: Cambridge University Press, 1996).

Clark, Ann Marie, *Diplomacy of Conscience: Amnesty International and Changing Human Rights Norms* (Princeton, NJ: Princeton University Press, 2001).

Clark, Ann Marie, Elisabeth J. Friedman, and Kathryn Hochstetler, "The Sovereign Limits of Global Civil Society: A Comparison of NGO Participation in UN World Conferences on the Environment, Human Rights, and Women," *World Politics*, Vol. 51, No. 1 (1998), pp. 1–35.

Cmiel, Kenneth, "The Emergence of Human Rights Politics in the United States," *The Journal of American History*, Vol. 86, No. 3 (1999), pp. 1231–50.

Cohen, Roberta, "Human Rights Decision-Making in the Executive Branch: Some Proposals for a Coordinated Strategy," in Donald P. Kommers and Gilburt D. Loescher (eds), *Human Rights and American Foreign Policy* (Notre Dame, IN: University of Notre Dame Press, 1979).

Cohen, Roberta and Francis Deng, *Masses in Flight: The Global Crisis of Internal Displacement* (Washington, DC: Brookings, 1998).

Cox, Robert W., "Gramsci, Hegemony, and International Relations: An Essay in Method," *Millennium: Journal of International Studies*, Vol. 12, No. 2 (1983), pp. 162–75.

Crahan, Margaret E., "Religion, Revolution, and Counterrevolution: The Role of the Religious Right in Central America," in Douglas A. Chalmers, Maria do Carmo Campello de Souza, and Atilio A. Boron (eds), *The Right and Democracy in Latin America* (New York: Praeger, 1992).

Crane, Barbara B., "The Transnational Politics of Abortion," in Jason L. Finkle and C. Alison McIntosh (eds), *The New Politics of Population: Conflict and Consensus in Family Planning* (New York: The Population Council, 1994).

Critchlow, Donald T., *Intended Consequences: Birth Control, Abortion, and the Federal Government in Modern America* (Oxford: Oxford University Press, 1999).

Crocker, Chester A., Fen Osler Hampson, and Pamela Aall (eds), *Managing Global Chaos: Sources and Responses to International Conflict* (Washington, DC: United States Institute of Peace Press, 1996).

Crow, Karim Douglas, "Islam, Peace and Nonviolence: A Select Bibliography," Nonviolence International (September 1998), <www.members.tripod.com/nviusa/islam.htm>.

Cusimano, Maryann K., *Beyond Sovereignty: Issues for a Global Agenda* (Boston, MA: Bedford/St. Martin's, 2000).

Davis, David Brion, *Slavery and Human Progress* (Oxford: Oxford University Press, 1984).

de Waal, Alex, *Evil Days: 30 Years of War and Famine in Ethiopia*, An Africa Watch Report (New York: Human Rights Watch, 1991).

de Waal, Alex, *Famine Crimes: Politics and the Disaster Relief Industry in Africa* (Oxford: James Currey, 1997).

de Waal, Alex and Rakiya Omaar, "Can Military Intervention be 'Humanitarian'?" *Middle East Report*, Vol. 187/188 (1994), pp. 3–8.

DeMars, William, "Waiting for Early Warning: Humanitarian Action After the Cold War," *Journal of Refugee Studies*, Vol. 8, No. 4 (1995), pp. 390–410.

DeMars, William, "Contending Neutralities: Humanitarian Organizations and War in the Horn of Africa," in Jackie Smith, Charles Chatfield, and Ron Pagnucco (eds), *Transnational Social Movements and Global Politics: Solidarity Beyond the State* (Syracuse, NY: Syracuse University Press, 1997).

DeMars, William, "War and Mercy in Africa," *World Policy Journal*, Vol. 17, No. 2 (2000), pp. 1–10.

DeMars, William E., "Hazardous Partnership: NGOs and United States Intelligence in Small Wars," *International Journal of Intelligence and CounterIntelligence*, Vol. 14, No. 2 (2001), pp. 193–222.

DeMars, William E., "Transnational Non-Governmental Organizations: The Edge of Innocence," in E. Wayne Nafziger and Raimo Väyrynen (eds), *The Prevention of Humanitarian Emergencies* (New York: Palgrave, 2002).

Des Forges, Alison, "Making Noise Effectively: Lessons from the Rwandan Catastrophe," in Robert I. Rotberg (ed.), *Vigilance and Vengeance: NGOs Preventing Ethnic Conflict in Divided Societies* (Washington, DC: Brookings, 1997).

Des Forges, Alison, *Leave None to Tell the Story: Genocide in Rwanda* (New York: Human Rights Watch, 1999).

Desai, Raj and Harry Eckstein, "Insurgency: The Transformation of Peasant Rebellion," *World Politics*, Vol. 42 (1990), pp. 441–66.

Devall, Bill and George Sessions, *Deep Ecology* (Salt Lake City, UT: Gibbs Smith, 1985).

Diamond, Larry, *Promoting Democracy in the 1990s: Actors and Instruments, Issues and Imperatives* (New York: Carnegie Commission of New York, 1995).

Dinges, John, *The Condor Years: How Pinochet and His Allies Brought Terrorism to Three Continents* (New York: The New Press, 2004).

Donnelly, Jack, "International Human Rights: A Regime Analysis," *International Organization*, Vol. 40 (1986) pp. 599–642.

Donnelly, Jack, *International Human Rights* (Boulder, CO: Westview, 1993).

Dougherty, James E. and Robert L. Pfaltzgraff, Jr., *Contending Theories of International Relations: A Comprehensive Survey*, 2nd edn (New York: Harper & Row, 1981).

Duffield, Mark, "The Symphony of the Damned: Racial Discourse, Complex Political Emergencies and Humanitarian Aid," *Disasters*, Vol. 20, No. 3 (1996), pp. 173–93.

Duffield, Mark R., *Global Governance and the New Wars: The Merging of Development and Security* (London: Zed Books, 2001).

Easterbrook, Gregg, "Forgotten Benefactor of Humanity," *The Atlantic Monthly* (January 1997), pp. 75–82.

Edwards, Michael and David Hulme (eds), *Beyond the Magic Bullet: NGO Performance and Accountability in the Post-Cold War World* (West Hartford, CT: Kumarian, 1996).

Egyptian Organization for Human Rights, "El Kusheh Village," 28 September 1998, Cairo (photocopy).

Elshtain, Jean Bethke, "The Mothers of the Disappeared," in Donna Bassin, Margaret Honey, and Marlyle Mohrer Kaplan (eds), *Representations of Motherhood* (New Haven, CT: Yale University Press, 1994).

Elshtain, Jean Bethke, "Exporting Feminism," *Journal of International Affairs*, Vol. 48, No. 2 (1995), pp. 541–58.

Erickson, Brad, *Call to Action: Handbook for Ecology, Peace and Justice* (San Francisco: Sierra Club Books, 1990).

Erlich, Paul R. and Anne H. Erlich, *The Population Explosion* (New York: Simon & Schuster, 1990).

Evans, L. T., *Feeding the Ten Billion: Plants and Population Growth* (Cambridge: Cambridge University Press, 1998).

Falk, Richard, *Predatory Globalization: A Critique* (Malden, MA: Polity Press, 1999).

Farer, Tom, "New Players in the Old Game: The De Facto Expansion of Standing to Participate in Global Security Negotiations," *American Behavioral Scientist*, Vol. 38, No. 6 (1995), pp. 842–66.

Fatton, Jr., Robert, *Predatory Rule: State and Civil Society in Africa* (Boulder, CO: Lynne Rienner, 1992).

Finkle, Jason L. and C. Alison McIntosh (eds), *The New Politics of Population: Conflict and Consensus in Family Planning* (New York: Oxford University Press, 1994).

Fischer, Julie, *Nongovernments: NGOs and the Political Development of the Third World* (West Hartford, CT: Kumarian Press, 1998).

Florini, Ann M. (ed.), *The Third Force: The Rise of Transnational Civil Society* (Washington, DC: Carnegie Endowment for International Peace, 2000).

Fogel, Robert William, *The Fourth Great Awakening and the Future of Egalitarianism* (Chicago, IL: University of Chicago Press, 2000).

Foreman, Dave (ed.), *Ecodefense: A Field Guide to Monkeywrenching* (Tucson, AZ: Ned Ludd Books, 1985).

Foreman, Dave, *Confessions of an Eco-Warrior* (New York: Harmony Books, 1991).

Forsythe, David P., *Human Rights and World Politics* (Lincoln, NE: University of Nebraska Press, 1983).

Forsythe, David P., "The United Nations and Human Rights, 1945–1985," *Political Science Quarterly*, Vol. 100, No. 1 (1985), pp. 249–69.

Forsythe, David P., *Human Rights in International Relations* (Cambridge: Cambridge University Press, 2000).

Fowler, Alan, "Distant Obligations: Speculations on NGO Funding and the Global Market," *Review of African Political Economy*, No. 55 (1992), pp. 9–29.

Fowler, Alan, "Non-governmental Organizations as Agents of Democratization: An African Perspective," *Journal of International Development*, Vol. 5, No. 3 (1993), pp. 325–39.

Frank, David John, Ann Hironka, John M. Meyer, Evan Shofer, and Nancy Brandon Tuma, "The Rationalization and Organization of Nature in World Culture," in John Boli and George M. Thomas (eds), *Constructing World Culture: International Nongovernmental Organizations since 1875* (Stanford, CA: Stanford University Press, 1999).

Fukuyama, Francis, *The End of History and the Last Man* (New York: Free Press, 1992).

Geertz, Clifford, *The Interpretation of Cultures* (New York: Basic Books, 1973).

Ghils, Paul, "International Civil Society: International Non-governmental Organizations in the International System," *International Social Science Journal*, Vol. 44, No. 133 (1992), pp. 417–29.

Gifford, Paul, "Some Recent Developments in African Christianity," *African Affairs*, Vol. 93, No. 373 (1994), pp. 513–34.

Gill, Peter, *A Year in the Death of Africa: Politics, Bureaucracy and the Famine* (London: Grafton Books, 1986).

Gladwell, Malcolm, "John Rock's Error," *New Yorker* (March 10, 2000).

Glasius, Marlies and Mary Kaldor, "The State of Global Civil Society: Before and After September 11," in Marlies Glasius, Mary Kaldor, and Helmut Anheier (eds), *Global Civil Society 2002* (Oxford University Press, 2003).

Glasius, Marlies, Mary Kaldor, and Helmut Anheier (eds), *Global Civil Society 2002* (Oxford: Oxford University Press, 2003).

Glendon, Mary Ann, *A World Made New: Eleanor Roosevelt and the Universal Declaration of Human Rights* (New York: Random House, 2001).

Goldstein, Judith and Robert E. Keohane (eds), *Ideas and Foreign Policy: Beliefs, Institutions, and Political Change* (Ithaca, NY: Cornell University Press, 1993).

Gordon, Linda, *Woman's Body, Woman's Right: A Social History of Birth Control in America* (New York: Grossman, 1976).

Goulet, Yves, "Washington's Freelance Advisors," *Jane's Intelligence Review*, Vol. 10, No. 7 (July 1998), pp. 38–41.

Gourevitch, Peter, "The Second Image Reversed: The International Sources of Domestic Politics," *International Organization*, Vol. 32, No. 4 (1978), pp. 881–912.

Gowing, Nik, "Real-Time Television Coverage of Armed Conflicts and Diplomatic Crises: Does It Pressure or Distort Foreign Policy Decisions?" The Joan Shorenstein Barone Center on the Press, Politics and Public Policy, Harvard University, Working Paper 94–1 (June 1994).

Griffiths, Hugh, "Evidence Gathering: The Role of NGOs," *The Tribunals, Magazine of the Crimes of War Project* (May 2001), <www.crimesofwar.org/tribun-mag/relate_ngo_print.html>.

GroupWatch, Profile of the Puebla Institute (Albuquerque, NM: Interhemispheric Resource Center, April 1989), <www.namebase.org/gw/puebla.txt>.

Guest, Iain, *Behind the Disappearances: Argentina's Dirty War Against Human Rights and the United Nations* (Philadelphia, PA: University of Pennsylvania Press, 1990).

Gunaratna, Rohan, *Inside Al Qaeda: Global Network of Terror* (New York: Columbia University Press, 2002).

Gutman, Roy, *A Witness to Genocide* (New York: Macmillan, 1993).

Haas, Peter M. and Ernst B. Haas, "Learning to Learn: Improving International Governance," *Global Governance*, Vol. 1 (1995), pp. 255–85.

Haglund, William D., Melissa Connor, and Douglas D. Scott, "The Archeology of Mass Graves," *Historical Archeology*, Vol. 35, No. 1 (2000), pp. 57–69.

Hartmann, Betsy, *Reproductive Rights and Wrongs: The Global Politics of Population Control* (Boston: South End Press, 1995).

Haskel, Barbara G., "Access to Society: A Neglected Dimension of Power," *International Organization*, Vol. 34, No. 1 (1980), pp. 89–120.

Haskell, Thomas L., "Capitalism and the Origins of the Humanitarian Sensibility, Part 1," *American Historical Review*, Vol. 90, No. 2 (1985), pp. 339–61.

Haskell, Thomas L., "Capitalism and the Origins of the Humanitarian Sensibility, Part 2," *American Historical Review*, Vol. 90, No. 3 (1985), pp. 547–66.

Hassan, Bahey el-Din (ed.), *Challenges Facing the Arab Human Rights Movement* (Cairo: Cairo Institute for Human Rights Studies, 1998).

Helsinki Watch, *War Crimes in Bosnia-Hercegovina* (New York: Human Rights Watch, August 1992).

Henderson, Simon (Saudi Strategies, London), "Institutionalized Islam: Saudi Arabia's Islamic Policies and the Threat They Pose," Testimony before the Senate Judiciary Committee, Subcommittee on Terrorism, United States Senate, September 10, 2003.

Hewit, Kenneth, *Interpretations of Calamity, from the Viewpoint of Human Ecology* (Boston, MA: Allen and Unwin, 1983).

Hoben, Allan, "The Cultural Construction of Environmental Policy: Paradigms and Politics in Ethiopia," in Melissa Leach and Robin Mearns (eds), *The Lie of the Land: Challenging Received Wisdom on the African Environment* (Oxford: James Currey, 1996).

Hochschild, Adam, *King Leopold's Ghost* (New York: Houghton Mifflin, 1998).

Hoeffel, Paul Heath and Peter Kornbluh, "The War At Home: Chile's Legacy in the United States," *NACLA Report on the Americas*, Vol. 17 (September–October, 1983), pp. 27–39.

Hoffmann, Stanley, "An American Social Science: International Relations," *Daedalus*, Vol. 106 (1977), pp. 41–60.

Holbrooke, Richard, *To End a War* (New York: Random House, 1998).

Holland, Jack, *The American Connection: U.S. Guns, Money, and Influence in Northern Ireland* (Lanham, MD: Roberts Rinehart, 1999).

"Human Rights: Egypt and the Arab World," Special Issue of *Cairo Papers in Social Science*, Vol. 17, No. 3 (Fall 1994), Cairo: American University in Cairo.

Human Rights Watch, "On the Precipice: Insecurity in Northern Afghanistan," Human Rights Watch Briefing Paper (June 2002).

Huntington, Samuel P., "Transnational Organizations in World Politics," *World Politics*, Vol. 25, No. 3 (1973), pp. 333–68.

Huntington, Samuel P., *The Third Wave: Democratization in the Late Twentieth Century* (Norman, OK: University of Oklahoma Press, 1991).

Hutchinson, John F., *Champions of Charity: War and the Rise of the Red Cross* (Boulder, CO: Westview, 1996).

Ibrahim, Saad Eddin, "Civil Society and Prospects of Democratization in the Arab World," in Augustus Richard Norton (ed.), *Civil Society in the Middle East*, Vol. 1 (Leiden: E. J. Brill, 1994).

Ibrahim, Saad Eddin, "A Reply to My Accusers," *Journal of Democracy*, Vol. 11, No. 4 (2000), pp. 58–63.

Ignatieff, Michael, *The Warrior's Honor: Ethnic War and the Modern Conscience* (New York: Henry Holt, 1997).

Ignatieff, Michael, *Virtual War: Kosovo and Beyond* (New York: Henry Holt: 2000).

International Crisis Group, Reality Demands: Documenting Violations of International Humanitarian Law in Kosovo 1999 (June 27, 2000), <www.crisisweb.org/projects/balkans/kosovo/reports/A400057_27062000.pdf>.

International Rescue Committee, "Mortality in the Democratic Republic of Congo: Results from a Nationwide Survey," International Rescue Committee (April 2003), <intranet.theirc.org/docs/drc_mortality_iii_full.pdf>.

Iriye, Akira, "A Century of NGOs," *Diplomatic History*, Vol. 23, No. 3 (1999), pp. 421–35.

Jacobson, Harold K., *Networks of Interdependence: International Organizations and the International Political System* (New York: Knopf, 1979).

Jacoby, Tamar, "The Reagan Turnaround on Human Rights," *Foreign Affairs*, Vol. 64 (Summer 1986), pp. 1066–86.

Jansson, Kurt, Michael Harris and Angela Penrose, *The Ethiopian Famine*, 2nd edn (London: Zed Books, 1990).

Jeal, Tim, *Livingstone* (New York: G. P. Putnam's Sons, 1973).

Johnson, Stanley, *Politics of Population: The International Conference on Population and Development, Cairo 1994* (London: Earthscan, 1995).

Joyce, Christopher and Eric Stover, *Witnesses from the Grave: The Stories Bones Tell* (Boston: Little, Brown, 1991).

Juergensmeyer, Mark, *Terror in the Mind of God: The Global Rise of Religious Violence* (Berkeley, CA: University of California, 2000).

Kacowitz, Arie M., "Latin America as an International Society," *International Politics*, Vol. 37 (2000), pp. 143–62.

Kaldor, Mary, *New and Old Wars: Organized Violence in a Global Era* (Stanford, CA: Stanford University Press, 1999).

Kaldor, Mary, Helmut Anheier, and Marlies Glasius (eds), *Global Civil Society 2003* (Oxford: Oxford University Press, 2004).

Kamrava, Mehran and Frank O. Mora, "Civil Society and Democratisation in Comparative Perspective: Latin America and the Middle East," *Third World Quarterly*, Vol. 19, No. 5 (1998), pp. 893–916.

Katzenstein, Peter (ed.), *The Culture of National Security* (New York: Columbia University Press, 1996).

Kaufman, Edy, "Prisoners of Conscience: The Shaping of a New Human Rights Concept," *Human Rights Quarterly*, Vol. 13 (1991), pp. 339–67.

Keck, Margaret E. and Kathryn Sikkink, *Activists Beyond Borders: Advocacy Networks in International Politics* (Ithaca, NY: Cornell University Press, 1998).

Keely, Charles B., "Limits to Papal Power: Vatican Inaction after Humanae Vitae," in Jason L. Finkle and C. Alison McIntosh (eds), *The New Politics of Population: Conflict and Consensus in Family Planning* (New York: The Population Council, 1994).

Keen, David and John Ryle, "Editorial: The Fate of Information in the Disaster Zone," *Disasters*, Vol. 20, No. 3 (1996), pp. 169–72.

Keohane, Robert O. and Joseph S. Nye, Jr. (eds), *Transnational Relations and World Politics* (Cambridge, MA: Harvard University Press, 1972).

Keohane, Robert O. and Joseph S. Nye, Jr., *Power and Interdependence: World Politics in Transition* (Boston: Little, Brown, 1977).

Kevles, Daniel J., *In the Name of Eugenics: Genetics and the Uses of Human Heredity* (New York: Alfred A. Knopf, 1985).

King, Jr., Martin Luther, "Letter From Birmingham Jail," in Martin Luther King, Jr., *Why We Can't Wait* (New York: Harper & Row, 1964).

Kirkpatrick, Jeane, "Dictatorships and Double Standards," *Commentary* (November 1979), pp. 34–45.

Kobrin, Stephen J., "The MAI and the Clash of Globalizations," *Foreign Policy*, No. 112 (Fall 1998), pp. 97–109.

Korany, Bahgat, "Restricted Democratization from Above: Egypt," in Bahgat Korany, Rex Brynen, and Paul Noble (eds), *Political Liberalization and Democratization in the Arab World, Vol. 2, Comparative Experiences* (Boulder, CO: Lynne Rienner, 1998).

Korey, William, *NGOs and the Universal Declaration of Human Rights* (New York: St. Martin's Press, 1998).

Kothari, Rajni, "On the Non-Party Political Process: The NGOs, the State and World Capitalism," *Lokayan Bulletin*, Vol. 4, No. 5 (1986), pp. 6–26.

Kothari, Rajni, *State Against Democracy: In Search of Humane Governance* (New Delhi: Ajanta, 1989).

Kothari, Rajni, "The Yawning Vacuum: A World without Alternatives," *Alternatives*, Vol. 18 (1993), pp. 119–39.

Krasner, Stephen D. (ed.), *International Regimes* (Ithaca, NY: Cornell University Press, 1983).

Krasner, Stephen D., "Sovereignty: An Institutional Perspective," in James A. Caporaso (ed.), *The Elusive State: International and Comparative Perspectives* (Newbury Park, CA: Sage, 1989).

Krasner, Stephen D., "Power Politics, Institutions, and Transnational Relations," in Thomas Risse-Kappen (ed.), *Bringing Transnational Relations Back In: Non-State Actors, Domestic Structures and International Institutions* (Cambridge: Cambridge University Press, 1995).

Kubalkova, Vendulka, Nicholas Onuf, and Paul Kowert (eds), *International Relations in a Constructed World* (Armonk, NY: M. E. Sharpe, 1998).

Kuperman, Alan J., "Transnational Causes of Genocide: How the West Inadvertently Exacerbates Ethnic Conflict," in Raju G. C. Thomas (ed.), *Yugoslavia Unraveled: Sovereignty, Self-Determination, Intervention* (Lanham, MD: Lexington Books, 2003).

Lane, Charles and Thom Shanker, "Bosnia: What the CIA Didn't Tell Us," *The New York Review of Books*, May 9, 1996.

Leach, Melissa and Robin Mearns (eds), *The Lie of the Land: Challenging Received Wisdom on the African Environment* (Oxford: James Currey, 1996).

Leatherman, Janie, William DeMars, Patrick Gaffney, and Raimo Väyrynen, *Breaking Cycles of Violence: Conflict Prevention in Intrastate Crises* (West Hartford, CT: Kumarian, 1999).

Lederach, John Paul, *Building Peace: Sustainable Reconciliation in Divided Societies* (Washington, DC: United States Institute of Peace Press, 1998).

Linz, Juan and Alfred Stepan, "Political Crafting of Democratic Consolidation or Destruction: European and South American Comparisons," in Robert A. Pastor (ed.), *Democracy in the Americas: Stopping the Pendulum* (New York: Holmes and Meier, 1989).

Lipschutz, Ronnie D., "Reconstructing World Politics: The Emergence of Global Civil Society," *Millennium: Journal of International Studies*, Vol. 21, No. 3 (1992), pp. 389–420.

Livezey, Lowell W., *Nongovernmental Organizations and the Ideas of Human Rights*, World Order Studies Program Occasional Paper No. 15 (Princeton University, Center of International Studies, 1988).

Loescher, Gil, *Beyond Charity: International Cooperation and the Global Refugee Crisis* (Oxford: Oxford University Press, 1993).

Lowe, David, "Idea to Reality: A Brief History of the National Endowment for Democracy" (Washington, DC: National Endowment for Democracy, 2001), <www.ned.org/about/nedhistory.html>.

Lyons, Gene M. and Michael Mastanduno (eds), *Beyond Westphalia? State Sovereignty and International Intervention* (Baltimore, MD: Johns Hopkins University Press, 1995).

MacDonald, Laura, "Globalising Civil Society: Interpreting International NGOs in Central America," *Millennium: Journal of International Studies*, Vol. 23, No. 2 (1994), pp. 267–85.

MacDonald, Laura, "A Mixed Blessing: The NGO Boom in Latin America," *NACLA Report on the Americas*, Vol. 28, No. 5 (1995), pp. 30–5.

MacDonald, Laura, *Supporting Civil Society: The Political Role of Non-Governmental Organizations in Central America* (New York: St. Martin's Press, 1995).

Mahoney, Liam and Luis Enrique Eguren, *Unarmed Bodyguards: Case Studies in Protective International Accompaniment* (West Hartford, CT: Kumarian Press, 1997).

Malin, Andrea, "Mothers Who Won't Disappear," *Human Rights Quarterly*, Vol. 15 (1994), pp. 187–213.

Manes, Christopher, *Green Rage: Radical Environmentalism and the Unmaking of Civilization* (Boston, MA: Little, Brown, 1990).

Manheim, Jarol B., *The Death of a Thousand Cuts: Corporate Campaigns and the Attack on the Corporation* (Mahwah, NJ: Lawrence Erlbaum Associates, 2001).

Mansbach, Richard W., Yale H. Ferguson, and Donald E. Lampert, *The Web of World Politics: Non-State Actors in the Global System* (Englewood Cliffs, NJ: Prentice Hall, 1976).

Marcus, George E., "Ethnography in/of the World System: The Emergence of Multi-Sited Ethnography," *Annual Review of Anthropology*, Vol. 24 (1995), pp. 95–117.

Martens, Kerstin, "NGO Participation at International Conferences: Assessing Theoretical Accounts," *Transnational Associations*, Vol. 3 (2000), pp. 115–26.

Martin, Lisa L. and Kathryn Sikkink, "U.S. Policy and Human Rights in Argentina and Guatemala, 1973–80," in Peter B. Evans, Harold K. Jacobson, and Robert D. Putnam (eds), *Double-Edged Diplomacy: International Bargaining and Domestic Politics* (Berkeley, CA: University of California Press, 1993).

Mathews, Jessica T., "Power Shift," *Foreign Affairs*, Vol. 76, No. 1 (1997), pp. 50–66.

Maynes, Charles William, "A New Strategy for Old Foes and New Friends," *World Policy Journal*, Vol. 17, No. 2 (2000), pp. 68–76.

McKay, Fiona, "Universal Jurisdiction in Europe," June 30, 1999, <www.redress.org/publications/UJEurope.pdf>, London, Redress.

Mearsheimer, John J., "The False Promise of International Institutions," *International Security*, Vol. 19, No. 3 (Winter 1994/95), pp. 5–49.

Melich, Tanya, *The Republican War Against Women: An Insider's Report from Behind the Lines* (New York: Bantam, 1996).

Mellibovsky, Matilde, translated by Maria and Matthew Proser, *Circle of Love over Death: Testimonies of the Mothers of the Plaza de Mayo* (Willimantic, CT: Curbstone Press, 1997).

Miers, Suzanne and Richard Roberts (eds), *The End of Slavery in Africa* (Madison, WI: University of Wisconsin Press, 1988).

Mignone, Emilio, *Derechos Humanos y Sociedad: El Caso Argentino* (Buenos Aires: Ediciones del Pensamiento Nacional and Centro de Estudios Legales y Sociales, 1991).

Minear, Larry and Thomas G. Weiss, *Mercy under Fire: War and the Global Humanitarian Community* (Boulder, CO: Westview Press, 1995).

Minear, Larry, Jeffrey Clark, Roberta Cohen, Dennis Gallagher, Iain Guest, and Thomas G. Weiss, *Humanitarian Action in the Former Yugoslavia: The U.N.'s Role 1991–1993* (Occasional Paper #18, Thomas J. Watson Jr. Institute for International Studies, Brown University, 1994).

Morgenthau, Hans J., *Politics Among Nations*, 2nd edn (New York: Alfred Knopf, 1954).

Moyano, María José, *Argentina's Lost Patrol: Armed Struggle, 1969–1979* (New Haven, CT: Yale University Press, 1995).

Murphy, Craig N., *International Organizations and Industrial Change: Global Governance Since 1850* (New York: Oxford University Press, 1994).

Nadelman, Ethan A., "Global Prohibition Regimes: The Evolution of Norms in International Society," *International Organization*, Vol. 44, No. 4 (1990), pp. 479–526.

Naess, Arne, "The Shallow and the Deep, Long Range Ecology Movements: A Summary," *Inquiry* 16 (Oslo, 1973), pp. 95–100.

Naim, Moisés, "Lori's War: The FP Interview," *Foreign Policy* (Spring 2000), pp. 29–55.

Nasr, Seyyed Hossein, *Traditional Islam in the Modern World* (London: Kegan Paul International, 1987).

Natisos, Andrew S., *The Great North Korean Famine: Famine, Politics, and Foreign Policy* (Washington, DC: United States Institute of Peace Press, 2001).

Ndegwa, Stephen N., *The Two Faces of Civil Society: NGOs and Politics in Africa* (West Hartford, CT: Kumarian Press, 1996).

Neier, Aryeh, "Human Rights in the Reagan Era: Acceptance in Principle," *The Annals of the American Academy of Political and Social Science*, Vol. 506 (November 1989), pp. 30–41.

Neier, Aryeh, *War Crimes: Brutality, Genocide, Terror, and the Struggle for Justice* (New York: Times Books, 1998).

Nelson, Joyce, "Great Global Greenwash: Burson-Marstellar, Pax Trilateral, and the Brundtland Gang vs. the Environment," *Covert Action Quarterly*, No. 44 (Spring 1993), pp. 26–33, 57–8.

Ness, Gayl D. and Steven R. Brechin, "Bridging the Gap: International Organizations as Organizations," *International Organization*, Vol. 42, No. 2 (1988), pp. 245–73.

Neuffer, Elizabeth, *The Key to My Neighbor's House: Seeking Justice in Bosnia and Rwanda* (New York: Picador, 2001).

Nicholas, Guy, "Victime ou Martyr," *Cultures et Conflits* 11 (Automne 1993).

Niebuhr, Reinhold, *The Children of Light and the Children of Darkness* (New York: Scribner, 1945).

Norton, Augustus R. (ed.), *Civil Society in the Middle East*, Vols. 1 and 2 (Leiden: E. J. Brill, 1994, 1995).

Nye, Joseph S., "The Changing Nature of World Power," *Political Science Quarterly*, Vol. 105, No. 2 (1990), pp. 177–92.

O'Brien, Robert, Anne Marie Goetz, Jan Aart Scholte, and Marc Williams, *Contesting Global Governance: Multilateral Economic Institutions and Global Social Movements* (Cambridge: Cambridge University Press, 2000).

O'Donnell, Guillermo and Philippe C. Schmitter, *Transitions from Authoritarian Rule: Tentative Conclusions about Uncertain Democracies* (Baltimore, MD: Johns Hopkins University Press, 1986).

Osorio, Carlos (ed.), "State Department Opens Files on Argentina's Dirty War," National Security Archive Briefing Book No. 73 (August 21, 2002), <www.gwu.edu/~nsarchiv/NSAEBB/NSAEBB73/>.

Ottaway, Marina, "Corporatism Goes Global: International Organizations, Nongovernmental Organization Networks, and Transnational Business," *Global Governance*, Vol. 7, No. 3 (2001), pp. 265–92.

Pagnucco, Ron, "The Transnational Strategies of the Service for Peace and Justice in Latin America," in Jackie Smith, Charles Chatfield, and Ron Pagnucco (eds), *Transnational Social Movements and Global Politics: Solidarity Beyond the State* (Syracuse, NY: Syracuse University Press, 1997).

Paige, Glenn D., Chaiwat Satha-Anand, and Sarah Gilliatt (eds), *Islam and Nonviolence* (Honolulu: Matsunaga Institute for Peace, University of Hawaii, 1993).

Pasic, Amir and Thomas Weiss, "The Politics of Rescue: Yugoslavia's Wars and the Humanitarian Impulse," *Ethics and International Affairs*, Vol. 11 (1997), pp. 105–31.

Pasic, Amir and Thomas G. Weiss, "Humanitarian Recognition in the Former Yugoslavia: The Limits of Non-State Politics," *Security Studies*, Vol. 7, No. 1 (1997), pp. 194–228.

Petras, James, "NGOs: In Service of Imperialism," *Journal of Contemporary Asia*, Vol. 29, No. 4 (1999), pp. 429–40.

Philpott, Daniel, *Revolutions in Sovereignty: How Ideas Shaped Modern International Relations* (Princeton, NJ: Princeton University Press, 2001).

Pollan, Michael, "An Animal's Place," *New York Times Magazine*, November 10, 2002.

Powell, Walter W., "Neither Market Nor Hierarchy: Network Forms of Organization," *Research in Organizational Behavior*, Vol. 12 (1990), pp. 295–336.

Power, Samantha, *"A Problem From Hell": America and the Age of Genocide* (New York: Basic Books, 2002).

Prendergast, John, *Frontline Diplomacy: Humanitarian Aid and Conflict in Africa* (Boulder, CO: Lynne Rienner, 1996).

Princen, Thomas and Matthias Finger, *Environmental NGOs in World Politics: Linking the Local and the Global* (New York: Routledge, 1994).

Rashid, Ahmed, *Taliban: Militant Islam, Oil and Fundamentalism in Central Asia* (New Haven, CT: Yale University Press, 2001).

Ray, James Lee, "The Abolition of Slavery and the End of International War," *International Organization*, Vol. 43, No. 3 (Summer 1989), pp. 405–39.

Reagan, Ronald, "Promoting Democracy and Peace," United States Department of State Bureau of Public Affairs, Washington, DC, Speech delivered before the British Parliament, London, June 8, 1982, <www.ned.org/about/reagan-060882.html>.

Reno, William, *Warlord Politics and African States* (Boulder, CO: Lynne Rienner, 1998).

Rich, Roland, "Bringing Democracy Into International Law," *Journal of Democracy*, Vol. 12, No. 3 (July 2001), pp. 20–34.

Rieff, David, *Slaughterhouse: Bosnia and the Failure of the West* (New York: Simon & Schuster, 1995).

Rieff, David, "A New Age of Liberal Imperialism?" *World Policy Journal*, Vol. 16, No. 2 (1999), pp. 1–10.

Risse, Thomas, Stephen C. Ropp, and Kathryn Sikkink (eds), *The Power of Human Rights: International Norms and Domestic Change* (Cambridge: Cambridge University Press, 1999).

Risse-Kappen, Thomas (ed.), *Bringing Transnational Relations Back In: Non-State Actors, Domestic Structures and International Institutions* (Cambridge: Cambridge University Press, 1995).

Ronfeldt, David and Cathryn L. Thorup, *North America in the Era of Citizen Networks: State, Society, and Security* (Santa Monica, CA: RAND, 1995).

Roth, Kenneth, "The Law of War in the War on Terror: Washington's Abuse of 'Enemy Combatants'," *Foreign Affairs*, Vol. 83, No. 1 (January/February 2004), pp. 2–7.

Rudolph, Susanne Hoeber and James Piscatori (eds), *Transnational Religion and Failing States* (Boulder, CO: Westview Press, 1997).

Ruggie, John Gerard, "global_governance.net: The Global Compact as Learning Network," *Global Governance*, Vol. 7, No. 4 (2001), pp. 371–8.

Sachedina, Abdulaziz, *The Islamic Roots of Democratic Pluralism* (New York: Oxford University Press, 2001).

Salamon, Lester M., "The Rise of the Nonprofit Sector," *Foreign Affairs*, Vol. 73, No. 4 (1994), pp. 109–22.

Salamon, Lester M. and Helmut K. Anheier, *The Emerging Sector: The Nonprofit Sector in Comparative Perspective—An Overview* (Baltimore, MD: Johns Hopkins University Institute for Policy Studies, 1994).

al-Sayyid, Mustapha Kamil, "A Civil Society in Egypt?" in Augustus Richard Norton (ed.), *Civil Society in the Middle East*, Vol. 1 (Leiden: E. J. Brill, 1995).

Scarce, Rik, *Eco-Warriors: Understanding the Radical Environmental Movement* (Chicago, Noble Press, 1990).

Schechter, Michael G. (ed.), *United Nations-Sponsored World Conferences: Focus on Impact and Follow-up* (New York: United Nations University Press, 2001).

Schwedler, Jillian (ed.), *Toward Civil Society in the Middle East? A Primer* (Boulder, CO: Lynne Rienner, 1995).

Selznick, Philip, *Leadership in Administration* (New York: Harper & Row, 1957).

Seuss, Dr, *The Lorax* (New York: Random House, 1971).

Shaw, Martin, "Civil Society and Global Politics: Beyond a Social Movements Approach," *Millennium: Journal of International Studies*, Vol. 23, No. 3 (1994), pp. 647–67.

Sikkink, Kathryn, "Human Rights, Principled Issue-Networks, and Sovereignty in Latin America," *International Organization*, Vol. 47, No. 3 (1993), pp. 411–41.

Sikkink, Kathryn, "The Emergence, Evolution, and Effectiveness of the Latin American Human Rights Network," in Elizabeth Jelin and Eric Hershberg (eds), *Constructing Democracy: Human Rights, Citizenship, and Society in Latin America* (Boulder, CO: Westview Press, 1996).

Simmons, P. J., "Learning to Live with NGOs," *Foreign Policy*, No. 112 (Fall 1998), pp. 82–96.

Sinnar, Shirin, "Mixed Blessing: The Growing Influence of NGOs," *Harvard International Review* (Winter 1995/96), pp. 54–7, 79.

Slim, Hugo, "The Continuing Metamorphosis of the Humanitarian Practitioner: Some New Colours for an Endangered Chameleon," *Disasters*, Vol. 19, No. 2 (1995), pp. 110–26.

Smillie, Ian, "NGOs in Complex Emergencies: The Case of Sierra Leone," Working Paper #1, CARE Canada, NGOs in Complex Emergencies Project (September 1996).

Smith, Brian H., *The Church and Politics in Chile* (Princeton, NJ: Princeton University Press, 1982).

Smith, Brian H., *More than Altruism: The Politics of Private Foreign Aid* (Princeton, NJ: Princeton University Press, 1990).

Smith, Jackie, Charles Chatfield, and Ron Pagnucco (eds), *Transnational Social Movements and Global Politics: Solidarity Beyond the State* (Syracuse, NY: Syracuse University Press, 1997).

Smith, Warren Thomas, *John Wesley and Slavery* (Nashville, TN: Abingdon Press, 1986).

Southern Poverty Law Center, "From Push to Shove," *Intelligence Report*, Issue 107 (Fall 2002), <www.splcenter.org/intelligenceproject/ip-4w3.html>.

Springborg, Robert, *Mubarak's Egypt: Fragmentation of the Political Order* (Boulder, CO: Westview, 1989).

Steinberg, James R., "International Involvement in the Yugoslav Conflict," in Lori Fisler Damrosch (ed.), *Enforcing Restraint: Collective Intervention in Internal Conflicts* (New York: Council on Foreign Relations Press, 1993).

Stern, Jessica, "The Protean Enemy," *Foreign Affairs*, Vol. 82, No. 4 (July/August 2003), pp. 27–40.

Stover, Eric and Gilles Peress, *The Graves: Srebrenica and Vukovar* (Berlin: Scalo, 1998).

"Strategic Nonviolent Action Key to Serbia's Revolution," *PeaceWatch*, Journal of the United States Institute of Peace, Vol. 7, No. 1 (December 2000).

Sullivan, Denis J., *Private Voluntary Organizations in Egypt* (Gainesville, FL: University Press of Florida, 1994).

SustainAbility, *The 21st Century NGO: In the Market for Change* (Brooklyn, NY: Sustainability, 2003).

SustainAbility, "The 21st Century NGO—White Paper" (Brooklyn, NY: Sustainability, 2003), <www.sustainability.com/programs/pressure-front/21-NGO-white-paper.pdf>.

Tarrow, Sidney, *Power in Movement: Social Movements and Contentious Politics*, 2nd edn (Cambridge: Cambridge University Press, 1998).

Tauran, Archbishop Jean-Louis, "The Presence of the Holy See in the International Organizations," Lecture at Catholic University of the Sacred Heart, Milan, Italy (April 22, 2002), <www.vatican.va/roman_curia/secretariat_state/documents/rc_seg-st_doc_20020422_tauran_en.html>.

Taylor, Lucy, "Exploring Civil Society in Post Authoritarian Regimes," in Ian Hampsher-Monk and Jeffery Stanyer (eds), *Contemporary Political Studies 1996*, Vol. II (Glasgow: Proceedings of the Annual Conference of the Political Studies Association of the United Kingdom, 1996).

Terry, Fiona, *Condemned to Repeat? The Paradox of Humanitarian Action* (Ithaca, NY: Cornell University Press, 2002).

Thomas, Daniel C., *The Helsinki Effect: International Norms, Human Rights, and the Demise of Communism* (Princeton, NJ: Princeton University Press, 2001).

Thomas, George M., John W. Meyer, Francisco O. Ramirez, and John Boli, *Institutional Structure: Constituting State, Society, and the Individual* (Beverly Hills, CA: Sage, 1987).

Thomas, Scott M., "Taking Religious and Cultural Pluralism Seriously: The Global Resurgence of Religion and the Transformation of International Society," *Millennium: Journal of International Studies*, Vol. 29, No. 3 (2000), pp. 815–41.

Thomson, Janice E., "State Sovereignty in International Relations," *International Studies Quarterly*, Vol. 39, No. 2 (1995), pp. 213–33.

Thropy, Miss Ann, "Population and AIDS," *EarthFirst! Journal*, Vol. 8, No. 2 (December 22, 1987).

Tilly, Charles, *Popular Contention in Great Britain, 1758–1834* (Cambridge, MA: Harvard University Press, 1995).

de Tocqueville, Alexis, edited by J. P. Mayer, translated by George Lawrence, *Democracy in America* (Garden City, NY: Doubleday, 1969).

Toulmin, Stephen, *Cosmopolis: The Hidden Agenda of Modernity* (New York: Free Press, 1990).

Turner, Frederick C. and José Enrique Miguens (eds), *Juan Perón and the Reshaping of Argentina* (Pittsburgh, PA: University of Pittsburgh Press, 1983).

Tvedt, Terje, *Angels of Mercy or Development Diplomats? NGOs and Foreign Aid* (Trenton, NJ: Africa World Press, 1998).

Villiamy, Ed, *Seasons in Hell: Understanding Bosnia's War* (London: Simon & Schuster, 1994).

Viotti, Paul R. and Mark V. Kauppi, *International Relations Theory* (New York: Macmillan, 1987).

Wapner, Paul, *Environmental Activism and World Civic Politics* (Albany, NY: SUNY Press, 1996).

Waterbury, John, *The Egypt of Nasser and Sadat* (Princeton, NJ: Princeton University Press, 1983).

Weaver, Mary Anne, "Egypt on Trial," *New York Times Magazine*, June 17, 2001.

Weber, Max, translated by Talcott Parsons, *The Protestant Ethic and the Spirit of Capitalism* (New York: Charles Scribner's Sons, 1958).

Weiss, Thomas G. (ed.), *Beyond UN Subcontracting: Task-Sharing with Regional Security Arrangements and Service-Providing NGOs* (London: Macmillan, 1998).

Weiss, Thomas G. and Leon Gordenker (eds), *NGOs, the UN, and Global Governance* (Boulder, CO: Lynne Rienner, 1996).

Weiss, Thomas G. and Amir Pasic, "Reinventing UNHCR: Enterprising Humanitarians in the Former Yugoslavia, 1991–1995," *Global Governance*, Vol. 3 (1997), pp. 41–57.

Weissman, Benjamin M., *Herbert Hoover and Famine Relief to Soviet Russia: 1921–1923* (Stanford, CA: Hoover Institution Press, 1974).

Weller, Marc, "Undoing the Global Constitution: UN Security Council Action on the International Criminal Court," *International Affairs*, Vol. 78, No. 4 (2002), pp. 693–712.

Wendt, Alexander, *Social Theory of International Politics* (Cambridge: Cambridge University Press, 1999).

Weschler, Lawrence, *A Miracle, A Universe: Settling Accounts With Torturers* (New York: Pantheon, 1990).

Westerlund, David (ed.), *Questioning the Secular State: The Worldwide Resurgence of Religion in Politics* (London: I. B. Tauris, 1996).

Whitman, Walt, "Democratic Vistas," in Walt Whitman, edited by Floyd Stoval, *Prose Works 1892*, Vol. II (New York: New York University Press, 1964).

Wickham-Crowley, Timothy P., "Winners, Losers, and Also-Rans: Toward a Comparative Sociology of Latin American Guerrilla Movements," in Susan Eckstein (ed.), *Power and Popular Protest* (Berkeley, CA: University of California Press, 1989).

Wickham-Crowley, Timothy P., "A Qualitative Comparative Approach to Latin American Revolutions," *International Journal of Comparative Sociology*, Vol. 32, Nos. 1–2 (1991), pp. 82–109.

Willets, Peter (ed.), *Pressure Groups in the Global System: The Transnational Relations of Issue-Oriented Non-Governmental Organizations* (London: Pinter, 1982).

Willetts, Peter (ed.), *"The Conscience of the World": The Influence of Non-Governmental Organizations in the UN System* (Washington, DC: Brookings, 1996).

Willetts, Peter, "Transnational Actors and International Organizations in Global Politics," in John Baylis and Steve Smith (eds), *The Globalization of World Politics*, 2nd edn (Oxford: Oxford University Press, 2001).

Williams, Phil, "Transnational Criminal Organizations: Strategic Alliances," *The Washington Quarterly*, Vol. 18, No. 1 (1995), pp. 57–72.

Williams, Phil, "The Nature of Drug-Trafficking Networks," *Current History* (April 1998), pp. 154–9.

Woodward, Susan, *Balkan Tragedy: Chaos and Dissolution After the Cold War* (Washington, DC: Brookings, 1995).

Woodward, Susan, "International Aspects of the Wars in Former Yugoslavia," in Jasminka Udovicki and James Ridgeway (eds), *Burn This House: The Making and Unmaking of Yugoslavia* (Durham, NC: Duke University Press, 1997).

Wright, Thomas C., *Latin America and the Cuban Revolution* (New York: Praeger, 1991).

Yamamoto, Tadashi (ed.), *Emerging Civil Society in the Asia Pacific Community*, 2nd edn (Seattle, WA: University of Washington Press, 1996).

Young, Helen and Susanne Jaspers, *Nutrition Matters: People, Food and Famine* (London: Intermediate Technology Publications, 1995).

Index

United Nations High Commissioner
    for Refugees (UNHCR), 138–9
United Nations Protection Force
    (UNPROFOR), 130, 139
United States Institute of Peace, 138
universal jurisdiction, 1, 184

Vienna World Conference on
    Human Rights, 19, 152

Walesa, Lech, 196 n8
war crimes, 1, 121–2, 128–34,
    136–7, 183–5
War Resisters League, 93
Washington Office on Latin
    America (WOLA), 94, 100
Wildlife Conservation Society, 167

William and Flora Hewlett
    Foundation, 152
Williams, Betty, 196 n8
Wipfler, William, 95
Women Acting Together for Change
    (WATCH), 164
Women's Campaign International,
    163
World Bank, 11, 21, 24, 145, 168
World Trade Organization (WTO),
    21–2, 85
World Transhumanist Association,
    171
World Wildlife Fund, 167
WorldWatch Institute, 150, 163

Yugoslavia, Former, chapter 5